THE STRENGTH OF OUR MOTHERS

AFRICAN & AFRICAN AMERICAN WOMEN & FAMILIES: ESSAYS AND SPEECHES

NIARA SUDARKASA

Africa World Press, Inc.

P.O. Box 1892
Trenton, NJ 08607

P.O. Box 48
Asmara, ERITREA

Africa World Press, Inc.

P.O. Box 1892

Trenton, NJ 08607

P.O. Box 48

Asmara, ERITREA

Copyright © 1996 Niara Sudarkasa

First Printing 1996

Book design: Jonathan Gullery

Cover design: Linda Nickens

Library of Congress Cataloging-in-Publication Data

Sudarkasa, Niara.
    The strength of our mothers : African & African American women & families : essays and speeches / Niara Sudarkasa.
      p.   cm.
    Includes bibliographical references (p.) and index.
    ISBN 0-86543-496-4 (cloth.) -- ISBN 0-86543-497-2 (pbk. : alk. paper)
    1. Afro-American women--Social conditions. 2. Afro-American families. 3. Women--Africa--Social conditions. 4. Family--Africa.
    I. Title.
    E185.86.S83   1996
    306.85'089'96073--dc20
                                    95-51294
                                       CIP

*In honor of generations past, this book is dedicated
to the memories of my mother,
Mrs. Rowena Marshall;
her mother, **Mrs. Tryphenia Evans;**
and
my "mothers" from Nigeria:
Chief (Mrs.) H.T. Soares of Ibadan
&
Mrs. Faderera Oparinde of Awe.

It is also dedicated to my son,
Michael Sudarkasa,
whose strength of character
and commitment to his family, immediate and extended,
are a source of pride
to his mother.*

CONTENTS

DEDICATION v

FOREWORD xi
by Harriette Pipes McAdoo

ACKNOWLEDGEMENTS xv

INTRODUCTION xvii
by Niara Sudarkasa

PART I: REASSESSING AFRICAN AMERICAN FAMILIES

1.   Value Premises Underlying Black Family Studies
     and Black Families 3

2.   Dispelling the Myths About Black Families 13

3.   Female-Headed African American Households—
     Some Neglected Dimensions 23

4.   Speaking Up for Single Mothers 35

5.   African American Families and Family Values 41

PART II: AFRICAN AND AFRICAN AMERICAN
FAMILIES: UNDERSTANDING THE LINKS

6. Roots of the Black Family:
    Observations on the Frazier-Herskovits Debate 77

7. African and African American Family Structure 89

8. Interpreting the African Heritage in
    African American Family Organization 123

9. Timeless Values for Troubled Times: Strengthening
    Today's African American Families 143

10. Planning *for* the Family versus "Family Planning"—
    The Case for National Action in Nigeria 149

PART III: AFRICAN WOMEN: PATTERNS OF
INDEPENDENCE, RESPONSIBILITY,
AND LEADERSHIP IN THEIR FAMILIES
AND COMMUNITIES

11. The "Status of Women" in Indigenous
    African Societies—Implications for the
    Study of African American Women's Roles 165

12. The Changing Roles of Women in
    Changing Family Structures in West Africa:
    Some Preliminary Observations 181

13. In a World of Women: Field Work
    in a Yoruba Community 191

14. Female Employment and Family Organization
    in West Africa 221

15. Women and Migration in
    Contemporary West Africa 237

16. The Effects of Twentieth-Century Social Change,
    Especially Migration, on Women of West Africa . . . 251

17. Gender Roles, Education,
    and Development in Africa 265

18. Male/Female Disparities in Education
    and Occupations in Nigeria: Implications for
    Technological Development 281

PART IV: AFRICAN AMERICAN WOMEN:
BUILDING ON THE STRENGTH
OF OUR MOTHERS

19. African American Women:
    A Legacy of Leadership 291

20. African American Women—
    A Case of Strength Without Power? 295

21. Black Women in Higher Education:
    Movin' Up But Payin' the Price 303

22. Comments on the National Centers for
    African American Women, with Special Reference
    to the International Development Center 309

23. Reflections on the Positions and Problems
    of Black Women in America 313

BIBLIOGRAPHY
    A. Articles Included in This Volume 323
    B. Works Cited in This Volume 326

FOREWORD

On the strength of its author's reputation alone, *The Strength of Our Mothers* by Niara Sudarkasa will recommend itself to many specialists in such diverse fields as anthropology, sociology, and political science. But let me list a few reasons why, at precisely this point in our history, this collection of Dr. Sudarkasa's essays and speeches should be broadcast far and wide in our society.

There are a number of enduring issues—originally and repeatedly addressed by Dr. Sudarkasa over the past three decades—which are daily becoming more and more important to our society *as a whole:*

- Which of the diverse traditions in American history and society will be accommodated in what is considered "normative"?
- Which family patterns actually—historically—have produced healthy and successful children and adults?
- In what ways have diverse family patterns nurtured those who have achieved their aspirations?
- How can the roles of women and men be transformed in our society into ones that are mutually empowering and complementary?
- How can the public debate on "Family Values" be informed by research and reporting that describe and analyze our society's rich diversity of family traditions in terms other than the two extremes of "pathological" and "non-pathological"?

- What is the actual—and the potential—role of mutually supportive African American males in this society?
- And, perhaps most important, what can this generation—in all its racial diversity—do *now* to ensure (or at least promote) the survival and success of *future* generations?

All these issues are ably addressed by Dr. Sudarkasa in the present work, which draws upon her in-depth anthropological training, her extensive field work, and her detailed knowledge of history to articulate a pattern of African American cultural resourcefulness and resilience. As a fellow researcher, it is with great pride that I note that that pattern is woven throughout with the life-experiences and family experiences of women of African descent—those women whom Maya Angelou has so aptly described as *"phenomenal women."*

The arguments made in this collection of Dr. Sudarkasa's writings, spanning as they do two tumultuous decades, still make a significant—and largely untapped—contribution to the field. The truth that Sudarkasa tells in this book is an important one for scholars and public policy makers to grasp: The lives of African American women are a fusion of cultural components, bridging the distinctly African and the uniquely American domains. Their lives are the "synthesis" that Herskovitz, Frazier, and Billingsley sought to describe. That synthesis consists of the African cultural patterns (of extended family, kinship networks, and polygynous family arrangements), put through the mill of Enslavement *and* the pressure-cooker of poverty which so many Black families have endured since our enslavement "officially" ended.

Many writers have felt compelled to defend either the view that our families are simply the result of African continuities, or the view that the formation and history of the Black family started with Enslavement. But we are much too complex to be confined to (or defined by) so narrow a view. Sudarkasa's synthesis has been too often overlooked by scholars schooled in that white orientation which views the African experience as insignificant, leaving only the experience of Enslavement as the formative one for those Africans born in America. Sudarkasa skillfully blends the African and the American experiences of women and their families into a coherent whole.

Sudarkasa describes the impact on her career of the policy writings of U.S. Senator Daniel Patrick Moynihan. Moynihan's contribution consisted not in what he actually wrote, but in the impetus that his comments gave to African American researchers and writers. His comments angered, yes, but also stimulated a "critical mass" of African Americans to begin to research and write on the subject of the Black family. Many mainstream scholars felt that Moynihan verbalized and vindicated what they themselves had long presupposed (i.e., that the Black condition is due to some deficiency in Blacks themselves), but his "research" was sheer polemic that merely echoed the prevailing white-oriented stereotypical view of Black families. Long before 1965, some African American scholars had been consistently writing about our families, but Moynihan's policy-paper propelled many more to debate, write, and begin major programs of research. Inadvertently, he did a service to us all, for a movement of historic proportions was stimulated. From the perspective of publishing history, the late 1960s was the turning point for the extensive non-pathologically-oriented study of African American families.

Fortunately, Dr. Sudarkasa was at a stage of her professional development to be able to respond, promptly and strongly, to the accusations that had been levelled against the Black family. Those responses included in this book are succinct statements of truths that are well known but ill acknowledged by non-black researchers and writers.

The traditional role of African women in the marketplace, in the wider world of work, and within the home has long been recognized on the Continent, in the Caribbean, and here in the U.S. Self-reliance and economic self-sufficiency are traditional African characteristics that have been undermined only by economic restructuring and impoverishment imposed from above.

Through it all, the Black Woman has been willing and ready to do the job of holding the Black family together.

The strength of Black women, however, need not detract from the role of the African American male. (That Black men constitute a powerful force within our communities was demonstrated dramatically by the recent "Million Man March" on Washington, D.C.) It is simply an acknowledgement of the central role that women have traditionally played in African American families. We have always had family patterns of flexible, inclusive, and cooperative families that go beyond actual blood lines. Our children may not always have been raised within the context of a marital union, but they *have* always grown up within a loving community of kin and fictive-kin. Our women have always played strong, independent, and loving roles that have brought their families through rough times and smooth. Black women of high achievement consistently report that their mothers gave them the strength to hold on, while both their parents, kin and fictive-kin alike, have given them love.

Unlike the patterns of patriarchy and male dominance so familiar in other families, the Black family reflects an egalitarian arrangement of complementary and mutually empowering roles for both genders that has endured across generations. This is the cultural continuity that allows families to function within an African context, whether in Africa or not. My own research in East Africa, Southern Africa, and particularly West Africa (whence so many of our ancestors originated), revealed family patterns that have women playing important roles in the family, in the community, and in the nation-state.

The ancestral African and African American women of Dr. Sudarkasa's own extended family (to whom she has dedicated this book) would surely be proud of her accomplishments. So, too, I know, are her descendants—her son (a fine example of African American manhood), his wife, and their three children—whom I can attest are surrounded by an extended family that will provide the love and strength to ensure generations upon generations of solid African American families in the days to come.

Harriette Pipes McAdoo
Lansing, Michigan

ACKNOWLEDGEMENTS

Over the years, my work on African and African American women and families has benefitted from the advice, counsel and support of teachers, colleagues, students and friends in the United States, Nigeria, Ghana, the Republic of Benin, various parts of the Caribbean and elsewhere. I cannot possibly name all those who helped me to develop the ideas in this book, but as the Nigerians say, "they know themselves," and I hope that they know that my gratitude is as deep now as it was when I thanked each of them personally as our paths crossed over the past thirty-odd years.

I must mention a few of the scholars who, over the years, have shown their support in very tangible ways: Bolanle Awe, Filomina Steady, Molara Ogundipe-Leslie, Ayo Ogundipe, Harriette McAdoo, Johnnetta Cole, Ruth Hamilton, Owodunni Teriba, Elliott P. Skinner, Maxwell Owusu, Ali Mazrui, John Igue, William Shack, and George Bond immediately come to mind as colleagues who have encouraged and assisted me in the areas of scholarship represented by the essays in this collection. Of course, I am very grateful to each of them, and I hope that they will feel that I have repaid them in some measure by finally collecting these essays in one place.

This leads me to confess that most of the essays in this book were published previously, and I gratefully acknowledge the permissions granted by the various original publishers to reprint them here. A detailed list of citations for the original publications and previous reprints is provided in section "A" of the Bibliography.

Of my friends and former students who helped me to sharpen my analyses of African and African American families, I am particularly grateful to Bamidele Agbasegbe Demerson, whose keen intellect and meticulous research habits made him an especially helpful critic. I hope the appearance of this volume will encourage him to collect and publish his own very important contributions to the study of African American culture.

In the early 1970s, when I started in earnest to lecture and write about the African origins of African American family structure, a group of us in Ann Arbor, Michigan, sought to make the principles of extended familyhood come alive through the relationships we created among ourselves and our children. Although more than two decades have passed since we started our Ujamaa Circle, I must acknowledge the value of this group that was dedicated to serious study as well as to providing mutual sustenance and support for the "family" members. The probing discussions that included Rasaba Sudarkasa, Joetta and Harry Mial, Don and Madeleine Coleman, Pat and Walter Rodney, Niyonu Benson, Mohammed Talballa, Esther Bright, Cheryl Murdock, and Janice Liddell, among others, helped me to clarify my thinking and deepen my understanding of the historical links between African and African American women and families.

There are always some people without whom an author literally could not have completed his or her book. For me, Diane Brown, Jody Brunner, and Frann Cooper, each of whom now works or has worked in the President's Office at Lincoln University, fall in this category. I extend my thanks to them for helping me to keep track of the articles and getting the manuscript in the form requested by the publisher. Most of all, I can say unequivocally that I could not have persevered with this project but for the total support of my husband, John L. Clark, who understood, or at least accepted, the tunnel vision and the odd hours that were required for me to be able to complete this book while attending to my myriad of responsibilities as President of Lincoln University.

THE STRENGTH OF OUR MOTHERS:
AN INTRODUCTION

This book might just as well have been titled "Strengths of our Families" because the themes woven throughout speak to those strengths. But the title has a more pointed reference. Within the constellation of African American families, historically, between one-fifth and one-fourth of them were female-headed. (The increased number and the changing composition of such households over the past three decades are noted and discussed in several of the essays in this book). Over the years, female-headed families have been among the most maligned and misunderstood of all Black families, being forced to bear the responsibility, as it were, for all the ills of Black America. Yet, in my personal experience and that of many other African American professionals, our successes could be attributed in large measure to the strength of our mothers, the stability of their households, and the support of the extended families around them.

Nevertheless, as an anthropologist specializing in African cultures, I probably would not have waded into the discussion on Black families in America had it not been for the undying furor created by Daniel Patrick Moynihan's 1965 publication, *The Negro Family: A Case for National Action*.[1] The previous year, I had completed my doctorate at Columbia University, with a dissertation entitled *Women, Trade and the Yoruba Family*, based on fieldwork in Nigeria.[2] As a new assistant professor at New York University, I fully expected to concentrate on teaching and continuing my research on Yoruba traders in Nigeria and other parts West Africa.

But the Moynihan report intervened. A major section of one of the courses I taught at NYU, titled "The Negro in the New World," was devoted to a comparison of Black families in the United States, Brazil, and the Caribbean. (When I moved to the University of Michigan in 1967, I renamed the course "African Peoples in the Americas.") As soon as the Moynihan report was published, it became the starting point for virtually all discussions of Black families in the United States. In fact, the Moynihan report immediately provided the terms of reference for public policy discussions on the Black family and—-whether acknowledged or not—-it has remained at the center of such discussions over the past three decades since it appeared.

Moynihan's central thesis was that: "At the heart of the deterioration of the fabric of Negro society is the deterioration of the Negro family."[3] (Does not this 1965 pronouncement have a familiar ring in 1996?) The report presented many statistical tables and charts, purporting to support his assertion that at least half of the Blacks in America were enmeshed in a "tangle of pathology" centered around their "matriarchial" family structure. Throughout the publication, Moynihan used terms such as "disorganized" and "highly unstable" in describing the Black family. Of the relationship between the "Negro middle class" and the "remaining half" of the Black population, he stated: "They are...constantly exposed to the pathology of the disturbed group and constantly in danger of being drawn into it."[4] Moynihan summarized his assessment of the "social pathology afflicting the Negro community" by stating that:

> ... at the center of the tangle of pathology is the weakness of the family structure. Once or twice removed, it will be found to be the principal source of most of the aberrant, inadequate or antisocial behavior that did not establish, but now serves to perpetuate, the cycle of poverty and deprivation.(5)

Moynihan's report evoked an avalanche of criticism from Black and white scholars familiar with Black families and their communities.[6] William Ryan was among the first to criticize the report for its "methodological weaknesses...manifest misstatements...and naive [interpretation] of statistical relationships in cause-and-effect terms."[7] Andrew Billingsley wrote a cogent and concise critique of Moynihan in his groundbreaking study *Black Families in White America* (1968). Of the various points Billingsley made, in my view, the most important was the observation that:

> A major distortion was [Moynihan's] singling out instability in the Negro family as the causal factor for the difficulties Negroes face in the white society. It is quite the other way round. But coming just at the time the nation was trying to find a single cause of the Watts riots, Moynihan's thesis struck a responsive chord in the collective American breast.[8]

Aside from the fact that I would have put "instability" in quotation marks to show that I did not accept Moynihan's cavalier characterization of Black families (in future articles, I was to argue that marital stability and family stability are not one and the same), I could not have agreed more with Billingsley's assessment.

A number of other very good articles and books were written in refutation of Moynihan's characterization of Black families as "pathological."[9] However, in 1970, not long after I had returned to the University of Michigan after a year-long study of Yoruba traders living in Ghana, I found myself increasingly drawn into debates concerning the Black family. My perspective on African American families was sufficiently different from that of most of those writing on this topic that I was soon sought out as a speaker in that area. I intensified my research and began to formulate a number of the themes that were developed in the essays that are now collected in this volume.

I refer to these and other essays that I have written on the African American family as "occasional papers" because they were written mainly as invited contributions to particular conferences and/or edited volumes. They are *essays in interpretation*, based on my examination of some of the vast body of literature in the area of Black family studies, not essays based on original research. In some key instances, however, they do draw on my own field researches in Nigeria, Ghana, and the Republic of Benin, as well as on my general knowledge of peoples and cultures of West Africa. I am very pleased to have them together and more accessible than they have ever been.

The first theme that emerges in my essays is that African American family structure is traceable to Africa, and not rooted in American slavery as Moynihan and, before him, E. Franklin Frazier had suggested. Slavery obviously had had an impact on this structure, but it was not the starting point for its development. Data in support of this view were provided by the spate of historical studies that appeared in the 1970s and 1980s providing details about the communities "the slaves made." Based on my knowledge of West African kinship, it was obvious to me that the family and kinship networks uncovered among enslaved Blacks by historians such as Blassingame, Genovese, Gutman, and others, had their origins in the extended family structures that already existed throughout West Africa.[10]

In his famous book entitled *Myth of the Negro Past* (1941), Melville Herskovits had presented considerable evidence for what he termed African "survivals" (and later, African "retentions" and "reinterpretations") in African American family life, religion, art, music, dance, dress, folklore, speech, and rites of passage and other ceremonials. Herskovits provided direct refutation of Frazier's view that "scraps of memories, which form only an insignificant part of the growing body of traditions in Negro families" were all that the enslaved Africans (whom he and those of his generation thought of simply as "Negro slaves") retained of their African heritage.[11]

In my essays on African American families, I examine the Herskovits-Frazier debate in light of the data provided by contemporary historians, such as those mentioned above. Although I did not accept every aspect of Herskovits' interpretation, I felt that he was generally right and Frazier generally wrong about the origins of African American family structure. On the other hand, I agreed with Frazier that the relatively large number of female-headed households among African Americans resulted from conditions imposed by the regime of slavery, not from retentions or reinterpretations of African family structures (*Infra*, chap. 6). I argued, however, that *both* Herskovits and Frazier had overlooked some important features of female-headed households that could be traced back to African kinship patterns (*Infra*, chaps. 6, 3).

A second theme in the papers collected here is that we should *go beyond* a refutation of Moynihan and others who saw Black families as "aberrant" and "abnormal," to an understanding of the tradition of scholarship that spawned such interpretations. Because of my extensive reading on kinship and marriage for my article titled "Marriage, Comparative Analysis," which I had been invited to write for the *International Encyclopedia of the Social Sciences* (Marshall 1968), I was well aware that in the development of comparative family studies, scholars had generally held high the standard of the conjugally-based, male-dominated nuclear families of the European tradition. In the late nineteenth century and throughout the twentieth century, sociologists and anthropologists tended to portray the nuclear family as the "highest," "best organized," "most stable," and "most functional" form of the family. Those that "deviated" from this model were viewed as "disorganized," "unstable," and "dysfunctional." Thus, as I said at a Conference of the National Medical Association in 1972, we had to expose and expunge the European-centered value premises underlying Black family studies before we could make headway in describing and assessing these institutions (*Infra*, chap. 1). A longer article on this topic, which I started years ago, unfortunately remains unfinished.

A third and related theme in my essays is that marital stability and family stability are not one and the same. I show that in the context of African domestic groups, marital dissolution did not lead to family dissolution. Lineages (i.e., descent groups based on consanguinity or "blood ties") rather than married couples formed the core around which typical African extended families were built. Polygyny (or plural wives) was an accepted form of marriage, but, regardless of whether a man had one wife or several wives, the dissolution of a marriage did not necessarily jeopardize the stability or continuity of the family unit (*Infra*, chap. 7).

In the case of African American families, I try to show that female-headed households were not and are not necessarily "unstable" just because the male spouse is absent. Historically, female-headed households were typically multigenerational units clustered around a core of consanguineally related adult women or adult women and men. The households would also include at least some of the dependent children of any or all of the women present. These female-headed households were linked to other households through extended family networks, and were generally stable over time (Johnson 1934; Powdermaker 1939; Stack 1974; Aschenbrenner 1975; Gutman 1976; Martin and Martin 1978; McAdoo 1983; *Infra*, chaps. 7, 5).

A fourth theme in my essays is that just as one must understand the value premises underlying Black family studies, one must also understand the values that have undergirded Black families over time. I note some values—such as the traditional value placed on having children—that help to explain certain patterns, such as that of mature women deciding to have children outside of marriage. I also put forth a set of values or general principles that have guided interpersonal relationships in African families and communities, and that carried over into African American families, particularly those of the past. These principles or values I at first termed the Four R's, and later expanded them to the Seven R's: respect, restraint, responsibility, reciprocity, reverence, reason and reconciliation, (Marshall 1970; *Infra*, chaps. 7, 5).[12]

I do not claim that the Seven R's are unique to African societies. In various formulations, and in conjunction with other principles, they are espoused in many of the world's religious and ethical systems. However, the specific combination of these seven values explains much of the interpersonal behavior traditionally found in African (and to some extent African American) families and wider communities.

The papers presented here show that just as my research on West Africa informed my writings on African American families, so too did my work on African American families influence the focus of my continuing research on West Africa. As I looked at the evolution of families in contemporary West Africa in response to urbanization, migration, and other factors, I was intrigued by the parallels with some of the changes that African American families had gone through in response to similar factors, and suggested on a number of occasions that this would be an important area for research. I was invited to write a paper on family policy for a national conference in Nigeria, and drew on my African American research to suggest that the country should embark on a program of planning for the family, not just "family planning" (*Infra*, chap. 10).

Given my continued interest in West African women's roles and responsibilities in the home and in the world of work, I began to explore the idea that understanding these roles might help to explain some of the roles and responsibilities that African American women assumed during slavery and beyond. After all, we know that in the precolonial period, West African women were active outside the home in various political and economic roles. All of their roles in the public domain were coordinated with their domestic roles as wives, mothers, sisters, and daughters within the families into which they were born and into which they married. We also know that during slavery, Black women not only had leadership roles in their homes and on the plantations generally, but, where permitted, they also pursued economic activities (such as trading and craft production) that they knew from Africa. The study of the linkage between African women's roles on the continent and those they created for themselves in America remains a fruitful area for research (*Infra*, chap. 11).

The essays and speeches on African and African American women contradict two prevailing stereotypes. First, the papers on *African* women collectively and separately show that they were not the "docile," "submissive," "downtrodden," powerless creatures they have often been portrayed to be. However, the papers also support Boserup's thesis that African women's roles in the public sphere were diminished and devalued by the colonial regimes with their male-oriented policies and preferences (Boserup 1970; *Infra*, chaps. 14, 16, 11).

Secondly, the papers on *African American* women suggest that there should be no negative connotation placed on the "strength" they are rightly thought to have. On the other hand, they also suggest (as have other scholars) that the strength of African American women has not been translated into commensurate power and authority in the public domain. If measured by participation in the highest levels of the professional, political, and economic sectors of our society, African American women may be the best examples of strength without power.

Yet, when we look back at the history of the African American struggle for survival in this country, it is clear that it is *our families themselves*, rather than institutions on the outside, that have been mainly responsible for our survival and success. Of necessity, African American women have been the bedrock of many, if not most, of those families, whether headed by one parent or two. It is appropriate, therefore, that we acknowledge and celebrate "the strength of our mothers," and that of *their* mothers in turn.

NOTES

1. Moynihan, Daniel Patrick. *The Negro Family: A Case for National Action* (1965)
2. Marshall (1964)
3. Moynihan, Daniel Patrick. *The Negro Family: A Case for National Action* (1965), reprinted in and quoted from Bracey, John H., August Meier, and Elliott Rudwick, èds. *Black Matriarchy: Myth or Reality,* Belmont, Calif.: Wadsworth Publishing Co., Inc., 1971, p. 128.
4. Ibid., p.141
5. Ibid., p. 142
6. See, for example, Ryan (1965); Carper (1966); Rainwater and Yancey (1967); Billingsley (1968); Valentine (1968), in References
7. Ryan, William, "Savage Discovery - The Moynihan Report" (1965), reprinted in and quoted from *The Black Family: Essays and Studies,* Robert Staples, ed., Belmont, Calif.: Wadsworth Publishing Co., Inc., 1971, p. 58.
8. Billingsley, Andrew, *Black Families in White America,* Englewood Cliffs, N.J.: Prentice Hall, Inc., 1968, pp. 199-200.
9. In addition to the authors cited in (6) above, see, for example, Young 1970; Hill, R. 1971; English 1974; Allen 1978; Staples 1978.
10. See, for example, Blassingame (1972); Genovese (1974); Gutman (1976); Owens (1976) and Perdue et al.(1980).
11. Frazier (1939), cited 1966 edition, p. 15.
12. I always emphasized the applicability of the Four R's (respect, restraint, responsibility, and reciprocity) beyond the context in which I used them, but I was very surprised to hear them used by General Alexander Haig in a foreign policy address in the early 1980s. I often wondered if a former student of mine was his speech writer!

REASSESSING AFRICAN AMERICAN FAMILIES

"As African American scholars, we must remind our communities and inform the wider society of the roles that our families have played in our survival in America. We cannot blame others for the perpetuation of stereotyped notions about African American families when we ourselves assume them to be inferior simply because they differ from family structures handed down from Europe. In form, African American families have been some of the most flexible, adaptable and inclusive kinship institutions in America. In function, they have been among the most accepting and nurturing of children, and the most supportive of adults."

Niara Sudarkasa, "African American Families and Family Values" (*Infra,* p. 82)

VALUE PREMISES UNDERLYING BLACK FAMILY STUDIES AND BLACK FAMILIES

INTRODUCTION

In recent years, a number of Black scholars have called attention to serious methodological, theoretical, and analytical flaws in many of the contemporary works on Black families in the United States. These scholars have criticized their white colleagues for centering their analyses around data that are selectively focused on the so-called "negative" or "pathological" aspects of Black family life; for committing a number of methodological errors in the presentation of data on Black families; and for misinterpreting assembled data on the verbal and nonverbal behavior of Black people in families. These scholars have suggested that whites promulgate, under the guise of theory, a number of distorted projections that only serve to buttress stereotypes created by whites about Blacks.

Underlying the specific criticisms that have been made is the general charge that Black families are seldom investigated as enduring institutions in their own right. Rather, Black families are usually measured against yardsticks that are reflective of the ideals (though not the actual behavior) of "middle class white America."

The central point of this paper is that despite the new trends in Black family studies, many students of Black families, including Blacks as well as whites, seem to accept the value premise that there is "more wrong" with Black families than with white families, and that Black families can only "improve" to the extent that they approximate the ideal of the nuclear family. The soundness of this value premise has never been demonstrated; in fact, a strong case can be made for the proposition that this premise concerning the superiority of the nuclear family must be exposed and expunged before genuinely useful work on Black family organization can be done.

This paper is developed as follows: *first*, the point is made that Black family studies must be examined in the context of the development of comparative family studies in general; *second*, documentation is provided for the view that existent Black family studies are based on the value premise that the nuclear family is superior to other types of family organization; *third*, some of the significant features of Black family organization are discussed, and the need for a full appreciation and understanding of these is pointed out.

The paper concludes with an elaboration of the comment that in the area of Black Family Studies, as in other areas of study, *Black people* must determine the value premises that will undergird scholarship by and about Blacks rather than accept—-explicitly or implicitly, knowingly or unknowingly—-the value premises of others whose interests have historically proven to be inimical to our own.

II

Comparative family studies developed in the late nineteenth and early twentieth centuries in the context of biological and social evolutionary theory. Anthropologists and sociologists of that time took for granted that the nuclear family, centered around a monogamous conjugal union, and comprised ideally of a married couple and their unmarried children, was the "highest" form of family organization that man had achieved to date.

European travellers, missionaries, and scholars of the nineteenth and early twentieth centuries were often preoccupied with describing those aspects of non-European family organization that contrasted with their own. They often expressed astonishment over the large number of persons non-white societies "lumped together" into a single family. Families built around polygamous unions, or large extended families built around consanguineal ("blood") kin groups such as lineages or clans, were the subject of many lectures, articles, and books. Of note is the fact that these families were considered to be less "advanced" types than the nuclear families (then termed "elementary" or "simple" families) of the West.

Examination of the "methodology" of the early comparative family studies reveals that the data on which they were based were often collected in a haphazard manner by untrained persons who often expressed "revulsion" at the customs of the people they met. Despite what one anthropologist admitted to be the defective knowledge upon which most studies of family organization among nonwhite peoples were based, a number of European and Euro-American scholars developed and disseminated "theories" about the nature of kinship and family organization in non-Western (so-called "primitive") societies. Of even greater consequence is the fact that these "theories" formed the basis of adverse moral and political judgements concerning the peoples described.

III

In today's social science, typological studies of the family have replaced the evolutionary studies of the nineteenth and the early twentieth centuries. However, comparative family studies still take the nuclear family as their point of departure and point of reference. The use of the term "nuclear" as a designation for the European (white) ideal type of family prejudices comparative study. The term "nuclear family" is meant to signify that this is the basic or primary form of family organization. George Peter Murdock in the book *Social Structure* (1949), and many other scholars following him, flatly maintain that the nuclear family is the building block of all other types of family structure.

According to Murdock, extended families are most appropriately described as two or more nuclear families linked through the parent-child relationship. Based on my study of the literature on traditional African extended families and upon my own fieldwork among the Yoruba living in Nigeria and in Ghana, it seems clear that many aspects of extended family organization are distorted by looking upon these groups as collections of nuclear families. Two salient features of African extended families should be noted. First, they were (and are) built around what Ralph Linton termed a "consanguineal core" of blood relatives rather than around a "conjugal core" (i.e., a married couple) as are nuclear families (Linton, 1936).

Secondly, even though extended families may be subdivided into constituent units comprising a male, his wife or wives, and children, it is erroneous to conceive and describe a polygamous family as comprised of distinct nuclear families with a husband/father "in common." In other words, a group comprised of a man, his three wives, and children, should not be construed to be three nuclear families with a husband/father in common. Before the advent of Europeans in Africa, and in most places even today, a man and his several wives are considered to be a single family, and all the women and children therein are united by ties of obligation and affection to one another as well as to the husband/father. In fact, traditionally it was only for specified occasions, such as those involving the division of certain types of property, that there was a division made between the children of the different wives. Even then, however, such divisions were not conceptualized as distinct families.

In recent years, the term "extended family" has been applied by Andrew Billingsley (1968) and others to various types of non-nuclear households found among Blacks in the United States. The growing tendency to use the term "extended family" as a generic contrast to the "nuclear family" makes it imperative that we not fall into the error of maintaining that the basic constituent unit of an extended family must be a nuclear family. Such a proposition only obfuscates the actual dynamics of family formation and of family group maintenance operative in many parts of the world, including those operative among Black people in the Americas.

A survey of the literature on comparative family organization shows that the emphasis on the nuclear family as the "basic" form of family organization does not derive from its universality or from its structural privacy, but rather from the value placed upon it in Western societies. What European (i.e., white) scholars did was to take the family type that existed in their own societies and rationalize its existence elsewhere. Where other types of family existed, they construed these to be "built upon" nuclear families. Moreover, where nuclear families did not exist as the normal or preferable form of family organization, they were promoted through the various propaganda agencies and techniques utilized by European missionaries, political officials, and scholars.

IV

What has been said so far should indicate that studies of Black families in the U.S. must be viewed in the general context of the development of comparative family studies. The value premise undergirding these comparative studies asserted (and still asserts) that the conjugally-based nuclear family is the "healthy," "normal," "organized," and "stable" form of family whereas families that depart from the nuclear family ideal are "unhealthy," "abnormal," "disorganized," and "unstable."

From the early twentieth century onward, most studies of Black families in the U.S. have conceptualized these institutions as aberrant forms of the nuclear family rather than as readaptions of the African extended families out of which they evolved. The conditions of "the slave plantation" made it impossible for Blacks to form African-type extended family households, however, the historical importance placed upon maintaining consanguineal kin ties that cut across "single-parent" and "two-parent" households indicates that a modified form of the extended family was very much alive in "plantation America." One fundamental task for those persons studying the history of Black families in America should be the investigation of the ways in which the African patterns of kinship organization persisted in and were adapted to a social and political environment totally inimical to their existence.

Although some recent studies of Black families in the U.S. have begun to characterize certain of these families as "extended families," the implications of this conceptualization have not been pursued. In fact, from some of the literature, one gets the impression that the term "extended family" is simply being used as a euphemism for terms such as "disorganized" family. Many Black writers still seem compelled to extol the virtues of Black nuclear families without looking at the strengths of other types.

What is needed in Black Family Studies is a perspective that will not only encompass the range of domestic groupings found among Blacks, but will also probe and pursue the implications of some of the fundamental structural differences between many forms of Black family organization and nuclear family organization. Observations such as the following should be taken as the basis for further study:

1) Whereas household and family are often conterminous where the nuclear family prevails (those kinsmen outside the household being considered as "relatives" rather than as "family" per se), among Blacks, family and household are not usually equated. Families cut across household divisions and, in many instances, single households are only part of larger family structures. One of the important implications of this fact is that census data collected for individual households cannot be taken as the most important source of information on Black family organization. Moreover, who is or is not the head of a family in terms of the role in decision making is not necessarily ascertainable by looking solely at isolated households.

2) Black families are not necessarily centered around conjugal unions, which are the *sine qua non* of the nuclear family. Among blacks, households centered around consanguineal relatives have as much legitimacy (and for most people, as much respectability) as family units as do households centered around conjugal unions. When this fact is understood, it becomes clear that *the instability of conjugal relations cannot be taken as the sole measure of the instability of the family.* That Black families exhibit considerable stability over time and space is evidenced by the enduring linkages and bonds of mutual obligation found among networks of consanguineal kin.

3) Adulthood for Black people does not necessarily entail the establishment of new households; one finds many single adults living with married and unmarried relatives. In fact, in some places it is considered highly preferable for unmarried adults to live with relatives than to live alone or to live outside the family with "roommates."

4) Family networks that link various households serve to make personnel and resources available to their members. They serve as virtual "mutual aid" societies, involving care for the young, aged, infirm, or homeless, as well as the provision of hospitality for kinsmen who are newcomers into an area.

In addition to probing the implications of the types of family organization found among Blacks, it is also important to realize that many of the values that underlie Black family organization are different from those that underlie nuclear family organization. In fact, the nuclear family is antithetical to many of the values held by Blacks. For example:

a) Many Blacks still feel that it is the duty of children to look after their aged parents rather than abandon them to "old folks" homes. Thus, many Black households are "extended" by the addition of one or more parents of one or more of the adults in them. It is important to note that Blacks cannot adhere to the value of personal care of the aged and at the same time aspire to establish or maintain nuclear families.

b) Many Blacks seem to hold onto the view that adult females have a right to motherhood if they choose it and to male companionship regardless of whether or not they are married. Blacks in the United States, as in Africa, seem to place a negative value on childlessness in females, and a positive value on having children. The implications of this are many. It appears, for example, that in any situation where there was a relative shortage of marriageable males to females, the positive value placed on having children, coupled with a realistic attitude toward the emotional and sexual needs of adults, would account for the accommodation by both females and males to the practice of males' having "women outside the home." In any case, the general observation can be made that the survival and expansion of the Black population in the Americas is directly linked to the fact that children were valued and legitimized regardless of whether or not they were "born out of wedlock." Moreover, it is also important to acknowledge that the positive value placed on motherhood for all adult females partly accounts for the historical development of a number of households comprised of mothers and their children. By and large, Black people accepted these as one of the normal variants of household organization rather than as "abnormal." What has not been sufficiently explored is the extent to which and the ways in which such "mother-centered" households were structurally linked to or incorporated in larger trans-residential family groupings.

c) Another pervasive value that seems to underlie Black family organization is that of cooperation within the family group.

Historically, generosity and reciprocity have been viewed as complementary values that should govern relations within the wider family network as well as within the household. The positive value placed upon cooperation and assistance to family members no doubt accounts in part for the fact, remarked upon earlier, that unmarried adults often live with parents or siblings. It was the positive value placed on inter-family cooperation that also accounted for the fact that people in urban areas took in their relatives who migrated to the city. Normally this behavior is attributed to the relatively high cost and/or shortage of living accommodations in the city. I am suggesting that there was more to it than that.

V

Today, Blacks are in a situation where their family networks have been undermined by urban living conditions, and by bombardment from propaganda agents (including schools, social workers, churches, etc.) that extol the virtues of the nuclear family. To the extent that Black scholars have supported the myth of the superiority of the nuclear family, they have also helped to obscure the importance and relevance of the types of family organization developed among Black people in the U.S.

Black scholars should not feel they have to apologize for or explain away patterns whose value they have not seriously examined. They need not provide sanctions for family patterns whose positive values have not been demonstrated. Black scholars, perhaps more than any others in the U.S., should take a very critical look at the nuclear family and its past and potential role in the evolution of Black communities. One thing is certain: the nuclear family of reality is significantly different from the ideal nuclear family projected by "social science fiction."

The nuclear family of reality is one in which (a) individualism and competition permeate the family, as they do all other aspects of Western society, and (b) selfishness and separateness rather than cooperation and communalism are taken as positive values. The nuclear family was a prime factor in the birth of the "generation gap." Within this family structure, it appears to be normal for children to "hate" and/or "reject" their parents and vice versa. Rivalry and discord among siblings is found in the extreme in nuclear family situations. The conjugal relationship emerges as the most valued relationship, and many people seem to aspire to a situation that might be characterized as "me and thee in our little box."

The survival of Blacks in America has demanded and will continue to demand cooperative family networks. These extensive, multi-purposed groups have served the welfare of their members when various other groups have proven unreliable. *Such groups deserve to be carefully studied with a view to improving upon them rather than deprecating them.*

In this connection, it would be important to study the various forms of extended family that existed in traditional (precolonial) Africa because all of these groupings incorporated realistic, adaptive, and enduring conjugal relationships while at the same time maintaining the continuity and cohesiveness of the consanguineal ("blood") kin group. Of course, the economic and political superstructure in which these families existed was fundamentally different from that in the U.S. today, and I am not suggesting that the institutions of precolonial Africa can be transplanted without modification to the U.S. today. What I am suggesting is that a study of the structural features of those institutions and of the values that supported them can help in the development of institutions that will serve our needs in the present context.

The important point is that in the area of family studies as in other areas of scholarship, Blacks must not allow others to dictate the questions they will study. It has been proven historically that in an effort to respond or react to publications about Blacks, many of our own scholars are led into pursuits that contribute little or nothing to our advancement or empowerment. Issues such as whether or not Blacks in the U.S. have historically lived mainly in nuclear families or in female-headed households are not the sort of issues that should be at the basis of our own studies of the Black family. *We must seek to understand and honestly assess the relative merit of the various types of family organization that have contributed to our survival in various socioeconomic and demographic contexts.* By so doing, we can try to institutionalize those new (or rediscovered) patterns that hold out the promise of helping us to overcome the myriad of problems facing Black communities and Black families today.

2

DISPELLING THE MYTHS
ABOUT BLACK FAMILIES

The Black family is seldom described, understood, or accepted on its own terms. For more than a century, it has been portrayed as "disorganized" and "unstable" because it has not conformed to the white American idealized model of what a family should be. In recent years, the term "pathological" has become the fashionable label to apply to Black families, but the term "pathological" more appropriately describes the social and economic conditions of poverty and degradation in which many of these families are forced to exist.

In the face of recent media attempts to portray the Black family as a chaotic and crumbling institution on the verge of collapse, it is vital that we have events such as the community-wide Black Family Reunion Celebrations sponsored by the National Council of Negro Women, Inc., to remind us of the critical role of families and kinship in the survival and success of Black people in America. Now more than ever, we also need Black scholars to provide the research and analyses that will put the one-sided and misguided interpretations of the Black family in their proper perspective. We must not allow the historical and continuing value and worth of Black families to be buried under a mountain of myths and misrepresentations. In this article, I will comment briefly on six myths that need to he exposed and expunged so that we may proceed with research and analyses of African American families that will help us better understand the changes they are undergoing and the reasons why.

Myth of the Superiority of the Nuclear Family

The first myth, and the one that undergirds all the others, is that the two-parent nuclear family is superior to all other forms of the family. Ever since comparative family studies began, the prevailing view in American and European scholarship has been that all other forms of the family are either "more primitive" or "less perfect" than the nuclear family. The myth of nuclear family superiority goes back to nineteenth-century social-evolutionary theory, which asserted that the types of families and other institutions found among white people were the most "advanced" and the most "civilized" on earth.

In 1949, the anthropologist George Peter Murdock coined the term "nuclear family" to refer to the monogamously married couple and their children. Murdock made the bold assertion that the nuclear family is the basic building block of all other forms of the family. In his view, other types of families were either extensions of the nuclear family or incomplete variants of it. The so called "primitive" extended families found in Africa were mistakenly viewed by Murdock as collections of nuclear families. However, Africans conceptualized their extended families not as collections of nuclear families, but rather as built around lineages, which were made up of consanguineal or "blood" relatives. It was the link between "blood" relatives, not the link between married couples that mainly gave African families their stability over time.

Having asserted that the nuclear family was the most basic form of the family, it was a short but equally arbitrary leap for some scholars to describe the nuclear family as the most perfect form of the family. Many scholars and members of the general public began to pass on the notion that the nuclear family represented the "complete," the "stable," the "healthy," the "normal" form of the family while other types were represented as "broken," "unstable," "unhealthy," or "abnormal." Scholars overlooked the strength and significance of African American extended families, which had their roots in Africa, while extolling the virtues of the nuclear family. Yet, as institutions, extended families proved in many ways *more* efficient and effective than nuclear families in rearing children, taking care of the elderly, and providing emotional and material support for their members.

There is only one irrefutable explanation for the claim for the superiority of the nuclear family. That is, it was the type of family found among the Europeans who colonized, subjugated, and enslaved many of the world's people of color in the period between 1500 and 1900. Where political and economic imperialism led, academic and intellectual colonialism followed.

Myth of the Inherent Instability of Black Families

Closely related to myths about the superiority of the nuclear family is the myth of the inherent instability and "pathology" of Black families, particularly those headed by women. Two points bear on this myth. First, as Andrew Billingsley demonstrated in his famous book entitled *Black Families in White America* (1968), historically most African American families *did* live in stable two-parent families. When Billingsley was writing, 75 percent of Black families were headed by married couples. Because of the extended family emphasis among blacks, many of these two-parent households included more relatives (such as mothers-in-law, sisters, cousins, etc.) than found in the prototypical nuclear family. To my knowledge, no one has demonstrated that these two-parent households were any less stable than their white counterparts. The women were more likely to end up as widows than were white women, but that is a form of marital dissolution over which they had no control. The incidence of divorce was not significantly different among Blacks and whites, especially when one controlled for social class.

The second point is that few scholars seriously considered the possibility that there could be stability in the female-headed households that constituted 25 percent of Black families. (This percentage has increased dramatically over the past two decades, a fact that will be discussed later.) However, *family stability should not be confused with marital stability*. In nuclear families, martial stability is the most important indicator of family stability.; however, in other types of family structures, marital stability may be less relevant to an assessment of family or household stability. In West Africa, for example, extended families living in large compounds were very stable over time even though divorce and remarriage occurred within the various polygamous families that made up the group.

Among Blacks in America there is also a tradition of stable family groupings that were not built around married couples. Typically, such households were built around a core of adult "blood relatives" such as a mother and her daughter(s), and sometimes, also, her grown son(s). Other males, such as "boyfriends" of the women, might reside with the group on an occasional or regular basis. Until recently, writers ignored the important roles of these men and concentrated only on the supposedly inevitably negative impact of the absent father. It is now acknowledged that various males in female-headed households have often been positive role models in the lives of the children they touch.

Until recently, female heads of households were mature women who were single mothers by choice or by force of circumstances (as in the case of widows or divorcees). The phenomenon of the teenage mother living alone with her children is recent among Black Americans. When I was a teenager in the 1950s, young women who had children out of wedlock usually remained in the families in which they themselves had been brought up or they went to live with relatives in other families. It is my belief that *the rise of isolated households headed by teenage mothers is directly related to public welfare policies and housing policies* that have discouraged and discriminated against the large, multi-generational black families that used to live together in a single household. Where formerly there might be one household with a mother and two teenage daughters with young children, now these women might make up three separate single-parent households. Obviously such circumstances that compel young single women to fend for themselves and their children predictably lead to family instability.

In rebuilding the extended family ties that once gave stability to single-parent and two-parent families, we must take the lead in acknowledging the demographic and economic realities that account for the large number of female-headed households in our communities, we must also stop apologizing for the fact that these have always been an accepted and acceptable form of domestic organization for Black Americans. Isolated female-headed households must become reconnected with supportive kinship and friendship networks which can help them survive and prosper despite the odds against them. We should acknowledge what the majority of Blacks in American have tacitly understood and accepted, namely, that some women have to conceive and rear children without husbands, if they are going to have children at all.

Generally, people of African descent place a high value on having children. More than 50 years ago, Charles S. Johnson, the eminent sociologist, pointed out that blacks did not stigmatize children as "illegitimate" simply because their parents were not married when they were born. (I might note, parenthetically, that white women are now demanding the same freedom from stigma for their children born outside of marriage.) Without being demographers, Blacks have traditionally understood that a number of factors mitigate against all women bearing and rearing children in the context of marriage. Differential birth rates for males and females; premature deaths and incarceration of many males in the years when they are most likely to father children; the migration of many males in search of work; and the fact that Black men have a shorter life span than Black women are all factors that contribute to the high incidence of female-headed households among Blacks.

Thus, having no options other than to live alone, many married women have tolerated their husbands' "outside affairs" and many single women have willingly established liaisons with married men. These are realities that must be taken into account when describing and assessing the phenomenon of single parenthood. We are rightly concerned about the rising numbers of teenage pregnancies, but we must remember that not all female-headed households are the result of teenage pregnancies. Many of these households are the result of rational choices made by adults who recognize the need for alternative forms of family organization in the face of the demographic, economic, and social realities that Black women (and Black men) confront in America.

Myth that Most Black Males Do Not Contribute to Their Families

The myth that most Black males are "no good" men who make few or no positive contributions to their families has already been alluded to. Because white American scholars studying male and female roles in Black families tend to concentrate only on the roles of husband and wife or father and mother, they miss a good deal of the behavior and responsibilities men and women take on in their roles as sisters and brothers, sons and daughters, and aunts and uncles.

There are very few working Black males who do not contribute to the upkeep of some households—oftentimes that of their mother or sister if not a wife or girlfriend. Those who live with their mothers or their female relatives usually have at least two households to which they have some obligations—that of a female relative and that of a girlfriend or a former wife. Nowadays, with the high rate of unemployment among Black males, some of these support patterns are breaking down, but it is erroneous to portray these men as "trifling" and "lazy" by nature. Those who do not have money to contribute often "do work around the house" or even help with the care of children in their extended families.

What many scholars of the nuclear family fail to understand is that some men give to their mothers even when they do not support their former wives or their girlfriends. This fact only serves to underscore the strength of consanguineal ("blood") ties in Black families. For Blacks in America as in Africa, the natal family—i.e., the one into which a person is born—is typically one with which ties are never broken. When the natal unit is female headed, many black males develop a deep and abiding loyalty to their mothers, whose sacrifices they extol. John H. Johnson, publisher of *Ebony* and *Jet*, for example, always speaks of the debt he owes his mother. Until her death, she had an office and a position in his corporation.

Myth of the Always Hostile Black Family

The Bill Cosby Show, Amen, 227, and other recent TV shows about Black families have done much to dispel the myth that hostile and combative behavior is ever- present in Black family relationships. This stereotype was epitomized in what I call the "J.J.-Thelma Syndrome" represented in the show *Good Times*. Between Thelma and J.J. (sister and brother on the show), every encounter was a confrontation, and every exchange a put-down. This stereotype may be changing on television, but it dies hard in the print media and in the scholarly literature.

No doubt, one reason why the image of a quarreling, fighting, unloving black family evolved in the first place was that historically, situations involving domestic violence presented virtually the only occasions when whites (in this case, in the person of the police) were allowed a close-up view of Black family life. Moreover, in the segregated South and in the early ghettos of the North, domestic violence and other crimes were often the only aspects of Black life that found their way into newspapers and other majority-controlled media. Only Black-owned newspapers and magazines carried positive (i.e., "regular") news about Black communities. When I was growing up in Florida in the 40s and 50s, we knew that when a Black person's picture appeared in the newspaper there was a 99 percent chance that he (for it was usually a male) had committed a crime. I can still recall the campaigns to force white newspapers to stop giving prominence to reports of crimes by Blacks (who were always identified by race, in words or in pictures) while those of whites were underplayed and written up without identifying racial labels.

To dispel the myth of the always-hostile Black family is not to say there is no violence in Black homes or that hostility where it exists should not be honestly reported, analyzed, and interpreted. What we must insist on is that the reverse is also true. Our own (and sometimes unique or special) ways of showing affection, support, and understanding must also be studied and described.

Myth that Black Families Do Not Value Education

The myth that Black parents do not value education and achievement for their children is perhaps the most pernicious of all. During slavery, many in the enslaved population literally stole "some learnin" from under the noses of their masters. In various cities, wherever free Blacks lived in relatively large numbers during slavery, they established schools for their children. After slavery, it has been said that an entire people sought to go to school, and the first of these schools were established by Blacks themselves. Within two decades after slavery, Blacks and their white benefactors had established hundreds of public and private grammar schools, high schools, normal schools, colleges, and universities to educate the free men and women in those parts of the country where they resided in large numbers.

Education has always been and still is considered by Blacks to be the surest route to upward mobility. It is a fact that many Black parents, who are themselves uneducated or poorly educated, cannot help their children with their homework, do not know what is required to make the children do their homework, and cannot otherwise motivate them by example. But the improved high school graduation rates among Blacks, and the large number of first generation Black college students in our institutions today, prove that the thirst for education still exists among low income Blacks as well as in the Black middle class.

Myth That Black Family Structure is the Cause of the Deplorable Conditions in Many Inner Cities

The myth that is hardest to overcome (because many Blacks themselves have become convinced that it is true) is the myth that Black family structure is the main cause of the high rates of crime, unemployment, school dropouts, teenage pregnancies, drug abuse, and disaffection among young people in many of our inner cities. Many scholars refuse to acknowledge that those Blacks whom Julius Wilson calls the "truly disadvantaged" are caught in a quagmire of poverty which is not of their own making, and which creates vicious cycles of depravity that most cannot escape. In desperation, many turn to drugs and/or crime.

Critics of my position will say, as they did in the 1960's: "Here you go again, claiming Blacks to be the victims and urging us to stop 'blaming the victim'." They will counter with the argument that the breakdown in Black family structure and morals make Blacks the perpetrators as well as the victims of their own crimes. If anyone is to blame, the argument goes, "Blacks must blame themselves." Of course, the African American family norms that reflect and are reinforced by the sub-culture of poverty become themselves a factor in the perpetuation of that sub-culture. But the structure of the Black family is not the root cause of the wretched conditions of poverty, nor will changing that structure eradicate those conditions. All evidence we have shows that the conditions that are allegedly due to family structure are rapidly improved when people in poverty are provided with skills and jobs to earn a decent living. The extraordinarily high rates of unemployment and despair among Black youth and the violent drug subculture that offers easy money and continuous highs are the root causes of crime and degradation in the inner cities. To eliminate these conditions, we must wage a relentless and total war on drugs and unemployment. We do not need a war on Black families.

Reclaiming Black Youth and Black Families

It goes without saying that although Black families are not the root cause of the problem, we are a part of that problem, and we must take the lead in attacking it. Causality is one thing, responsibility is another. We must take the responsibility of forcing the country's leadership to use the political and economic weapons necessary to wage a total war on the international drug cartel. We must also take responsibility for fighting to rescue our youth even in the face of these forces that will take their lives without so much as a backward look.

We cannot wait for the political and economic situation to improve before we escalate our crusade against inferior schools, high dropout rates, teenage pregnancies, disease, drugs, crime and other causes and consequences of misery in our inner cities. As we did during our enslavement, we must once again use our families and our organizing power as instruments of our own liberation. We need to encourage our organizations, especially the wealthy churches, to work with our architects to construct new types of housing to accommodate new types of multi-generational living units. For example, these dwellings could put young single mothers living alone with their children in proximity with elderly mothers and grandmothers living alone with time on their hands, wanting to be useful. Like generations of Black women before them, the older women could tend the children to enable the younger women (and their men) to go out to work.

The key to African American survival has been the flexibility of our family organization. Historically, we accepted one-parent as well as two-parent households. The first networks we used for liberation as well as for support were our extended families. We must now systematically plan and create new kinship networks and new types of families for the new age—networks that will once again embrace and affirm families whether they are headed by women, by men, or both.

21

FEMALE-HEADED AFRICAN AMERICAN HOUSEHOLDS— SOME NEGLECTED DIMENSIONS

There has been considerable speculation and misinformation in the scholarly literature as well as in the popular media about the causes and consequences of female-headed households among African Americans. Amid the confusion and controversy, over the years, policymakers have proposed and developed various "solutions" to the "problems" supposedly embodied in and engendered by Black families headed by women. Such "solutions" have been well intentioned but often misguided because they attempted to address problems and issues that were only half-understood. A sound analysis is not only relevant to the formulation of policy, it is indispensable to it. If we are to develop a program of action to assist female-headed households, we must have a clear conception and complete analysis of the circumstances of their development as well as their form and function.

In this paper, I will comment on the following six points, which I feel are important to keep in mind as we seek to clarify, amplify, and demystify the data on households headed by African American women:

1. A key to understanding contemporary African American family structure, whether headed by women, by men, or by couples, is a knowledge of the earlier structure of African extended

families out of which they evolved. It is particularly important to understand that as these African-derived extended families evolved in America, they embraced households headed by single parents, most of whom were women, as well as households headed by married couples.

2. Female-headed households are not all the same. They differ in terms of the dynamics of their formation and their functioning.

3. Marital stability and family stability are not one and the same. Female-headed households have been and can be stable over time.

4. There are demographic and socioeconomic reasons why many African American female-headed households are now and have always been predictable and accepted forms of household organization.

5. There is a need to appreciate that women may be primary providers and heads of households in families with both parents present as well as in situations where they are the only parent in the home.

6. It is necessary to refute the notion that female-headed households are the main cause of the deplorable conditions of poverty, crime, and hopelessness found among Blacks in many inner cities.

First, in order to understand families and households among African Americans, one must realize that *these groupings evolved from African family structure, in which co-residential extended families were the norm* (*Infra,* chaps. 7, 8, 2). To varying degrees in different parts of the United States, the organization of many African American households and families still reflects that extended family background. It is important to mention this because many researchers and policymakers studying Black families look only at individual households and therefore miss the "web of kinship" (Fortes 1949) and patterns of cooperation that tie these households together.

Historically, in parts of America where conditions permitted it, different constituent families within large Black extended families built their houses near each other on commonly owned land, thereby creating living areas resembling African compounds. Two of my former students, Dr. Mary Faith Mitchell and Mr. Bamidele Agbasegbe Demerson, found such patterns in the Sea Islands off the coast of South Carolina in the early 1970s (Demerson 1991). In fact, such clusters of individual households, headed by couples and by single women, could be found in various parts of the South before African Americans began to lose control over much of the land they had acquired after slavery.

In many places, even where households were or are spatially separated from one another, cross-residential or transresidential cooperation was and continues to be an important factor in rearing children, providing financial support in times of need, caring for aged family members, and providing shelter for various kinfolk who need it from time to time. These patterns of cross-residential cooperation are not static. They have changed over time, but the work of contemporary scholars such as Carol Stack (1974) and Joyce Aschenbrenner (1975) shows that these patterns of cooperation have been a very important factor in the survival of Black families in cities as well as in rural areas throughout America. Thus many female-headed households have had bases of support in other households. Unfortunately, however, in the United States today, the poverty that engulfs the majority of African Americans is threatening the very survival of these traditional self-help extended family networks. This sea of poverty has a particularly negative impact on households headed by women. Yet, we must not forget that most female-headed households among the poor would be in an even worse condition without the extended family networks and patterns of cross-residential cooperation that still exist.

The second point to be stressed in this paper is the need to understand that *different dynamics underlie the formation and functioning of different types of female-headed households*. These households may represent entirely different phases in the developmental cycle of a family group. For example, households headed by young, never-married women are different from households headed by widows. The latter are appropriately understood as a phase in the life-cycle of what was a two-parent household. The former may be an incipient two-parent household or it may remain a female-headed household throughout the life of the mother. Households headed by widows and older mature women who are divorced or separated from their husbands or mates predictably function differently from those headed by younger mothers. Thus, age as well as maturity and previous marital status of the household head need to be taken into consideration in any discussion of households and families headed by women.

In this connection, it is very important to note that the pattern of young mothers living alone with their children, a pattern discussed a great deal today, is a relatively recent phenomenon among African Americans. In the 1950s, when I was a teenager, young Black women who had children outside of wedlock usually lived in households headed by their mothers, grandmothers, parents, grandparents, or other senior relatives. They did not live alone. The younger the mother, the longer she would probably live with other adults. It is my hypothesis that *the phenomenal rise in the number of single-parent households among African Americans is as much a consequence of a change in residential patterns as it is the result of a higher incidence of teenage pregnancies.* The large number of isolated households headed by young single mothers today is directly related to public welfare policies and public housing policies that, over the years, discouraged and/or disallowed the multi-generational households that were characteristic of Black families, whether they were headed by women or by married couples (*Infra*, chap. 7; Jewell 1988). The breakup of multi-generational female-headed households and multi-generational two-parent-headed households automatically results in a higher incidence of households headed by young women. Where, for example, in the past a woman, her adult son, two adult daughters, and the daughters' children might have been found living in one household, we now might find the mother and the son in one household and each of the daughters and their children living in separate households. Thus, we have three female-headed households to be counted by the census takers, where 30 or 40 years ago we probably would have had only one.

My third point relates to the *need to expunge the misconception that marital stability and family stability are one and the same,* and that family stability can be found only in two-parent households. In several of my earlier papers, I stressed that traditional Black female-headed households were built around several adult consanguineal or "blood" relatives rather that around a single adult woman (*Infra*, chaps. 7, 8, 2). Such consanguineally-based households typically included a woman, some of her adult children, perhaps a sister, and the dependent children of one or more of the women. The core of adult relatives was often a stable unit that remained together over time and provided an environment for bringing up children that could be just as supportive as an environment provided by a two-parent family. Many writers have tended to focus on the absent father in such households, while neglecting the *critical support provided by adult males in the roles of sons, brothers, and uncles.* Some of these men lived with their mothers or sisters in female-headed households. Others headed households that were a part of the extended family network on which their mothers or sisters depended. In both circumstances, *these men provided important role models for the children as well as financial and emotional support for their kinswomen.* Although today many Black males do not have jobs that would enable them to continue this pattern of support for their female relatives, some still provide financial assistance to their mothers and sisters as well as to their wives or girlfriends.

The main point here is that discussions of family stability that focus only on the roles of husband and wife or father and mother overlook the stability and support that traditionally have been provided by a nucleus of consanguineal relatives in African American households headed by women. The instability of the marital bond cannot be taken as an infallible barometer of family instability among African Americans because they have main-tained the African commitment to "blood" kin and have used those bonds of kinship as building blocks for a significant pro-portion of their households and families (McAdoo [J.] 1988; Manns 1988).

A fourth point that needs to be addressed concerns *the legit-imacy of female-headed households as an alternative form of domes-tic organization among Blacks.* Andrew Billingsley (1968) pointed out more than two decades ago that, historically, about 25 per-cent of Black families had been headed by women—a minority to be sure, but a significant number. In 1985, the proportion of Black families headed by women approached 50 percent. As African American scholars and professionals, we must acknowl-edge, unequivocally, that *female-headed households have been—and are—one accepted form of domestic organization in our communities.* Such households have always been a "legitimate" (though not necessarily the most preferred) family form among African Americans. Blacks have historically understood and accepted that some women had to conceive and/or rear children without husbands if they were going to have children at all.

Underlying this acceptance was and is the fundamental fact that African Americans, like their African ancestors, still place a high value on having children. As I said in a paper published more than 15 years ago, the maiden aunt is a rarity, almost an anomaly, among Africans and peoples of African descent (*Infra*, ch. 1). The high value we place on children has always meant that African American women could have children out of wedlock without the stigma placed on many white women in the same situation. Charles S. Johnson (1934:66-69), the eminent sociologist of the first half of the twentieth century, long ago pointed out that Blacks did not stigmatize children as "illegitimate" simply because their parents were not married when they were born. (Parenthetically, I might note that white women are now demanding the right to be single mothers and to rear their children without stigma.)[1]

African Americans understood that a number of factors made it impossible for all women to have or to rear children within the framework of marriage. Unlike Africa, where polygamy (or, more technically, polygyny) was sanctioned, in the United States a man could have only one wife at a time. Yet, factors such as the higher birthrate of females over males, earlier deaths of males, the migration of males in search of work, and the incarceration and execution of large numbers of Black males during their prime reproductive years, converged to cause a relative scarcity of males in relation to females in many Black communities. Some men responded to the realities of this unequal sex ratio by having serial marriages and/or common-law living arrangements with various women. Other men remained legally monogamous while maintaining liaisons with other women. But we cannot "blame" men, as many are wont to do, for these domestic patterns, any more that we can "blame" women for their behavioral responses to the shortage of men. Many women have sought the companionship of married men because they saw themselves as having no other options. Moreover, many African American wives have accepted the pattern of what contemporary Africans now call "outside wives," because they know they have to share their husbands or risk losing them altogether. Among African Americans, as among ostensibly monogamous Africans, as long as the husbands give public respect and recognition to their legal wives, many of these women tolerate their husbands' infidelities as an option preferable to divorce.

These realities must be taken into account when we analyze the phenomenon of single motherhood. Of course, we are rightly concerned about curbing the rising number of teenage pregnancies and the consequent number of households headed by young single women. But we must be realistic about the totality of the phenomenon we are addressing. *Female-headed households are not just the consequence or the result of teenage pregnancies. Many are alternative forms of family organization that mature Black women have adopted in the face of the demographic, economic, political, and social realities* of Black life in America.[2]

The fifth point that needs to be clarified concerns the role of women as co-providers or sole providers in households where both husbands and wives are present. Because most of the discussion of family and household dynamics assumes male headship whenever a male is present, the female-headed household with a male spouse present is virtually unexplored in the literature.[3] Yet we know that the unemployment of Black males has led to the existence of a number of households where wives or girlfriends are the sole providers and the *de facto* heads of "two- parent" households.

This raises the more general point of a need to understand all types of domestic arrangements in which women assume all or most of the responsibility for providing for themselves and their children. The anthropological and historical data show that, *regardless of household structure, in most parts of the world in most social classes, women have been co-providers or primary providers* for themselves and their children. We have not sufficiently focused our attention on this fact under conditions where women live with their husbands. We are unable, therefore, to understand what is different when they live alone with their children or with their children and other family members.

As female scholars, we should be the last to be seduced by the myth of the male provider, if by that is meant "sole provider." Historically, women have worked in the fields, in the marketplace, in factories, and in the home to shoulder much of the responsibility for the support of their children and themselves. It is equally true, historically, that much of the wealth generated by men has gone to support and validate their political, social, economic, and military positions in society, rather than solely or even mainly toward the ongoing material needs of their families. It is only within a relatively brief period of Western history that women and children in the privileged classes have been supported more or less entirely by men. And even there, researchers in women's studies have shown that the value of the in-kind contribution of these women to their domestic units has been greatly underrated. Moreover, for women in the very elite classes, it is not so much their husbands who have supported them as it is the masses of people in the lower classes whose work has supported them both.

The more typical pattern that we find in the world is not one of male providers but of male and female co-providers of support for their families. Women have usually been and will continue to be a major source of material and financial support—as well as the major source of emotional support—for their children. In the case of African American women, if we want to explore fully their contributions as heads of households, we need to include an examination of their economic roles in families where they live with their husbands or mates as well as those in which they live as single parents.

My last point in this chapter focuses on the need to expose *the myth that female-headed households are the root cause of the deplorable conditions in which many Blacks find themselves in urban ghettos.* As I wrote in an article in *Sisters* magazine, this myth is hardest to overcome because many Blacks themselves have accepted it as truth (*Infra,* chap. 2). They have been led to believe that Black family structure is the main cause of the high rates of crime, unemployment, school dropouts, teenage pregnancies, drug abuse, and disaffection among young people in many of our inner cities. Their views are shaped by scholars and journalists who refuse to acknowledge that those African Americans whom William Julius Wilson (1987) calls the "truly disadvantaged" are caught in a black hole of poverty that is not of their own making and that creates vicious cycles of deprivation that most cannot escape. Of course, some of the African American family patterns developed in response to abject poverty have themselves become factors in perpetuating the distressing conditions in many inner cities. But the structure of the Black family (which in this context usually refers to female-headed households) cannot be labeled the root cause of the wretched conditions of poverty; the reverse is more probably the case. In fact, it is virtually impossible to envision a change in family structure so long as the systemic unemployment of males and other conditions of poverty and deprivation persist. Moreover, the evidence is unequivocal that most *two-parent* families in the ghettos are often powerless to combat the drugs, crime, and degradation that grow out of the conditions of poverty in which they live.

Ironically and sadly, one reason it is difficult to wipe out drug-related crime in Black communities is that some families, particularly those headed by women, have come to depend on the income they receive from the young men who are the ones mainly involved in illicit drug traffic. In the face of the chronic and systemic unemployment of young Black males, drug money becomes the alternative to no money at all. Too often, the relatives of young drug dealers look the other way when members of their community seek to mobilize to stamp out narcotics. This dependence on the underground economy, which of course is not unique to African Americans, is one of the patterns that must be broken if we are to rescue Black families who are long-term victims, even if they think of themselves as short-term beneficiaries, of the illegal drug traffic and the violence it breeds.

All the evidence we have shows that the social pathologies that are allegedly caused by Black family structure rapidly improve when people in poverty are provided with skills and jobs to earn a decent living. William Julius Wilson's book *The Truly Disadvantaged* (1987) demonstrates that the extraordinarily high rates of unemployment and despair among young Black males, along with the violent drug subculture that offers them easy money and continuous highs, are the root causes of crime and degradation in the inner cities. Eliminating these conditions will require a relentless and total war on drugs and unemployment, not a war on Black families.

CONCLUSION

As we formulate plans and seek models for improving African American families, we must not be seduced by the myth that only the nuclear family can provide the stability and support necessary to ensure the survival and success of our communities in the twenty-first century. Rather, we should explore ways in which the values of cooperation and reciprocity that allowed female-headed households to thrive within the context of the extended family can be revived and rekindled in the context of the realities of family organization of the present day. In the arena of public housing, we need to call for policies that do not disallow or discriminate against extended family households. These multi-generational domestic units can be an answer to the problems facing young single mothers living alone, struggling to find the support that would enable them to go out to work to sustain themselves and their children. Elderly mothers and grandmothers now living alone with time on their hands could look after the children of these young working mothers, as elderly Black women did in the past.

We also need to use African American institutions such as churches, sororities, fraternities, and other community groups to begin private initiatives to bring together adults from different generations and both genders to discuss and plan for the African American family of the future. These organizations can mobilize financial resources to design and build new types of housing units that would accommodate families of varying sizes and configurations. Rather than assume that a family unit must be the proverbial nuclear family of husband, wife, and two children, we must recognize that the key to the survival of African Americans has always been the flexibility and adaptability of our family organization. We must remember that our first effective economic and social networks were extended family networks. We can now use ties of kinship and friendship to create new domestic networks for the new age, networks that will embrace and affirm families that are headed by women, by men, or by both.

NOTES

1. A 1995 Report to Congress by the U.S. Department of Health and Human Services (HHS), entitled *Out-of-Wedlock Childbearing,* confirms the growth in the numbers of births to unmarried white women, a trend that was obvious in 1987 when this paper was first presented. According to the report, in 1993, white women gave birth to 60 percent of the babies born outside of marriage (DHHS Pub. No. PHS 95-1257, September 1995).
2. The aforementioned HHS Report also shows that teenage pregnancies do not account for most of the births outside of marriage. In 1993, single women over twenty years old gave birth to 70 percent of the babies born out of wedlock (DHHS Pub. No. PHS 95-1257, September 1995).
3. A very important paper on the concept of provider and co-provider was

brought to my attention after this paper was presented (Hood 1986). It explores a number of the points I raised on this subject.

Speaking Up
for Single Mothers

Isn't it about time that African Americans demanded a halt to the derogatory characterizations of single mothers and female-headed households that abound in the scholarly literature as well as in the popular press? How many of us owe our success to mothers who struggled to bring us up by themselves or with the help of their mothers and other women? Would we characterize our families as "unstable" or "pathological" simply because they were headed by women? Have we ever stopped to think that people who do so are talking about our Mamas?

Historically, the adaptability and flexibility of African American families has been one of our community's strengths. Households headed by women as well as those headed by married couples were accepted as a part of the normal pattern of everyday life, even by those whose preference was for the two-parent family. Without being sociologists, African Americans understood that many factors contributed to the relatively high incidence of female-headed households in the Black community. In many places, there was a shortage of Black males in relation to females because of the greater number of women born in the population, the shorter natural life span of Black men, the migration of some Black men in search of work, and the incarceration and execution of large numbers of Black males during their prime reproductive years. Given these demographic realities and the strong traditionally African value placed on having children, African Americans understood and accepted that some women had to *bear* children without husbands, if they were going to have children at all. The same demographic realities also contributed to relatively high rates of marital separation and widowhood, hence, some women also had to *rear* children without husbands, whether they wanted to or not.

Historians and sociologists have pointed out that from the period of slavery through the early 1960s, female-headed households constituted between 20 percent and 25 percent of all Black family households. By 1985, according to the U.S. Census Bureau, a total of 43 percent of Black households were headed by women, and of these, 28 percent were comprised of mothers living with their children. The remaining 15 percent were various other combinations such as grandmothers and their grandchildren or women heading households that included their brothers and sisters, cousins, or other relatives. It is important to recognize that, until recently, virtually all female-headed households in the Black community were headed by mature women, not by teenagers. The younger mothers lived in households with their parents or other adults. Although some female heads of households never married, most of them were separated or widowed. (Legal divorce was not common, particularly in the working class.) Usually, these households had three or more generations in them. For example, they might include a woman, an adult or teenage daughter or sister and their children as well as the dependent children of the woman herself. It was also common for a woman's adult sons to live with her until they got married, which could be well into their twenties or thirties. Together, the adults in the house provided for its upkeep as well as for the children in their care. The respect accorded women in the community did not depend on whether they were married or not. Many female heads of households were leaders in their churches, lodges, and other community organizations.

Contrary to prevailing views outside the Black community, *households headed by women were not inherently unstable, nor were the children in them necessarily disadvantaged.* Most single mothers worked for a living, owned or rented their homes, and made many sacrifices in order to give their children more education than they had had. When I was growing up, this often meant just getting the children through high school, but many women, like my own mother, put their children through college as well. Relatives residing in different households were usually closely linked together in extended family networks that helped to provide child care as well as financial assistance when needed. The children in some of these households may not have had fathers in the home, but they had brothers, uncles, grandfathers, and other male relatives who served as role models and took an active part in their upbringing. And, in fact, the fathers themselves often helped to take care of their children even though they resided elsewhere. Moreover, the pattern of teenage mothers living alone with their children, which people nowadays tend to think of when they think of single mothers, is something relatively new in the Black community. When I was a teenager in the 1950s, and before that when my mother was growing up, young Black women who had children outside of wedlock did not move into separate households. They lived with their parents or other adults until they got married or reached a level of self-sufficiency to move out on their own. In some cases they lived with their mothers until the older women died, and then carried on as heads of households started generations before.

It is my hypothesis that the phenomenal rise in the number of Black female-headed households over the past two decades is more a consequence of changing residential patterns than it is the result of an increase in the incidence of teenage pregnancies. The large number of isolated households headed by young single mothers stems in part from public welfare policies and public housing regulations which, over the years, discouraged or disallowed the multi-generational households that were characteristic of Black families of the past. The incidence of young mothers living alone with their children is also due to the generally smaller size of apartments available for rent, particularly in cities, and to the growing acceptance by African Americans of the Euro-American notion that the "need for privacy" takes precedence over the need for family.

If we look at residential patterns of Black women living in cities today, we might find a mother in her early forties living in an apartment with her dependent children, while two of her daughters in their late teens or early twenties are living in separate apartments with their children. Thirty years ago all three women and their children would have been under one roof, constituting one female-headed household. The 1990 census takers would have enumerated three separate female-headed households. The problems faced by many of these young women living alone with their children are monumental. Not only are they poor, but they lack the security and support of the multi-generational households and extended family networks that provided for generations of single mothers before them. One of the solutions we ought to consider as a matter of public policy, is to provide adequate housing and monetary assistance to allow young single mothers to remain in households with their mothers, parents, or other adult relatives.

Even as we seek solutions to the problems facing teenage mothers, it is important to remember that these young women are still the minority of women who head households in African American communities today. There are still many mature Black women who are heading families by necessity or by choice. To characterize their families as "unstable" or "pathological" simply because they do not conform to the nuclear family ideal of a married couple and their children is unfounded and irresponsible. Despite the fact that the nuclear family is rapidly disappearing as the norm in most ethnic groups and social classes in America, its proponents still proclaim it as the most stable form of the family. Despite the increase in the incidence of divorce over the past few decades, many people still equate family stability with marital stability. Children living with single parents continue to have their households stigmatized as "broken homes," even though continuity and stability may be provided by a core of adult "blood relatives" living in the home.

It is about time that we insist that a good family—a stable family—cannot be determined by looking at the gender of its head nor by counting the number of people at its helm. Stability is determined by the nature of the relationships within the family; by the commitment and concern its members demonstrate for one another; by the values that are passed on from one generation to the next; and by the continuity that is evident when one looks at the composition and organization of the family over time. From this perspective, we see the need to understand and appreciate the stability in African American families headed by women as well as in families headed by married couples or by men. From this point of view, we must commend not condemn the many single mothers who made these families among the most respectable and respected in many of our communities. We cannot allow detractors to make us forget this fact.

AFRICAN AMERICAN FAMILIES
AND FAMILY VALUES

INTRODUCTION

All over America, families are changing. The American ideal of the
nuclear family, comprised of two parents and their children, is
only one of many different types of family grouping likely to
occupy a single household today. Various permutations of the
"step-family"—resulting from the marriage of couples with children from previous marriages—are commonplace. Households
comprised of single mothers and their children have increased
dramatically over the past 25 years. Single parenting by men is also
on the rise, as is the incidence of parenting by couples of the same
gender. Public policy discussions and debate over these changes,
however, have focused not on the economic, demographic, and
sociological forces underlying them; rather, these discussions have
tended to portray changes in family structure as *moral* failures that
signal a breakdown in the fabric of our society. Thus, instead of
being urged to understand and assess these emerging forms of the
family in order to influence their development, the public is
warned against (1) the "alarming disintegration" of the nuclear
family, and (2) the "loss of traditional family values."

No less than three Presidents have identified the "disintegration of the family" and the "loss of family values" as issues of
national concern. Former Presidents Ronald Reagan and George
Bush (along with former Vice President Dan Quayle) exhorted

the country to "return to traditional family values." Currently, President Bill Clinton is focusing his efforts on restoring and-strengthening the nuclear family. An attentive observer recognizes right away that these different emphases are actually two stanzas of the same lament for the "demise" of the American family. And no matter what particular "spin" is given to this theme, the stated or unstated premise is the same: something is "wrong" with families throughout America, but there is "more wrong" with Black families than with any others. Although families in various ethnic groups and at various income levels are recognized as undergoing change, *only* the *African American* family is consistently described as being *"in crisis."* Other families are "in transition"—African American families are portrayed as being "on the brink of collapse."

Starting from this premise, a number of journalists, scholars, and public officials proceed to lay the blame for the relatively high incidence of crime that occurs in certain Black neighborhoods on the "disintegration of the Black family" and the "absence of family values" in the African American community at large. Despite the persuasive evidence and arguments presented by William Julius Wilson in his book *The Truly Disadvantaged* (1987) that poverty and unemployment are the fundamental causes and predictors of high crime rates among African Americans, we still hear that the Black family is the "root cause" of these social problems. This notion of the "pathological" Black family, traceable to Daniel Patrick Monyihan (1965) and others, still dominates thinking about the form and function of African American families, and still misinforms makers of public policies supposedly designed to assist those families.

The primary goal of the present essay is to place the recent changes in African American family structures in their historical context in order to better understand and interpret these changes. The essay asks: What do we know about the earliest African American families, and what do we know about the changes that these families have undergone from the period of slavery to the present day? The discussion begins with an overview of West African family structure, because most of the enslaved population came from this region. Understanding the family structure brought by the Africans who came to America in chains is essential to an understanding of what happened to these families as they adapted and evolved during slavery and afterward.

Obviously, we cannot explain African American families *only* by reference to their West African cultural antecedents. By the same token, we cannot understand African American families *without* taking into account the West African family structures out of which they evolved. Scholars from E. Franklin Frazier (1939) to Andrew Billingsley (1992) have emphasized the adaptive nature of African American families. Indeed, African American families, like all families, are by their very nature *adaptive institutions*. Thus, in analyzing the changing structure of African American families, one must examine the contexts and conditions that influenced those changes. Slavery, segregation, urbanization, changing economic conditions, changing educational opportunities, changing demographics, housing options, welfare restrictions and other public policies—all must be taken into account. Yet, one cannot begin to speak of the adaptation of any structure to any condition unless one knows *what the structure was to begin with*. Thus, in the case of African American families, we must first understand the African family structures that were brought to America in order to analyze, assess, and appreciate how those structures adapted and changed over time. In that way, we can better interpret what we see today.

The first part of this essay provides an overview of the African extended family out of which African American families evolved, and discusses some aspects of the transformation of African families into African American families during the period of slavery and beyond. In reviewing African family structures, and in seeking to interpret some of the changes in them that occurred in America, many complex aspects of family organization are greatly simplified, and lengthy scholarly debates abbreviated or only alluded to. Readers are encouraged, therefore, to trace the various arguments back to the publications in which they were first set forth. The second and third sections of this essay call attention to special aspects of African American household and family organization, and outline the changes that have occurred in these structures in the past thirty years. Drawing on data in Billingsley's recent book *Climbing Jacob's Ladder*, the paper highlights the extraordinary decline in two-parent households, the phenomenal increase in female-headed households, and the increase in households with individuals living by themselves (Billingsley 1992, chap. 1).

In this connection, the book *Survival of the Black Family: The Institutional Impact of U.S. Social Policy*, by K. Sue Jewell, is often cited to support the view that many of the changes in African American family structure that have occurred in the past thirty years are directly linked to welfare policies and programs, especially the program known as Aid to Families with Dependent Children (AFDC). The central argument in this copiously documented and cogently argued book is that female-headed households have proliferated as a result of welfare policies that discouraged or disallowed males in the home (see also *Infra*, chaps. 3, 8).

Of the various changes in family structure documented by Billingsley and Jewell, the most far-reaching is the proliferation of female-headed households, especially two-generational households in which women are living alone with their children. Most writers, including Billingsley (1992) and Jewell (1988), attribute the phenomenal increase in this type of household to the *break-down* of the nuclear family. I suggest that this is also the result of the *break-up* of the multi-generational, female-headed household that was common before the welfare system encouraged and enabled young mothers to live alone with their children (*Infra*, chap. 3). The implications of this point are very important. Instead of focusing solely on strengthening and rebuilding nuclear families, we would also acknowledge the benefit of reconnecting and strengthening multi-generational female-headed households that have proven in the past that they too could be a source of stability and upward mobility within the African American community.

Part four of this essay takes up the issue of "family values" from an African American perspective. Virtually every historian or sociologist—Black or White—writing on the African American experience, has remarked on the importance of families in the life of African Americans. Many scholars, including myself, consider the family, especially the extended family, to have been the institution most responsible for the survival of African people in the United States and elsewhere in the Americas. Some might argue for the primacy of the church because of its centrality in the life of African American families, but even they would have to acknowledge the more pervasive role of immediate and extended families themselves in providing for the well-being of their members.

How could these families so revered by African Americans become so reviled by our White American compatriots? *How could anyone who knows the historical (and the present day) dynamics in African American families maintain that they have no "family values"?* One part of the answer is clear. Most White Americans know little or nothing about African American families beyond the negative stereotypes portrayed in the visual media and sensationalized in the press. Another part of the answer is that many White Americans, like many other people of European descent, still cling to nineteenth-century notions about the racial superiority of their group and the cultural superiority of their institutions. Simply because African families and those of their descendants differ from the European ideal of the nuclear family, they have been denigrated by many with no thought that there might be something to gain by studying these institutions.

In discussing African American family values, I first survey some of the values other scholars of Black family life have identified as important through their research. Then I discuss seven values that emerged from my own research as constituting seven guiding principles for interpersonal relations within African families, both of the past and, to some extent, of the present. I suggest that these "Seven Rs" (as I call them)—respect, responsibility, reciprocity, restraint, reverence, reason, and reconciliation—are principles that can be universally embraced by those seeking ways to strengthen African American families and communities today.

This essay concludes by reiterating the need to shun the pejorative in describing and analyzing African American families and focus instead on understanding their dynamics in order to develop and implement policies that will have a truly positive impact on the family's future. My final point is that all social ills in the Black community cannot and should not be laid at the doorstep of the African American family. As many persons have observed, and as Andrew Billingsley puts it in Climbing Jacob's Ladder, "societies make families" just as "families make societies." Billingsley also points out: "The so-called black family crisis is not of their own making; nor is it the worst crisis they ever faced and survived" (Billingsley 1992:79). In my judgment, this is both a justifiable conclusion from the evidence on the history of Black families in America and an appropriate starting point for analyses and action that would address the problems Black families face.

AFRICAN ROOTS OF THE AFRICAN AMERICAN FAMILY

To understand African American families today, one must understand their evolution over time. Fundamentally, they grew out of African institutions, brought to the Americas by enslaved populations over a period of centuries. Over time, the transplanted African families evolved into African American families, Afro-Caribbean families, Afro-Brazilian families, etc. In the various countries or regions where the enslaved Africans were settled, they were forced to accommodate and adapt to whatever European laws and traditions prevailed. Nevertheless, the similarities evident in family life among people of African descent throughout the Americas are a testament to the strength and viability of the extended family, which is one of the two most important kinship groupings throughout Sub-Saharan Africa, the other being the lineage.

Not surprisingly, throughout the Americas, surviving features of African family structure tend to be strongest among the lower income segments of the Black population. The greater the income and the higher the formal education of Africa's descendants, the more their family organization and other socio-cultural attributes are intentionally or unintentionally patterned after the European-derived dominant group. Everywhere, formal education and exposure to the dominant group have tended to validate and reinforce the culture and lifestyles of that group.

African extended families were (and are) large, multi-generational groupings of relatives built around a core group known as a "lineage." What is a lineage? This may be described as a group of "blood relatives" who trace their descent back to a common male ancestor through a line of males (in societies such as the Yoruba of Nigeria) or back to a female ancestor through a line of females (in societies such as the Ashanti of Ghana) (see Figures 1 and 2). Those lineages that trace descent through the father-line are termed patrilineages and those that trace descent through the mother-line are termed matrilineages. Because lineage members are prohibited from marrying each other, they must take their

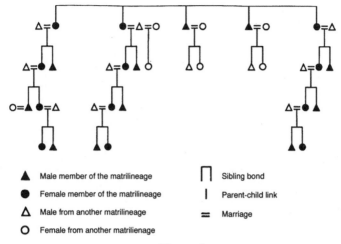

▲ Male member of the matrilineage   ⊓ Sibling bond

● Female member of the matrilineage | Parent-child link

△ Male from another matrilineage   = Marriage

○ Female from another matrilienage

Figure 1.
Schematic View of a Matrilineage

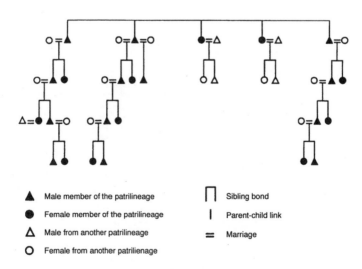

▲ Male member of the patrilineage   ⊓ Sibling bond

● Female member of the patrilineage | Parent-child link

△ Male from another patrilineage   = Marriage

○ Female from another patrilienage

Figure 2.
Schematic View of a Patrilineage

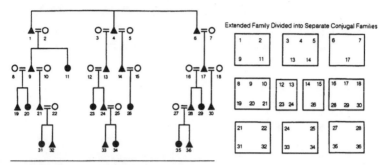

Extended Family Divided into Separate Conjugal Families

Extended families showing division into lineage members (dark) and wives who come from other lineages (uncolored)

▲ Male member of the patrilineal core of the extended family

● Female member of the patrilineal core of the extended family

○ "Wives of the Compound" (wives who marry in from other lineages)

∏ Sibling bond

| Parent-child link

= Marriage

Schematic Compound
Showing Rooms Occupied by Extended Family Members on Kinship Diagram Above

Compound
Entrance

Figure 3.
Schematic View of an Extended Family
Occupying a Single Compound

spouses from other lineages. In this way, extended families are created. The adult members of an extended family consist of the lineage members who form the core group, and their spouses who "marry-in" from different lineages. According to whether the rule of descent was patrilineal or matrilineal, the children (both male and female) are considered to be born into the lineage of their fathers (in patrilineal societies such as the Yoruba) or that of their mothers (in matrilineal societies such as the Ashanti).

Traditionally, extended families lived together in residential units we term compounds. In the countryside, a compound might be a collection of small conically shaped, one room mud-brick (i.e., adobe) houses facing inward around a large circular courtyard. To visualize a compound within the towns, imagine a series of one-story or two-story houses built adjacent to one another and enclosed with a large fence or wall; or picture a one-story structure built in a square, facing inward onto a large courtyard. Each side of the square-shaped building would be divided up into adjacent rooms facing a veranda or corridor that opens onto the courtyard. Members of the compound might use the courtyard for recreation, for outdoor cooking, for meetings, etc. The back walls of such compounds would have small, highly situated windows, forming a continuous barrier to the outside. One enters the compound through centrally located gates or large heavy doors (see Figure 3).

Many families were (and are) so large that their compounds are made up of not just one, but several such square buildings and the entire cluster of dwellings might be enclosed by a wall. A compound might house 30 or 40 people, or its residents could number in the hundreds. Royal compounds might have thousands of members. Each compound, whether made up of one large dwelling or several such dwellings, is named after the lineage that forms the core of the extended family occupying the compound. The land on which a compound is built is collectively owned by a lineage, and lineage members build and own the houses themselves. The oldest member of the lineage is its head, and all important decisions concerning the lineage or the compound must be made or approved by the lineage head and the other elders.

From this brief description of West African extended families, it may be deduced that each extended family occupying a compound may be looked at from two perspectives. From the perspective of the lineage, the extended family consists of their own lineage members, as one component, and their in-marrying spouses as the other component (see Figure 3). Lineage members are related by "blood" ties that are perceived to exist in perpetuity. Spouses are "in-laws" whose relations can be broken "by law," hence they are portrayed as an "outsider group" on certain ceremonial occasions (Marshall 1968; *Infra*, chap. 7).

From the perspective of the individual families created by marriage, the extended family in a compound can be viewed as a group of related conjugal families (see Figure 3). Each of these conjugal families would be made up of a man and his wife or wives and their children. These conjugally based families differed from typical "nuclear families" in several respects (*Infra*, chap. 8). First of all, even when a man has only one wife, the possibility of plural wives was always there. Secondly, because of the lineage principle that linked members of the various conjugal families, children in the same generation grew up more or less like sisters and brothers, rather than strictly separating themselves into siblings versus cousins. In some languages, such as that of the Yoruba, there is not even a word for "cousin," only words for older or younger sibling, and these terms are used for both males and females. Thus, the strength of the lineage principle made the boundaries of African conjugal families far less rigid than those that delineate nuclear families. For example, "uncles" might raise their "nephews" as their "sons" without any mechanism such as formal adoption. Usually, only in legal matters would questions of precise kinship relationships arise.

In describing what happened to African family structure when Africans were captured and enslaved in America, we must acknowledge that the family structures on plantations, as reconstructed from written records and oral history, cannot be viewed as examples of direct *institutional transfer* from Africa to America, but rather as examples of *institutional transformation* that took place from Africa to America (*Infra*, chap. 8). As I have stated previously:

> The extended family networks that were formed during slavery by Africans *and their descendants* were based on the institutional heritage which the Africans

had brought with them to this continent, and the specific forms [these families] took reflected the influence
of European-derived institutions as well as the political and economic circumstances in which the enslaved
population found itself. (infra. chap. 8, pp. 41–42)

The conditions of slavery did not allow the enslaved Africans to
replicate or re-create the compounds and extended families they
had left behind on the African continent. However, even in the
small, cramped slave quarters, one could find multigenerational
families comprised of couples or single mothers their children,
some grandchildren, other relatives and even non-kin. The influence of European norms, as well as the demographics of the plantations, ensured that marriage was usually monogamous, but
several historians have noted instances of polygamy (the commonly used term) where the wives lived in separate houses
(Gutman 1976:59, 158; Blassingame 1972:171; Perdue et al.
1980:209).

Despite the fact that Africans enslaved in America were forced
to compartmentalize their extended families, the importance of
their kinship networks on the plantations and across plantations
has been noted by many historians. Moreover, the continuing
strength of the lineage principle was manifest through the strong
sense of obligations to consanguineal ("blood") relatives. Gutman
put it this way: "the pull between ties to an immediate family and
to an enlarged kin network sometimes strained husbands and
wives" (1976:202; see also Frazier 1966:2).

After slavery, wherever African Americans had access to large
parcels of land, they recreated kin networks that resembled African
extended families and compounds. Parents and their married children lived in houses built in close proximity to one another, and
three and four generations of kin typically resided together in
these houses. Two of my former students, Dr. Mary Faith
Mitchell and Mr. Bamidele Agbasegbe Demerson studied such
compounds in the Sea Islands off the coast of South Carolina in
the early 1970s (Demerson 1991). Even where relatives did not
live in spatial proximity, the extended family ties linked people
across households and even across states, so that relatives could
turn to each other not only for assistance in childrearing, but in
caring for the sick and the aged, in providing accommodations for

51

those who migrated from one state to the other, and in rendering financial support in times of need. Such patterns of transresidential extended family cooperation and support have been reported by contemporary writers such as Stack (1974) and Aschenbrenner (1975), and Billingsley (1992), as well as by many historians and sociologists writing about earlier periods.

To summarize: Enslaved Africans living on plantations could not replicate African compounds. However, their households were often "extended" beyond the nuclear family. Most importantly, they maintained *transresidential kinship networks* that had many of the features of extended families that had resided together in a single compound in West Africa. When we speak of extended families among African Americans, we must always recognize that these are kin groups that transcend individual households. Billingsley (1968 and 1992) uses the term "extended family" to refer to households in which family members such as grandparents reside with nuclear families. Such households do not, in and of themselves, constitute entire extended families. African American extended families embrace many households, some with two generations, some with three or more, and some of these households are headed by women, some by men, and some by both.

HOUSEHOLD FORMATION
AMONG AFRICAN AMERICANS

Several points concerning household formation among African Americans must be made before we examine recent trends in Black family organization.

The first and most general observation is that *family* and *household* are *not the same thing*. (Indeed, in all societies, the notion of family embraces more than a single household.) In contemporary America, however, there is a tendency to treat the concepts of family and household as if they are co-terminus. This tendency stems from the fact that the majority culture in America views the nuclear family formed at marriage as *the* most important family (some would say the "real" family, in comparison to other relatives), and one which ideally should occupy a household separate and apart from that of others. Thus, in many instances, family and household are used interchangeably. For example, the concepts of "two-parent families" and "two-parent households" tend to be used interchangeably. So, too, are the concepts of "single-parent families" and "single-parent households."

Historically, among African Americans, it has always been important to recognize that the term "family" refers not only to family members resident in particular households, but includes extended family members living in other households. Because of the strength of consanguineal ties, particularly those between mothers and children but sometimes also among siblings, one cannot conclude that the nuclear family built around the marital relationship is conceived of as "the" primary family. For many African Americans, marriage does not mean that the husband-wife relationship will "replace" the mother-daughter or mother-son relationship as the primary relationship in the newly married person's life. In the best of circumstances, these relationships become complementary; in the worst of circumstances, as Gutman points out, the consanguineal ties may place a "strain" on the husband-wife relationship. In any case, where these consanguineal ties are very strong, in order to understand the form and functioning of the "immediate" family among African Americans, one would have to study a cluster of related households, not simply any single, isolated "nuclear family" household.

A second general observation to be made concerning household formation among African Americans is that historically, although female-headed households were a minority of the households in the Black community, they were an accepted form of household organization. In fact, because of the general acceptance of female-headed households during slavery and afterward, some writers erroneously proclaimed this to be the typical or normative form of the African American family. Frazier's characterization of *some* Black families as "matriarchal" was generalized by others to refer to "most" Black families. The publication of Herbert Gutman's monumental book, *The Black Family in Slavery and Freedom* (1976), dispelled the myth of the Black family as predominantly "matriarchal" (or "matrifocal," which was the newer and more descriptive characterization). Gutman reported that from the mid-1700s through the mid-1920s, less than one-fourth of African American households were headed by single women. As recently as 1960, only 22 percent of African American families were female headed (Jewell 1988:17; Billingsley 1992:36).

Thus, the incidence of female-headed households did not change much in two hundred years. These data show that, *contrary to popular belief, historically, African American women—like their African "fore-mothers"—typically gave birth to children within the context of marriage.*

The point must be made, however, that a rate of 20 to 25 percent female-headed households within the African American population was still high in comparison with that of the Euro-American population. Billingsley reported that in 1960 only 6 percent of white families with children were headed by women (1968:14). To understand why a larger percentage of African American women were single heads of households, a number of cultural, demographic, and economic factors must be taken into consideration.

First, it must be understood that, historically, African American women, like their African ancestors, placed a very high value on having children, and most of them wanted to have their own children even if they adopted or reared others (*Infra*, chap. 1). Although this has changed somewhat under the influence of "radical feminism," even today very few African American women want to be childless throughout their lives.

Secondly, it must be understood that since polygamy (or, more technically, poly*gyny*, or a plurality of *wives*) was not and still is not a legal form of marriage in the United States, unequal gender ratios among African Americans living in many areas meant that not all marriageable women would be able to find husbands during their prime childbearing years. Some of the factors that contributed (and still contribute) to the preponderance of women over men in many localities include: the death or incarceration of males in their prime reproductive years; the migration of males in search of work; high male unemployment rates, which reduce the number of men available for or interested in, the responsibilities of marriage; the overall higher birth rate of females; and the shorter lifespan of males. Given these factors, and the high value placed on children, it is not surprising that historically nearly one-fourth of all African American families were headed by single women (*Infra*, chap. 3). This does not mean that the incidence of female-headed households was or is solely due to the birth of children out of wedlock. Some of the same factors mentioned above as contributing to the gender imbalance between males and females in some localities also contribute to a relatively high incidence of divorce, separation, and widowhood among African Americans. Thus, now and in the past, many mature, previously married women are among those heading single-parent households (Billingsley 1968, 1993; Jewell 1988; *Infra*, chap. 3).

Turning from the issues surrounding the formation of female-headed households, the third point I want to make concerning household formation among African Americans relates to the notion of the "household head" itself. In the sociological literature and in the media in this country, considerable emphasis is placed on the question of who heads a household or who heads a family. In fact, the way the question is asked presumes that the answer is a straightforward, easily discernible fact. In the case of African American households, however, several caveats need to be raised concerning the concept of "household headship." (1) The answer to the question, "Who heads a household?" may differ depending on whether one is thinking about the primary decision maker or the primary provider. (2) Key decision makers for a given household may not even reside in that household. This is especially true nowadays when households are headed by young single mothers who are dependent on other adults for advice and various forms of support. (3) In order to understand the functioning of a household, it is sometimes more important to understand who are the core adults in the household, rather who "heads" it. Historically, this was particularly the case in multi-generational female-headed households. The oldest adults in the house (who might be two or three sisters, a sister and a brother, or an older woman and her mature daughters) might share the responsibilities of headship, both in terms of decision making and in terms of financial support.

The fourth and final point I wish to make concerning household formation among African Americans is that historically, when we look at *households headed by married couples*, we see that they (*like female-headed households*) *also typically included relatives other than parents and children* (see, e.g., Billingsley 1968; Stack 1974; Aschenbrenner 1975). Many of these two parent households were multi-generational through the inclusion of grandchildren or a parent or parents of one of the spouses. Many of them were also "extended" laterally to include an uncle, aunt, cousin, niece, or nephew. In other words, *even these two-parent families were not typical nuclear families.* In the section that follows, I observe that the break-up of multi-generational households headed by women and by married couples subsumes and accounts for all the major trends that have been identified in Black family and household organization over the past few decades.

RECENT CHANGES IN AFRICAN AMERICAN FAMILY AND HOUSEHOLD ORGANIZATION

Without question, *the major change that has occurred in Black family organization in the last three decades has been the rise in the number of female-headed households.* The percentage of female-headed households among African Americans has almost tripled in thirty years, a phenomenal increase that we are only beginning to understand. Billingsley notes:

> ...the incidence of one of the alternatives to the traditional family, the female-headed single-parent family, has escalated enormously over the past generation. Consisting of a minority of 20 percent [actually 22 percent] of families with children in 1960, this family form had increased to 33 percent by 1970, to 49 percent by 1980, and to a whopping 57 percent by 1990. Over the same period single fathers bringing up their own children increased from 2 percent to 4 percent. (Billingsley 1992:36-37)

Billingsley goes on to make the very interesting point that the change in household headship is mainly a reflection of changing marriage patterns rather than an indication of a diminishing commitment to family or to family living.

> The major observation here is that both black men and women have been avoiding or abandoning marriage in record numbers during recent years. *But this is more a shift in the marriage relation than in the family"* [emphasis added]. Marriage, as has been pointed out above, is only one of several bases for family formation and endurance. The allegiance to families is still so strong that on any given day the overwhelming majority of African-American people will be found living in families of one type or another. In 1990, for example,

70 percent of the 10.5 million African-American households were family households with persons related by
blood, marriage, or adoption. (Billingsley 1992:37)

This observation supports a point that cannot be overem-
phasized, namely, that *marital stability and family stability are not
one and the same.* Twenty years ago, I noted that:

Black families are not necessarily centered around conjugal unions, which are the *sine qua non* of the nuclear
family. Among blacks, households centered around
consanguineal relatives have as much legitimacy (and
for most people, as much respectability) *as family units*
as do households centered around conjugal unions.
When this fact is understood, it becomes clear that the
instability of conjugal relations cannot be taken as the
sole measure of the instability of the family. That black
families exhibit considerable stability over time and
space is evidenced by the enduring linkages and bonds
of mutual obligation found among networks of consanguineal kin. (*Infra*, chap. 1, p. 8)

In the case of nuclear families, divorce signals "the breakdown"
of at least one family, but where consanguineal relationships form
the core of the family, the failure of a marriage or a companionate relationship does not necessarily have a disruptive effect on the
unit, although it might have emotional effects on individuals concerned.

As stated earlier, in my view, the African American commitment to consanguineal ("blood") relatives is traceable back to
Africa where lineage ties based on descent (rather than marital ties
based "in-law") provided the primary source of stability within
extended families living together in compounds (Sudarkasa
1980:47-48, 1981:43-44). In the United States, the dependence
on "blood relatives" as a source of support and stability in the
family remained strong among African Americans, even in the
face of the white American idea that the primary source of family stability was the marriage bond that formed the core of the
nuclear family. The strength and stability of these consanguineal
ties, as Gutman suggested, could be one cause of the fragility of
marriage bonds noted among African Americans. Obligations to

the extended family could be a source of dissension between couples, particularly when these obligations appeared to consume resources and time that could be devoted to the spouse and the conjugal family. Moreover, because the extended family was present as a source of support when a divorce or separation did occur, marital dissolution was less threatening and less traumatic for the partners involved (*Infra*, chap. 8).

Now, in the 1990s, we are facing a situation in which a great increase in the percentage of female-headed households, particularly among the working and non-working poor where they constitute upwards of 70 percent of all households, means that these single parents must depend on their "blood" relatives for stability and support if there is to be any family stability at all. Yet, one of the most alarming changes that has occurred since 1960 renders this support less readily available to them than it was in the past. I refer to the fact that *nowadays many young single mothers are living alone with their children, whereas in the past most of them would have been living in households with other adult relatives* who could provide economic assistance, emotional support, and most importantly, advice and assistance in the rearing of their children.

It is very important to point out that the pattern of single mothers living alone with their children is a recent phenomenon among African Americans. As a teenager in the 1950s, I witnessed a relatively high dropout rate among girls in junior high school and high school, who left school because they became pregnant. These young women never set up households of their own. They lived with their mothers, with both parents, grandmothers, grandparents, or other senior relatives. And the younger the mother, the longer she would probably reside with other adults. Households headed by mature mothers and grandmothers were usually as stable as two-parent families in terms of their longevity and their ability to provide adequately for the needs of the adults and children within them.

Most of the discussion concerning the rise in the numbers of female-headed households among African Americans has focused on the so-called "breakdown" of the nuclear family. Jewell's book *Survival of the Black Family* is especially detailed in attributing the increase in divorce, separation, and births out of wedlock to welfare policies which started in the 1950s, and began to show serious effects in the 1960s, '70s, and '80s. She also points out that from the 1950s onward, as more Black males shifted their occupation from farm worker to unskilled laborer, more of the Black elderly became eligible for social security benefits and therefore were less dependent on their children. With this came "the establishment of [more] independent living arrangements," as indicated by the decrease in the number of "sub-families" living in the one household between 1950 and 1960 (Jewell 1988:24).

In her own words, Jewell summarizes the impact of social welfare policy on the structure of African American families as follows:

> Although liberal social welfare legislation created economic independence for the elderly, conservative administration of social welfare programs, especially in the Aid to Families with Dependent Children program, promoted marital conflict, as welfare policies and practices required male absence as a condition for eligibility. Hence, through overt and covert practices, social welfare agencies, not black wives, forced men out of the home. Thus, the black female-headed household, created through separation, divorce, or non-marriage, has been system-precipitated. Thus, one could expect an escalation in the dissolution of marriages among blacks and an increase in the number of black women with children who choose to permanently forego marriage. The trends in both of these areas was [sic] initiated in the 1950s and became firmly established by the 1980s. By excluding black males through the institution of the "man-in-the-house" policy in the 1950s and maintaining this policy in the 1960s and 1970s and by systematically entitling women, and not their husbands, to benefits, black two-parent families were undermined. (Jewell 1988:24-25)

Even though Billingsley and Jewell emphasize the *"breakdown"* in the nuclear family as a result of economic, demographic and policy factors previously mentioned, both sets of data demonstrate that another important trend is in evidence. I am referring to *the break-up of multi-generational female-headed households*, formerly the most common type of household headed by women. In the past, female-headed households usually included at least three generations, and sometimes four. Women normally started having children at an early age (i.e., in their teens or early twenties) and might continue having them into their late thirties or forties. Thus, it was not uncommon for women to be rearing their own children while assisting their daughters with the upbringing of theirs.

Not only were these female-headed households extended lineally (i.e., by including a woman, her children, grandchildren, and possibly great-grandchildren), often they were also extended laterally to include never-married, widowed, or divorced sisters or brothers of the head of the household. For example, such households might include a woman, an adult sister or brother, her adult daughter(s), her adult unmarried son(s), and the dependent children of any or all of the women in the house, including any minor children the woman herself might have. Nowadays, owing to the impact of social welfare policies (as delineated by Jewell) and as a result of the skyrocketing unemployment of Black males since the late 1970s and 1980s, what would have been a single, multigenerational female-headed household in the 1950s or early 1960s is likely to be several separate female-headed households today. For example, a woman's unmarried daughters would probably be living alone with their dependent children, creating three or four female-headed households where previously there would have been one.

Reflecting on the data presented by Billingsley, Jewell, and others, I conclude that *the major trend among African American families over the past thirty years is the increasing disaggregation of households, whether headed by married couples or by women.* In other words, we see more separate households in relation to population size than ever before. It is not surprising that the majority of those households are female-headed, since many Black males are either incarcerated, unemployed and "on the streets," unemployed and living in dependent relationships with their mothers or girlfriends, or otherwise unable to assume the responsibility of household headship.

The trend toward the disaggregation (and hence diminishing size) of households is evidenced not only by the proliferation of two-generational female-headed households; it is also evidenced by the increase in the number of elderly persons living alone or in couples, as noted by Jewell, and by the substantial increase in the number and percentage of single persons living alone (Billingsley 1992:37-38, 47-48). As of 1990, 25 percent of all African American households were occupied by single adults, and most of these were single women.

Historically, for economic reasons as well as for reasons that relate to cultural traditions, unmarried African American adults lived with their parents or other relatives. In 1975, I cited this as one of the "fundamental structural differences" between Black families and traditional nuclear families.

> Adulthood for black people does not necessarily entail the establishment of new households; therefore one finds many single adults living with married and unmarried relatives. In fact, in some places it is considered highly preferable for unmarried adults to live with relatives than to live alone or to live outside the family with "roommates." (*Infra*, chap. 1, p. 8)

The rise in the number of households occupied by one person living alone represents a dramatic shift in patterns of residence over a twenty-year period.

IMPLICATIONS OF THE RECENT CHANGES IN FAMILY AND HOUSEHOLD

The question might be asked: what are some of the consequences of the disaggregation of African American family households? In particular, does the proliferation of female-headed households signal a "crisis" in the Black family?

I have stressed that most young single mothers used to live in multi-generational households, whose members provided a wide range of mutual support to one another. Such households were particularly important for the rearing of children. To the extent that the break-up of these units has left many inexperienced mothers alone to cope with the rearing of their children, there is no question but that this creates serious problems. One of the often cited signs of "crisis" in the Black family is the inability of some single mothers to "control" their children, particularly their male children. When single mothers lived with their adult relatives, they could rely on these adults (male as well as female) to assist them in establishing and enforcing the rules by which children were brought up. The impact of a father's absence could be compensated for by the presence of a maternal grandfather, mother's brothers, and other male figures living in, or frequenting, a household. Today, even when these relatives play a supporting role in the life of a single mother and her children, the fact that they live in different residences, sometimes great distances apart, means that they cannot have the continuous influence on the children that they would have had in the past.

Adults as well as children are inevitably affected by the disaggregation of African American family households. On a very practical level, the economic support and sharing of resources that were a feature of the multi-generational households will be unavailable to the same degree as in the past. In addition to in-kind services to one another, borrowing among relatives was a major feature of African American households of the past. Without other adults in the house today, single mothers have no one to turn to borrow small amounts of cash, personal items (such as toiletries, clothing, or jewelry), housewares, or food items. In the past, different members of the household would buy different appliances for the house, or they might all "chip in" to purchase what was needed. The loss of such material support cannot be underestimated, and no doubt explains why single parents may decide to "look the other way" when their children get involved in illegal activities that bring much needed cash into the home.

The absence of the adult companionship provided by African American households of the past makes the life of single mothers harder to bear. When a woman did not have a husband or "boyfriend," she could turn to her relatives in the household for companionship and support. Today, without the presence of adult relatives in the home, the burden of rearing children alone may be compounded by the fact of loneliness, or worse, by despair.

Even if we agree with Billingsley that "the so-called Black family crisis is not of their own making [and] is not the worst crisis they ever faced and survived," we have to acknowledge that this is the first time since the break-up of families during slavery that external factors have had such a profound impact on African American family structure. To overcome what could become a crisis, it is necessary to consciously strengthen and augment the extended family networks which have been the key to the survival of Blacks in America, and to which people still turn for support (see, e.g.,

Harriette McAdoo 1978 and 1983, and Hatchett and Jackson 1993).

It must be noted that the changes we have been discussing have already sent an alarm through the African American community nationwide. Various initiatives to rekindle the commitment to kin, and provide support to female-headed households are being undertaken by churches and other religious groups, and by civic and service organizations such as the National Council of Negro Women (NCNW), the Coalition of 100 Black Men, national sororities and fraternities, etc. Support is given to children and young adults in the form of tutoring, mentoring, and guided recreational activities, and help is also given directly to single mothers to enable them to better cope with their responsibilities. The NCNW's annual "Black Family Reunion Day" observed in over 200 cities and towns serves as an occasion to re-dedicate to familyhood, and to demonstrate to the nation that the Black family is in much better condition than the media would have us believe.

In a recent paper on female-headed households, I suggested that we also need to call for the building of public and private housing units that are large enough to accommodate multi-generational kinship and friendship groupings, which can provide single mothers with the help they need to be able to go to work to support themselves and their children. One way in which the government could assist welfare mothers to become working mothers would be through support to elderly women who now live alone, but who might be persuaded to live with or near young working mothers, helping them with their children as African American grandmothers did in the past. In short, we need to strengthen and expand existing trans-residential kinship and friendship networks and develop new types of extended residential arrangements in order to reverse the debilitating effects of the break-up of the multi-generational households of the past (*Infra*, chap. 3).

One thing is certain, we must be realistic about the trends we are seeing, and about the best ways to respond to them. It is futile to think that the "salvation" of the Black family lies in the revival of the nuclear family when the nuclear family per se has never been the dominant pattern in the African American community. It is true that most households were headed by married couples, but as has already been noted, at various phases in their domestic cycle, they took in grandchildren, elderly parents, and other relatives. In other words, both two-parent and single-parent households among African Americans were more inclusive than the typical nuclear family. It was these multi-generational households and the extended families that linked them together that enabled African Americans to survive and thrive in this country.

Rather than look to the nuclear family, with its ideology of isolationism and self-centeredness, as the building block for African American communities of the future, we need to look to the inclusive, mutually supportive household and family structures that proved their effectiveness in the past. We know that some of these households were successfully headed by women. As we seek to reconnect the disaggregated households that have become the reality of the nineties, we need to accept the fact that in the twenty-first century, many if not most of the households that will emerge will still be headed by women. As in the past, women will have to rely on male relatives and friends, wherever they reside, to play the supportive roles that will enable these households to thrive and succeed, just as they did in the past.

AFRICAN AMERICAN FAMILY VALUES

If our families are to play the constructive roles they have in the past, rebuilding and redesigning their structures is only one task we must confront. Equally important is the task of rediscovering and instilling the values that made it possible for these families to persist and prevail in the past. The preceding sections of this paper should have demonstrated that the most fundamental of these values was the commitment to the family itself (DuBois 1908, Frazier 1939, Herskovits 1941, Billingsley 1968 and 1993, Hill 1971, Blassingame 1972, Stack 1974, Gutman 1976, and others). This sense of commitment to kin, and the values that were taught to children as a way of instilling and reinforcing this commitment, were brought to America by the enslaved population just as they brought memories of the African family structures they would seek to recreate in America.

Various writers have sought to delineate additional values that have been paramount in African American families. Drawing on the works of various scholars, Billingsley developed a list of African

American family values, some of which are: a commitment to education, a commitment to self-help, service to others, a strong religious orientation, and a strong work orientation (Billingsley 1992:328-333). Few, if any, who have studied African American families would dispute this listing of values encouraged through these institutions. However, given the stereotype that women on welfare "do not want to work" and that large numbers of Black males are unemployed because they are "lazy," I am sure that some would question whether a "strong work orientation" is indeed a value promoted within the Black families. Two points are relevant here. First, most women on welfare would work if they could earn enough to eke out a living and afford child care, transportation, and other job-related expenses. If they earn a minimum wage, their disposable income is no higher than what they would receive from public assistance, and hence they could not afford the additional cost of working. Those who earn more than the minimum wage risk losing their medical protection (Medicaid) if they earn in the upwards of $10,000 annually (Jaynes and Williams 1989). The fact that recent programs to put welfare mothers in the workforce include provisions for day care and health care is a noteworthy development.

The second point concerns the stereotype that "Black men are lazy and do not want to work." Studies of employment trends in the African American community show that for more than fifty years, the rate of unemployment for African American males has been more than twice that of white males (Jaynes and Williams, p. 308). The actual rates of unemployment of Black males are even higher, because many of them are "defined" out of the work force simply because they recognize the futility of looking for work. Anyone who skips one month of looking for work, is "classified as not in the labor force" (Jaynes and Williams 1989:301). Thus, through a statistical sleight of hand, actual unemployment statistics are under-reported for many in the population, including Black males. These high unemployment rates reflect a number of factors, notably the *unavailability of opportunities* for males looking for assembly-line work and other semi-skilled jobs that have declined dramatically over the last two decades. Even the menial jobs that Black males could depend on in the past may be no longer available to them as competition has increased from other groups seeking to make a living in difficult economic times.

Thus, the high rates of unemployment of Black males certainly cannot be attributed to their "laziness," nor can that unemployment be taken as a lack of commitment to the strong work ethic cited as a value in Black families by various scholars (Billingsley 1992:331, 332).

My own effort to identify traditional values in African American families has taken a somewhat different approach than that of scholars who sought to uncover the tenets that encouraged achievement and upward mobility (commitment to education, work, self-help, service to others, and a strong religious orientation). All these I acknowledge as important values in Black family life. However, I have been particularly interested in setting forth the basic precepts or values that were taught to children and expected of adults in order to achieve the patterns of cooperation and self-help exemplified in the extended family.

As I read the historical accounts of African American family life during slavery and afterward, it was clear that the values taught and promoted in these families were very similar to those I had found in my readings and research on various societies in West Africa. In 1970, I first proposed that the principles of respect, responsibility, restraint, and reciprocity were four "cardinal values" undergirding African family life that had been retained in the family life of African Americans (Marshall 1970; *Infra*, chap. 7). Over the years, as I continued to read about and reflect on these values in African family life, it became clear that some key tenets of behavior were not covered by the above-cited "Four Rs." In an effort to incorporate into my teachings and writings these other principles, I added three additional "Rs"—*reverence, reason and reconciliation*—making a total of "Seven Rs."

The first five "Rs" seem clearly to have been carried over into African American family life. The latter two, reason and reconciliation, which were important in African families and communities in settling disputes, may have diminished in importance in the United States because African Americans looked to America's legal system rather than their own authority structures for settling major disputes within their communities and even within their own families. Thus, reason and reconciliation were no longer key mechanisms in preserving social order as they had been in indigenous African societies. (Today, we see that these values have also been lost in parts of contemporary Africa where indigenous precepts no longer govern behavior).

In setting forth my "Seven Rs," I do not mean to suggest that these are the only values that were traditionally promoted in African families. Nor is it implied that these values are unique to Africa. Indeed, to some degree they are embraced by cultures in most, if not all, parts of the world. But the same can be said of the values contained in the doctrines of many of the world's religions. Thus, it would not surprise me if people other than Africans identify the Seven Rs as values taught in their own families or communities.

The reason for discussing these values here is two-fold. First, it is to provide an understanding of why the extended family structures described in the previous sections could be sustained in Africa and in America and other parts of the African diaspora over hundreds and hundreds of years. It is my view that the African form of family organization was reinforced by precepts such as the ones enumerated here. These precepts or values were passed on through oral tradition and exemplified in the behavior of family members in their day-to-day relationships. The second reason for focusing on these values is that they can be helpful to African American families coping with the troubled circumstances in which many of them find themselves today. In the face of poverty, homelessness, drugs, violence, crime, disease and other problems that are threatening to destroy the family structures that have been the bedrock of our survival in America, it is important to recognize these and other values that might help us rescue our families and save our communities.

It is understood, of course, that values alone are not sufficient to overcome the misery that poverty, crime, and disease create in too many African American communities. The long-term sustained improvement of these communities requires economic changes as well as social changes. The creation of jobs and the establishment of local businesses that will re-invest in the community; the improvement of schools and opportunities for higher education; and the genuine empowerment of the people are some of what is required to make these communities come alive with promise and hope. Nevertheless, values are also important because they instill the principles that guide the choices people make. It is suggested, therefore, that we take another look at the specific family values that enabled African Americans to persevere and prevail in the face of unbelievable obstacles in the past.

Respect is the first of the cardinal values that guided behavior within African families and communities. It not only governed the behavior of children toward their parents, but toward all elders with whom one came in contact. In fact, because seniority conferred rank and status within the African extended family, respect and deference were due to all persons who were senior to oneself. When Africans came to America, they retained 'respect' as a fundamental precept on which their families and communities were built. Respect was shown by forms of address—with older people being called by kinship terms such as "Uncle" or "Aunt," or by titles such as "Mister" or "Miss." Respect was also shown by the way younger people treated their elders—through greetings, bows, curtsies, and other gestures that they learned early. Among Africans and African Americans, it was considered impolite for younger people to "look their elders dead in the eye." The emphasis on respect was widely reported from the period of slavery to as recently as thirty or forty years ago. Obviously, many of the specific ways of showing respect would be considered old-fashioned and inappropriate today. Yet, one of the ways in which *we can strengthen our families* is *through the teaching of respect*. If our children are once again taught the importance of respecting others, they will be in a better position to demand and command respect for themselves.

Responsibility is the value that required members of African extended families to be their brothers' and sisters' keepers. Studies of African American families have shown that they too accept responsibilities for a wide range of kin, even if for no other reason than they consider it their duty to do so. Of course, in every society kinship imposes some responsibility, but societies differ in defining the limits of that responsibility. Africans and African Americans traditionally accepted responsibility for a much wider network of kin than is typical of Americans with a nuclear family orientation, who consider "real" responsibility to kin to extend mainly to spouses, parents and children. Among Americans committed to nuclear families and nuclear family values, even siblings can make only "so many" demands on each other. Relatives outside the nuclear families into which people are born or which they form at marriage, are helped only if people do not have to "put themselves out" in order to do so. By contrast, African

Americans typically housed and fed distant relatives who migrated into their areas looking for work; helped their sisters and brothers provide for their children; cared for parents and other aging relatives who did not have children to look after them. If African Americans are to prosper in the twenty-first century, particularly in the face of the large numbers of people who lack the education and the economic wherewithal to "fend for themselves," we must once again be prepared to accept responsibility for the less fortunate in our extended families and our communities.

Reciprocity is the principle that compelled Africans and African Americans to give back to their families and communities in return for what had been given them. Entire treatises have been written on the principle of reciprocity in human societies (Mauss 1954; Sahlins 1972, chap. 5), hence, we do not claim that this is a value exclusive to Africans or African Americans. The point is that Africans placed a very high premium on mutual assistance, especially among relatives, and they expected that good deeds would be reciprocated either in the short run or in the distant future. Even if obligations were carried from one generation to the next, they should not be abrogated. The data on cooperation within the African American family indicate that the commitment to reciprocity remained an important family value. Today, many civic and service organizations, as well as historically and predominantly Black colleges and universities, are stressing the importance of "giving back to the community." It is a principle that will have to be reinforced within the family if self-help is to become once again the primary instrument of African American survival and success.

Restraint is probably the most difficult of African values to teach or accept in today's highly individualistic and materialistic society. In America "me and mine" always take precedence over "thee and thine." Everyone wants to "do his or her own thang." But within African families, when personal decisions had implications for the group as a whole (whether that was the immediate family, the lineage, or the extended family), a person had to give due consideration to the group when making those decisions. Of course, even the definition of what should be considered a "personal decision" was different in African and African American families of the past. Many such decisions were made by, or in consultation with, family elders. Restraint was manifest in many ways—parents went without so that their children might have; adult sons and daughters returned the sacrifice by putting the needs of their elderly parents before they own desires. An oft-cited example of the principle of restraint or sacrifice in African and African American communities is that of a sister or brother who did not to school, but helped to pay for a sibling's education. This sacrifice was repaid when the educated sibling assumed responsibility for educating his or her brother's or sister's children. In this example, the principles of reciprocity, responsibility, and restraint are all manifest, but that of restraint (or sacrifice) is especially important to emphasize in an age where everyone is taught to "look out for Number One."

Reverence is the value emphasized by those who recognize a "strong religious orientation" among African Americans. This orientation is directly traceable to Africa, whose sons and daughters are known to be a spiritual people. In Africa, children were taught to revere the God of the Universe as well as lesser gods. They were also taught reverence for the ancestors as well as for many things in nature. Both Christianity and Islam spread easily through Africa because of the people's predisposition to embrace religions that seemed to empower their adherents (Herskovits 1941). Among African Americans, with the exception of the family, the Church has been the strongest institution, and continues to be one of the anchors of African American communities today. Islam is also spreading among African Americans, who welcome its uplifting influence among many of the youth. It is no accident that over the years, many of our most prominent national or community leaders have had a base in the Church, or in a few notable instances, in the Mosque.

The third stanza of the "Negro National Anthem," *Lift Ev'ry Voice and Sing* by James Weldon Johnson, begins:

God of our weary years, God of our silent tears,
Thou who has brought us thus far on the way;
Thou who has by Thy might, led us into the light,
Keep us forever in the path, we pray.

Such unabashed, and some would say sentimental, spirituality may be too old-fashioned for many people today. Yet, the appeal to a higher power, the reverence and respect for a high God, by whatever name, has been an indispensable part of the survival of Blacks in America. The belief in God has given hope in situations that otherwise would have been hopeless, and as the Reverend

Jesse Jackson has said, today more than ever, African Americans need to "keep hope alive." If reverence for a higher power can continue to sustain African Americans in our fight for empowerment here on earth, it is one of those values that should be retained in our twenty-first-century "survival kit."

Reason is a value that is often invoked in many African contexts. As African Americans, however, we are often portrayed (and portray ourselves) as emotional people, characterized by spontaneity and expressiveness. We see ourselves as a people with rhythm. Indeed, as a people we have all these attributes, but historically, *reason* was more important than all of them in maintaining social order in African communities. I saw the importance placed on reason in human affairs when I was conducting anthropological research in the towns and villages of Nigeria and Ghana in the 1960s. I was always impressed by the premium that Africans placed on reasonableness in the settling of disputes within the family and within the wider community. When disputes broke out, elders appealed to reason, not to emotion, to settle the matter. In the small Yoruba town in Nigeria where I lived in the early 1960s, most disputes and breaches of the law were settled by elders within the compounds or by the traditional chiefs in the town. In Ghana, where I studied Yoruba traders in the late sixties, the Yoruba umbrella organizations, known as Parapos, tried to settle all matters that arose within the Yoruba communities throughout Ghana without going to court. When Elders convened to adjudicate matters brought before them, moreover, they took as much time as necessary to persuade the parties concerned to come to a reasonable settlement. Sometimes I was amazed at how much people were willing to compromise to reach agreement on a fair and reasonable settlement. I often thought that Americans, including African Americans, would have done far less. The art of reason and compromise can be taught, and it seems to me that efforts should be made in our families, as well as through the churches, mosques, schools, and other institutions, to teach the importance of taking a reasoned approach to settling differences.

Reconciliation is a value that was also essential to the maintenance of social order in African extended families and in the wider communities. When I reflect on what I have seen in the decades that I have been in and out of West Africa, I realize that

71

one of the most important lessons taught through the family is the importance of forgiveness and reconciliation. The ultimate sign of respect among the Yoruba is for a woman to kneel and a man to prostrate himself before another person. Inevitably, when a person goes before another to "beg" forgiveness, he or she will prostrate or will kneel, as required. It is virtually unthinkable that anyone would be so hard hearted as to ignore or rebuff such a gesture. It is considered uncultured to fail to reconcile with a relative or friend, or even an adversary, who begs to put the matter to rest. When asked about disputes or dissension within the family or the community, one often hears people say: "We have settled the matter." After that, nothing more needs to be said. Although the art of reconciliation appears to have been lost or cast aside in the evolution of African families transplanted and transformed in America, it is a value that should be reclaimed as we seek to strengthen our domestic institutions. By emphasizing the importance of reconciliation, hostilities can be diffused and quarrels de-escalated. The more easily this can be accomplished, the more likely it is that households and families will be able to focus on the larger goals they wish to achieve.

The "Seven Rs" enumerated above—*respect, responsibility, restraint, reciprocity, reverence, reason and reconciliation*—represent *African family values* that supported kinship structures (lineages, compounds, and extended families) that lasted for hundreds, perhaps even thousands, of years. The strength of these values is indicated by the fact that most of them were retained and passed on in America, thereby enabling African Americans to create and maintain extended family networks that sustained them here as their prototypes had sustained their ancestors on the African continent. Today, in the face of circumstances that threaten the existence of these extended family structures, it is suggested that a revival of the values that allowed them to persist could strengthen the family and community structures on which African Americans must depend in the twenty-first century.

CONCLUSION

There have been profound changes in African American household and family organization over the past three decades. The four most impactful of these are: the decline in the number of two-parent households, the proliferation of female-headed households, the increase in the percentage of single persons living alone, and the increase in the number of elderly persons living alone or as couples apart from any other relatives. *Together these changes add up to an overall trend toward the break-up or disaggregation of the large multi-generational households in which most African Americans used to live.* The most serious consequence of this trend is that nowadays we see many single mothers living alone with their children (i.e., in two-generational households), whereas in the past most of them would have been in households with their mothers and/or other kin who could provide assistance with the upbringing of their children and with other aspects of their lives.

Recognizing that demographic, social, and economic realities make it likely that these female-headed households are here to stay, in one form or another, I suggest an all-out effort to re-build extended family support systems for these single mothers rather than hold out the unrealistic expectation that two-parent families will reemerge as the predominant household structure in the Black community. In the past, African American households organized around core groups of consangunieal kin ("blood relatives"), could be just as stable as those organized around married couples. A similar flexibility in household structures will be required if we are to build strong family networks for the future. In the meantime, as African American scholars, we must not be seduced by the myth that female-headed households are the cause of the deplorable social conditions that exist in the poverty-stricken communities in which most of these households are found. Unemployment, dilapidated schools, drug infestation, and violent crimes have increased during the same period when female-headed households were tripling in response to deliberate decisions by public officials. But that does not mean that there is a causal relationship between family organization and the social pathologies with which they have to cope.

This is not to say that family structures and relationships have no effect on the behavior of those within them. The question is whether changing family structure will make as much of a difference in the lives of people as would intervention to change the deplorable conditions in which they live. There is no evidence that two-parent families living in drug- and crime-infested neighborhoods are significantly better off than those with single parents.

The evidence available indicates that by expanding the opportunities for the poor (providing them with jobs, access to better schools, caring and concerned role models who can help the young people on the road to a better life) we go a long way toward changing behavior that is allegedly due to family structure. To address the root cause of the violence and despair we see among the youth in many of our inner cities, we must advocate a *genuine* "war on poverty," one that will eliminate rather than mask unemployment, and one that will make an all-out assault on drugs.

Finally, as African American scholars, we must remind our communities and inform the wider society of the roles that our families have played in our survival in America. We cannot blame others for the perpetuation of stereotyped notions about African American families when we ourselves assume them to be inferior simply because they differ from family structures handed down from Europe. In form, African American families have been some of the most flexible, adaptable, and inclusive kinship institutions in America. In function, they have been among the most accepting and nurturing of children, and the most supportive of adults. These are institutions for which we should be grateful rather than apologetic.

PART II

AFRICAN AND AFRICAN AMERICAN FAMILIES: UNDERSTANDING THE LINKS

"It is time to move beyond the debate over whether it was slavery or the African heritage which 'determined' Black family organization. Instead, I have proposed a synthesis which looks at institutional transformation as well as institutional transfer for the interplay between Africa and America in shaping the family structures of African Americans."

Niara Sudarkasa, "Interpreting the African Heritage in African American Family Organization" (*Infra*, pp. 145–146)

ROOTS OF THE BLACK FAMILY:
OBSERVATIONS ON THE FRAZIER-
HERSKOVITS DEBATE

In the wake of the *Roots* phenomenon (i.e. the Alex Haley novel
and its televised dramatization which popularized the notion of
a traceable genealogical link between contemporary African
Americans and Africans), it might surprise many to learn that
there is considerable controversy among scholars over the question of whether there are any recognizably African elements in the
institutions, behavior, attitudes, or values of contemporary Black
Americans. Nowhere have the disagreements been more strongly
stated or more continuously aired than in the literature on the
Black American family. The issue is not simply whether elements
of African family organization persist as "survivals," "retentions,"
or "reinterpretations" in contemporary Black family life. More
fundamentally, it is a question of whether the Black families that
developed *during slavery* were essentially African institutions
adapted to the American context or new, "slave" institutions that
bore traces of African influences but were unquestionably rooted
in America.

The strands of argument in this debate are labyrinthine, but
the parameters were drawn some fifty-odd years ago when E.
Franklin Frazier, the sociologist, and Melville J. Herskovits, the
anthropologist, confronted each other over the issue of African

survivals in Black American family life.[1]

In *The Negro Family in the United States* (1939), Frazier outlined a thesis that was to be echoed for decades:

> . . . scraps of memories, which form only an insignificant part of the growing body of traditions in Negro families, are what remain of the African heritage. Probably never before in history has a people been so nearly stripped of its social heritage as the Negroes who were brought to America. . . [where] there was no social organization to sustain whatever conceptions of life the Negro slave might have retained of his African heritage.

Herskovits' counter-argument was set forth in an equally famous book, *The Myth of the Negro Past* (1941), which sought to document the presence of Africanisms in Black American family life and in various other aspects of Black culture.

Interestingly, the question of the link between African and African American family organization was never fully explored by Frazier, Herskovits, or the other scholars who subsequently contributed to the debate. Instead, following Frazier's lead, they focused on only a few characteristics that were typical of less than one-fourth of the Black families in America. Specifically, the debate centered on the origin of female-headed households, the "dominant" position of the mother within the family, the "high rate" of illegitimate birth, and the "ease" of separation and divorce. Although these features were not found in the majority of Black families, they were taken as the ones that most sharply distinguished these families from their white counterparts. Over the years, these few characteristics of a *minority* of Black families came to be regarded by many as the *defining* attributes of Black American family organization.

Frazier traced the origin of female-headed households, or maternal families, as he called them, to the conditions of slavery which made the mother "mistress of the cabin and head of the family." He also attributed the relative ease of separation and divorce, and the "high rate" of illegitimacy (which he estimated as ten to twenty percent of all births) to the "breakdown" of institutions and morals caused by slavery and by the "disruptive" processes of urbanization after emancipation. Although Herskovits echoed Frazier's contention that the main contrast between Black and white families derived from a "higher illegitimacy rate and the particular role played by the mother" among Blacks, he disputed the notion that these features were signs of Black family disorganization. Instead, he maintained that they represented New World variants of African family practices. In his view, the central role of the mother in Black American families was traceable to bonds fostered between mothers and their children in polygynous families (i.e., those where men had more than one wife) in Africa. He argued that the concept of illegitimacy was inappropriate in describing Black children born outside of wedlock, because many African Americans sanctioned unions by consent as well as by law, and children born to both types of union were considered to be legitimate offspring. Thus, in Herskovits' view the concept of illegitimacy was appropriate only if one applied the norms of the dominant society, not those of the Black community, in defining the legal status of children. According to Herskovits, the survival of the African custom of marriage by consent also explained the informality of divorce among some African Americans.

In the years since the appearance of the works of Frazier and Herskovits, a number of historians have clarified some of the issues by using plantation records, early census data, and other public documents to refine the picture of Black family life in the 17th, 18th, and 19th centuries. Over the past decade, the publications of John Blassingame, Eugene Genovese, Herbert Gutman, and others have greatly expanded our knowledge of the major patterns and variations in types of African American households and wider family groups. Gutman's *The Black Family in Slavery and Freedom* (1976) is particularly significant for understanding Black family organization in the periods about which Frazier and Herskovits had written. Gutman's study shows that despite the ban on legal marriages among enslaved Blacks, the conjugal unions entered into by Black men and women were normally sanctified by ritual and approved by plantation owners as well as by relatives of the couples concerned. These unions were often terminated only by death or by the sale of one of the partners. *In most plantations, fewer than one-fifth of all Black households were headed by single women, and most of those were widows or women forcibly separated from their mates.* A young woman who had a child before marriage usually continued to live with her parents, and customarily got married before the birth of a second child. *Thus, Gutman demonstrates that despite the restrictions of slavery, marriages were the norm among Blacks, and two-parent households had considerable stability over time.* These findings contradict Frazier's claim that "maternal" family organization predominated among enslaved Blacks. They also show that the percentage of female-headed households in the Black population remained relatively constant between the period of slavery and the 1930s and early 1940s when Frazier wrote.

On the issue of the *origin* of Black family structure, Gutman's interpretation of the evidence follows the mainstream view of Frazier and others, that Black family organization was fashioned in America in response to American conditions, with relatively insignificant connections to patterns of family life in Africa. In his endeavor to build the case for the historical predominance of two-parent families among blacks, Gutman did not fully explore the significance of the extraordinary data he had uncovered on extended family organization among blacks. To be sure, Gutman describes black family networks and recognizes the strength of kinship ties beyond the conjugal family, but he is content to explain these "affective familial and kin arrangements" as "adaptations" to slavery. He failed to ask *what* was being adapted or why Black extended families took the form they did—questions that would have led inevitably to an examination of the link with the African past. Instead, Gutman ridicules the notion of trying to "collect" African survivals in Black family structure. He acknowledges that some African patterns persisted in marriage ritual, in names and naming patterns, and in some other relatively minor areas of black family life, but he did not see continuities in the fundamental areas of structure, values, or interpersonal behavior. Apparently, Gutman took the existence of marital stability and two-parent households, Black family features that resembled Western nuclear family organization, as proof that Black family organization developed in America, and that there was no need to look beyond the plantation to explain this structure.

Paradoxically, it is the data on Black family life provided by Gutman more than any other scholar that enables the student of African kinship and family organization to identify evidence of what I have termed *institutional transformation* as well as *institutional transfer* in the kinship and family organization of the early African American population. The picture of early African American families that emerges from the narratives by the Blacks themselves and from the descriptions given by others is that of essentially African family structure, behavior, and values being adapted to the political, economic, and social conditions and constraints imposed by slavery and by the conditions of subjugation under which most "free" Blacks lived. Of course, a key component of this American environment was the complex of laws, values, and attitudes of white Americans concerning their own family organization and that of the Blacks.

In order to adequately analyze the process of adaptation in early Black families, one must understand the West African family organization out of which they derived. This type of family organization differed fundamentally from that of early white Americans and their Western European forebears. The major contrast was in the different emphasis which the two traditions placed on conjugality (relationships based on marriage) and consanguinity (relationships based on descent, i.e., on "blood ties"). The tendency for people in different parts of the world to emphasize one or the other of these principles in their family organization was first elaborated by Ralph Linton in *The Study of Man* (1936). Even though African families, like those in other parts of the world, included relationships based on both conjugality and consanguinity, they emphasized the latter. By contrast, European families tended to emphasize the conjugal relationship in matters of household formation, decision making, property transmission, and socialization of the young.

In West Africa, the basic residential unit was an extended family occupying a cluster of dwellings known as a *compound*. Upon marriage, couples did not normally establish separate households, but rather joined the compound of either the groom or the bride, depending on the prevailing rules of descent and residence. In societies with a rule of patrilineal descent (i.e., where membership in the lineage and the inheritance of property passed through the father line), the core group of the compound consisted of a group of brothers, their adult sons, and grandsons. This group along with their wives and children made up the co-residential extended family. The adult sisters and daughters of the group would still belong to the compound and lineage, but they resided in their husbands' compounds as part of their husbands' co-residential extended families. In the relatively few matrilineal societies found in the West African regions from which most American Blacks were taken, the residence patterns were more complex, with spouses sometimes residing in separate compounds. The situation was also complicated by the fact that in these societies, as in patrilineal ones, males held major leadership roles in the domestic groups. However, in matrilineal societies, as in patrilineal ones, the core of the co-residential extended family was composed of "blood relatives" (in this case, groups of sisters or groups or brothers and sisters along with the sisters' children). Throughout West Africa, the spouses in the extended families were conceptualized as "outsiders" *vis-a-vis* the core consanguineal group members.

The stability of the extended family did not depend on the stability of the marriages of the core group members. Divorce did not signal the "dissolution of the family," as in the case of families built around married couples. Each partner remained a life-long member of the lineage and extended family into which he or she was born. When divorce occurred, the in-marrying spouse returned to his or her natal compound until he or she remarried. Children of divorced couples normally continued to reside in their natal compounds except under special circumstances. For example, in a patrilineal society, a divorced woman normally left her older children in their father's compound but kept the very young ones with her until they were of an age when they could return to their father's compound to be reared by his mother (i.e., their paternal grandmother), one of their father's wives, or one of his brothers' wives. No doubt, the practice of polygyny complemented the emphasis on consanguinity in the African family, because it freed the male member of the family core group from dependence on any one wife. It also promoted the independence of women in some societies and strengthened their attachment to their own natal families.

The stability of the African extended family also derived from the corporate and communal nature of its consanguineal core group, which collectively owned land and other properties, including hereditary titles. The group also cooperated in food and craft production and shared responsibility for the well-being of the entire membership of the compound. The elder who headed the group was its official representative in the community.

The conjugal families within the African extended family differed significantly from typical nuclear families of Western tradition. First, the institution of polygyny created a number of roles and relationships, such as those of co-wife and "co-mother," that are not found in typical nuclear families. Secondly, the conjugal families had responsibilities for persons outside their immediate group. To some extent, all children of the compound were the responsibility of all the adults in it, and husbands and wives often took care of their nephews and nieces (who were usually termed sons and daughters) as well as their own children. Thirdly, these families did not have the rigid boundaries characteristic of nuclear families. African conjugal families did not usually live together in a bounded space within the compound. Customarily, wives had their own rooms and husbands theirs. Young children slept in their mothers' rooms, while older children slept in communal rooms set aside for boys or girls, respectively. Fourth, conjugal families were in many ways under the influence or control of the wider extended family. Decisions made by the elders of the compound often determined what would happen within the conjugal units.

The student of West African family organization cannot fail to see African patterns in early Black American kinship. Such patterns become apparent when one looks beyond the issue of household headship (to which more attention will be given later) to the detailed descriptions of the structure of early African American kin networks and patterns of mutual obligation; relationships between husbands and wives, parents and children, brothers and sisters, and grandparents and grandchildren; child-rearing practices; patterns of respect and deference among kin and the extension of kinship behavior to elders outside the family group. The retention of African patterns in these areas is more significant and just as obvious as that which Gutman and others have acknowledged in the areas of courtship, marriage rules and rituals, and naming patterns and ceremonies.

Data from the various collections of "slave narratives" and those provided by Gutman and others also show that consanguineally based extended families persisted among Blacks in America. The political, economic, and social conditions of slavery did not permit the replication of African families, but neither did they prevent the *transformation* of these institutions to serve the needs of the new environment. In fact, the conditions of slavery fostered the persistence of these groups, which emphasized collective responsibility and reciprocity in the face of adversity. In fact, it was the extended families (not the two-parent households existing in isolation)that enabled Blacks to bear the pain of forcible separation from loved ones; obtain help in bringing up their children, attending their sick, and mourning their dead; form cooperative work groups; "cover" for each other at critical times; plot insurrections and escape from bondage; and generally persevere despite the oppression of slavery. Contrary to Gutman's view, these networks did not develop *sui generis* in America in response to the conditions of slavery. They were re-creations, albeit with modifications, of groups that had existed in Africa and that had served many of the same purposes they would later serve in the United States.

The existence of two-parent households among enslaved Blacks does not negate the significance of the African heritage in their kinship structure. Marriage was virtually universal in Africa, and widowed or divorced persons normally remarried without much delay. Given the size and arrangement of the "cabins" in which enslaved Blacks had to live, and given the proscriptions against polygyny, it is hardly surprising that a single conjugal pair formed the core of most residential units. What is interesting is that despite the circumstances, polygyny was sometimes practiced (the co-wives usually lived in separate cabins and often on separate plantations); relatives beyond the nuclear family often lived together in one cabin; and on some plantations, groups of cabins formed kinship clusters similar to African compounds.

Interestingly, the pattern that was assumed to be African did not originate there. *The development of isolated female-headed households among enslaved Blacks did not grow out of African traditions.* There were very few isolated female-headed households in West Africa, even in matrilineal societies, and certainly the mother-child dyads within polygynous families were not independent households. Herskovits may have been right about some of the similarities in the relationship between mothers and children in the African polygynous family and in the Black American "maternal" family. However, he could not possibly account for the incidence of such groups in America by labelling them "retentions" or "reinterpretations" of African institutions. Frazier rightly traces the origin of these groups to the restrictive conditions of slavery. African American households headed by widows, by women forcibly separated from their mates, and by unmarried mothers represented new formations explainable by demographic conditions, negative sanctions on polygyny, decisions by the "masters," the existence of sexual liaisons between the "masters" and enslaved Black women, and by other factors in the political economy of slavery.

Even though these female-headed households were not African in origin, an understanding of the importance of consanguinity in African kinship helps to explain why they persisted among Black Americans as an alternative form of household organization. First of all, it is necessary to focus on household composition as well as household headship as a defining characteristics of these groups. Given what we know about trans-residential cooperation among Blacks during slavery and in later periods, it is not always possible to ascertain who was or was not the head of a household by simply looking at isolated dwellings. The essential characteristic of these households is that they were (and are) usually composed of a core of consanguineally related adults with some dependent children attached. For example, they might include a woman, her adult daughter(s), and the children of one or all of them; a woman, her son and daughter, and daughter's children: or two sisters, a brother, and the children of one or both of the women, etc. The incidence and distribution of such groups among Black Americans must be attributed to political and economic factors that fostered their development. However, their persistence must also be related to the fact that they have always been regarded as a legitimate form of household structure by some segments of the Black population. In other words, it appears that the African values sanctioning household groupings built around consanguineal relatives were not obliterated despite the overwhelming preference of the American majority population for households and families based on conjugality.

The data on family organization among enslaved Blacks show that the African institutional heritage, the Euro-American family codes and practices that were promoted by the whites, *and* the conditions of enslavement must all be taken into account when explaining the patterns that emerged among African Americans. Several factors seem to account for the failure of various scholars studying the problem to develop an analytical framework encompassing *both* the institutional matrix from which these families evolved *and* the political economy of slavery and "freedom" in which they developed.

First is the fact that both Herskovits and Frazier along with their respective supporters have tended to follow the epistemological tradition that explains a given phenomenon by reference to a single cause. Hence, they juxtapose the *experience* of slavery and the *heritage* of Africa as if only *one* could be *the* explanation of the emergence of the patterns in question.

Second is the fact that after Herskovits, very few Africanists have entered the debate on the origin of African American family patterns. Most of those who have written on the relevance of the African background have had the disadvantage of knowing little about that background. Few of the scholars had read extensively enough in the historical and anthropological literature to go beyond superficial and facile observations that the "diversity" of the backgrounds of the Blacks enslaved in America preclude generalizations about their background. Additionally, scholars have focused their attention on marriage and courtship in Africa rather than delve into the structure and functioning of kin groups, which would have afforded deeper insight into the possible linkage between African and African American institutions in question. (Indeed, few of Herskovits' critics seem to have carefully read his book, which provides an impressive compendium of data on social organization in the West African regions from which most Afro-Americans descended.)

Third, and perhaps most pernicious, has been the persistence of what might be termed the "Myth of the Deculturating Middle Passage," which insists that Africans arrived on these shores stripped of virtually all of their culture. Closely related to this is the myth that what they did retain scarcely lasted the lifetime of the bearers, and certainly could not have been passed on to successive generations.

The rapid accumulation of new data on Black families in different time periods and different geographic regions demands that scholars put aside these contrived positions and begin the process of serious collaboration that is required to provide an analysis of the evolution of Black family organization from Africa to America and within America itself.

NOTES

1. In addition to the books by Frazier, Herskovits, and Gutman mentioned in the text, the following references may be consulted for further discussons on this topic: John A. Bracey, A. Meier, and E. Rudwick, (1970); *Infra*, chaps. 7 & 8; and R.L. Watson (1978).

AFRICAN AND AFRICAN AMERICAN FAMILY STRUCTURE*

INTRODUCTION

Not since the publication of Herskovits's *Myth of the Negro Past* in 1941 has there been such an interest as there is today in the relationship between Black American family structure and indigenous African family structure. The writings of a number of scholars, including Ladner (1971), Nobles (1974a, 1974b, 1978), and Shimkin and Uchendu (1978), essentially reaffirm the position articulated by DuBois in his pioneering study *The Negro American Family,* first published in 1908. Noting that he had made an attempt "to connect present conditions with the African past," DuBois stated:

> This is not because Negro-Americans are Africans, or can trace an unbroken social history from Africa, but because there is a distinct nexus between Africa and America, which, though broken and perverted, is nevertheless not to be neglected by the careful student. (DuBois 1908:9)

---

*This essay is not intended as an exhaustive treatment of African kinship. The analyses and interpretations presented should enable scholars from various disciplines to delve into the anthropological and historical literature for further information specific to their research needs. It should be noted also that the paper does not deal with the important subject of African kinship terminology.

It should not be necessary at this juncture in the study of the Black family to argue anew for the significance of the linkage between African and Black American families. The early historical and sociological writings of DuBois (1908), Woodson (1936), and Herskovits (1941), and the recent historical studies of Blassingame (1972), Genovese (1974), Owens (1976), Haley (1976), Gutman (1976), and others knowingly or unknowingly reveal many of the continuities as well as the changes in African family structure that resulted from the descent into slavery. Nevertheless, in view of some of the generalizations that have been put forth concerning African family patterns and the principles that are said to link African American family structure to its African antecedents (Nobles 1974a, 1974b, 1978), it seems appropriate for a student of continental African societies to help shed light on some of the issues that have been raised.[1]

The purpose of the present paper is twofold: (1) to analyze and interpret the structure of African families, with the aim of clarifying the operation of the principles of consanguinity and conjugality in the formation and maintenance of these groups, and (2) to show how the data on African family structure point to a need for studying the process by which, in the changing socioeconomic and political contexts of the United States, African American family organization evolved from the African patterns re-created by the first Blacks brought here in captivity.

It is important to note, by way of a preface, that when the concept of "African family structure" is used, it implies generalization along two dimensions. First, there is an attempt to delineate those features of African family organization that underlie and unify the variety of specific familial patterns and kinship ideologies that exist among the indigenous peoples of the African continent. Secondly, there is an attempt to describe those features of African family organization that have had relative *permanence or persistence* over time, so that they represent aspects of kinship that are legitimately termed a part of the African heritage. This is not to say that such structural features are unchanging, but rather that, whether one studies African families of the sixteenth century or the twentieth century, one would find remarkable similarities in the institutional features described.

AFRICAN KIN GROUPS DEFINED

Basic to an understanding of African kinship is an understanding of (1) the composition of the *lineage* and the *extended family;* (2) the differences between these two kin groupings and their relationship to one another; and (3) the relationship of the lineage and the extended family to the typical African residential grouping known as the *compound.*

The lineage is a kin group in which the members, living and deceased, are related to each other and to a common ancestor through a line of descent traced through mothers or through fathers, but not through both. In the case of a matrilineage, the males and females who belong to it trace their kinship to each other and to their common female ancestor through their mothers, their mothers' mothers, their mothers' mothers' mothers, and so on. In the case of a patrilineage, the males and females who belong to it trace their kinship to each other and to their common male ancestor through their fathers, their fathers' fathers, their fathers' fathers' fathers, and so on. Stated another way, this means that *in a matrilineal society, a woman's children, male and female, belong to the lineage to which she herself belongs.* That lineage would also include her brothers and sisters born of the same

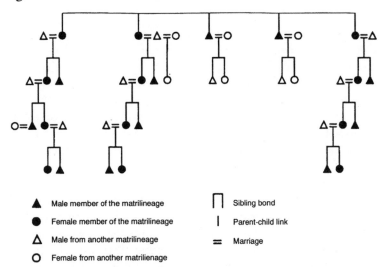

FIGURE 1. Schematic view of a matrilineage.

mother; her mother and her mother's brothers and sisters born of the same mother; her mother's mother, and so on. By the same principle, it follows that children of uterine sisters also belong to the same matrilineage (see Figure 1).

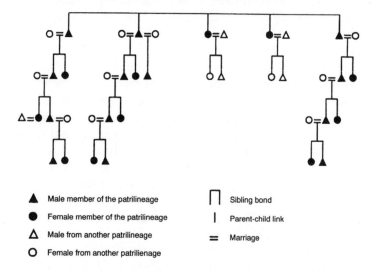

FIGURE 2. Schematic view of a patrilineage.

In a patrilineal society, a woman's children, male and female, belong to the lineage to which their respective fathers belong. They do not belong to the lineage to which their mother belongs. A woman's children would belong to a lineage comprising their father and his sisters and brothers by the same father; their father's father and his sisters and brothers of the same father, and so on. By extension of this principle, it follows that all children of a set of paternally-linked brothers belong to the same patrilineage (see Figure 2).

Two points are immediately apparent regarding the concept of "brothers and sisters" in societies where people are born into lineages. First, in a matrilineal society, children of the same mother belong to the same matrilineage, regardless of differences in paternity. Correspondingly, in a patrilineal society, children of the same father are members of the same patrilineage, without regard to differences in maternity.

Although it is beyond the scope of this paper to discuss all the functions of lineages in African societies, suffice it to say that, where they existed *in precolonial times, lineages were landholding corporate entities charged with the allocation of land, titles, and other properties among their members.* In virtually all cases, lineages were identified with particular ancestral homelands; in some instances, they had special deities as well. Although there have been some changes in the function of lineages in contemporary Africa, where they exist they are still a vital part of the social structure. Ultimately, because of the actual and fictive links that connect the living members to the founding ancestor, *lineages were and are the kin groups that signify and symbolize social continuity in African societies.*

Through rules of lineage exogamy, i.e., rules that mandate marriages outside the lineage,[2] African lineages become linked with one another in networks of alliance and cooperation (see Marshall 1968). Traditionally, through ties of marriage, members of different lineages are drawn together into extended families. Even though marriage is not necessarily expected of all members of contemporary African communities, in traditional African societies it was customary for all adults except holders of certain offices and persons with severe mental or physical disabilities to get married and have children (see, e.g., Kenyatta 1938; Mbiti 1969 and 1973; Radcliffe-Brown and Forde 1950). It is important to note that *when Africans got married, they did not "start families," they joined existing families.* Upon marriage, a couple joined a cluster of related families who resided together in a single compound. This extended family comprised resident members of a lineage, their spouses (from other lineages), and children (who, of course, were also members of the resident lineage).

Depending upon the prevailing rules governing residence after marriage, the newly married couple joined either an extended family where the groom's relatives formed the core of the group, or one where the bride's relatives formed the core of the group. In actuality, only one of the spouses normally changed residence at marriage, because the other was usually already living in the compound of the extended family which they would join.

It is important to understand *the differences between the lineage and the extended family in African kinship,* for although the two groupings are closely related, they are not the same. From what I have said so far, it should be apparent first of all that *extended families are based on marriage and descent, whereas lineages are based solely on descent.* It is important to realize also that *the living adult members of a lineage form the core of consanguineal ("blood") relatives around whom the extended family is built.*[3] Furthermore, as Uchendu notes, even in those African societies where corporate lineages are absent or exist only in rudimentary form, the extended families are still based around consanguineal cores, that is, around persons linked by parent-child and/or sibling ties (Shimkin and Uchendu 1978).

A second difference between the lineage and the extended family concerns the manner in which descent is reckoned in the two groupings. *In the lineage, descent is traced through one line only, whereas in the extended family descent (or more technically, filiation) is traced bilaterally, through both parents.* Thus, in a patrilineal or matrilineal society, from the point of view of any given person, the lineage comprises relatives linked through the father-line or the mother-line, as the case may be. In both types of society, however, the extended family comprises relatives on both the mother- and the father-side.

A third point of contrast between the lineage and the extended family is that *lineage membership is discrete and non-overlapping whereas extended family membership is always overlapping.* Ideally, a society can be divided into a finite number of lineages, and each person in the society would be a member of only one of those lineages.[4] The situation is different with extended families. Given the different marital connections of the various members of the lineage, it is obvious that even brothers and sisters do not have precisely the same constellation of relatives in their extended families. African extended families were and are transresidential groupings, even though in day-to-day affairs the particular extended family constellation that actually resides together in the same compound is the group that carries out most of the mutual aid and socialization functions normally ascribed to African extended families.

A fourth distinction between the lineage and the extended family concerns the relative permanence and the generational depth of the two types of groups. *Lineages are conceptualized as existing in perpetuity, involving the living and the dead, going back to the founding ancestor. Extended families are essentially constellations of living relatives.* Their precise composition will vary

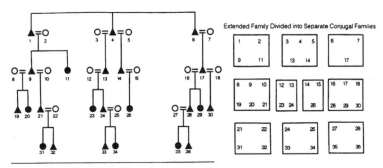

Extended Family Divided into Separate Conjugal Families

Extended families showing division into lineage members (dark) and wives who come from other lineages (uncolored)

▲ Male member of the patrilineal core of the extended family

● Female member of the patrilineal core of the extended family

○ "Wives of the Compound" (wives who marry in from other lineages)

⊓ Sibling bond

| Parent-child link

＝ Marriage

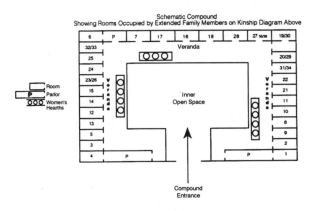

Schematic Compound
Showing Rooms Occupied by Extended Family Members on Kinship Diagram Above

Figure 3.
Schematic View of an Extended Family
Occupying a Single Compound

depending upon the person who is taken as the "central ego" from whom the extended family is being reckoned. When deceased persons are remembered, they are always identified by their lineage (or compound) affiliation, not simply by their extended family connections to some living person. For example, one's deceased maternal grandfather would be remembered as a son of a particular lineage and compound rather than recalled simply as one's "mother's father."

Although African extended families tend to be large, labyrinthine groupings, for illustrative purposes an extended family occupying a single compound in a patrilineal society (such as that of the Yoruba of Nigeria) might be diagrammed as a group of brothers, their wives, their adult sons and grandsons and their wives, and any unmarried children in the groups (see Figure 3).

The married daughters and sisters of the adult males would be resident in the compounds of their husbands. Thus, the consanguineal core of the domiciled extended family consists of the adult males and their unmarried children. The core might also include a divorced or widowed sister or daughter who has returned to live in her father's compound until such time as she remarries.

From one perspective, members of the patrilineage view the wives collectively as the "in-law" (affinal) component of the resident extended family. That is, the wives represent the component of the domiciled extended family that is created "by law" rather than "by blood" (see Sudarkasa 1973, ch. 5). And whereas only in the most extraordinary circumstances do African societies provide for the legal severance of consanguineal kinship bonds, they all provide for the "severance by law" of those bonds that are based "in law" (Marshall 1968:9).

From another very important perspective, however, *as mothers* of children of their husbands' lineage, the women married into the compound are the very persons through whom the patrilineage achieves continuity. Hence, as the "mothers of the lineage" they have a significance that transcends their relationship to the particular men who happen to be their husbands. Moreover, the wives and mothers of a lineage constitute connecting links with other lineages and as such are very important to their husbands and their husbands' kin. Understanding these linkages helps to explain why divorce was discouraged in most indigenous African societies. It also helps to understand in many African societies the custom whereby widows were "inherited" by men from their deceased husbands' lineages.

In this paper I cannot go into the differences in structure and functioning between lineages and extended families in patrilineal societies and those in matrilineal societies. A moment's reflection should reveal that males in matrilineal societies cannot occupy roles that are strictly analogous to those of females in patrilineal societies. In both instances, it is the women who bear the children, and that in itself has important implications.

I have already noted that in day-to-day affairs it is the co-residential extended family that carries out most of the functions normally associated with African extended families. These compound-based groupings vary considerably in size within the same society and across different societies. In the small town of Awe, Nigeria, I studied Yoruba compounds that had as few fifteen and as many as sixty adults in them (Sudarkasa 1973). In large Yoruba cities, many compounds, especially those headed by indigenous rulers, had hundreds of adults living in them. The number of dependent children in the compounds was difficult to obtain, but in most compounds they outnumbered the adults.

SUBDIVISIONS OF THE AFRICAN EXTENDED FAMILY

Having described the structure of the lineage and its relationship to the compound and the extended family, we turn now to an examination of the marriage-based families within the traditional extended family. The first point to be made is that these conjugal families are not "nuclear families" in the common usage of the term. They were actually or potentially polygamous families (usually involving polygyny, i.e., a plurality of wives, but in some societies polyandry, i.e., a plurality of husbands, was permitted). The data suggest that most men in traditional African societies were involved in a polygynous marriage for a least some part of their married life. Thus, traditionally the normal developmental cycle of a conjugal family would involve a monogamous phase and then a polygamous phase. But even when a couple had a monogamous union throughout their married life, in the context of the extended family, where many people were involved in polygamous unions and where everyone had obligations to their own lineages as well as to their conjugal families, the monogamous family was not the insular type of institution implied in the Western concept of the nuclear family.

A second and equally important point concerning conjugal

families within the extended family is that from the perspective of the larger family group the monogamous and polygamous families within it were structurally equivalent to each other. In other words, whether a man had one wife and children, two wives and children, or many wives and children, his was only one family. This very important point concerning the structural equivalence of monogamous and polygamous families within the extended family has been overlooked in many discussions of African families. The Western preoccupation with "reducing" polygamous families to their "minimal constituents" has led various writers, including W.H.R. Rivers (1924:12) and Murdock (1949:2) to propose that these families be viewed as "multiple families" with a husband-father in common. Elizabeth Colson even went so far as to maintain that a mother and her children constituted the nuclear family in traditional Africa, and that this "nuclear" family could best be viewed as having been incorporated into various types of larger units.[5] If one logically pursued these arguments, the monogamous family would be one family, and the polygamous family many families within the extended family.

Although Africans recognize the mother-child dyad as a primary social and affective unit (as do most of the world's peoples), it is erroneous to characterize this unit as a separate "nuclear family" within the African extended family. Such a formulation has no explanatory value since none of the normal functions of a family were traditionally performed by this unit in isolation. It was not a unit of socialization in and of itself; it was not a unit of economic production or consumption in and of itself; it was not an isolated unit of emotional support or mutual aid; it obviously was not a procreative unit. Why then term it a "nuclear family"?

The obsession of some anthropologists with nucleation within the extended family stems from the *a priori* assumption of Westerners that anything larger than the nuclear family must be reducible to it or to something smaller. It is undeniable that in all societies, including those of Africa, the procreative unit is normally a male and a female, and that this unit, together with its offspring, can be profitably isolated for study or analysis. It does not follow, however, that this unit should be conceptualized as the building block for families in every society where it is found. Labeling the father-mother-child unit as the "nuclear family" does not make it invariably so. Other role configurations are sometimes more appropriately designated as the nuclear family in a given society. Depending on the purpose of the division, there can be said to be two nuclear groups within the African extended family. The consanguineal core (excluding spouses) forms one nucleus of the African extended family. The "nuclear" *families* (including spouses) within the traditional African extended family normally would be built around polygamous marriages, not monogamous ones as is the case in Western nuclear families.

If there is one thing that anthropologists should have learned from the study of African societies, it is that large and complex family groupings do not present to Africans the "problems" that they present to Europeans. In fact, what P.A. Tetteh observes concerning Ghana is true of indigenous Africa in general; "when the word 'family' is used, it does not usually refer to the nuclear or elementary family based on the husband-wife relationship but to the extended family based on descent" (Tetteh 1967:201). Given the "naturalness" of the extended family to Africans, one would have thought that anthropologists would have sought to explore the implications of this reality rather than obscure it by conceptual analyses that seek to reduce it to Western-derived paradigms.

The polygamous families that form one of the basic subdivisions of the extended family can indeed be further subdivided for certain purposes, but the occasions for these divisions vary from case to case. My own researches among the Yoruba provide one illustration of the way in which the polygynous family may be subdivided. (It should be noted that the practice of polygyny as described below is disappearing in Nigeria and elsewhere under the impact of Christianity, Western education, demographic and economic changes, and so on.)

In a typical traditional Yoruba compound, each man had a section of the dwelling, or a separate dwelling, for himself and his family. Whether he was married monogamously or polygynously, he had a separate room apart from his wife or wives. Each wife also had her own room, her own household furnishings, cooking utensils, and so forth. Nevertheless, each polygynous family was one family. Any other interpretation misrepresents the structure and functioning of the unit. To speak of separate families with a husband/father in common would overlook, for example, the important integrative role of the senior wife. Traditionally, the Yoruba expected the senior wife to be a companion and confidante to her co-wives, as well as to her husband (Mabagunje 1958). She was often called upon to intercede with her husband on behalf of a co-wife. Wives of the same husband often cooperated in domestic activities and sometimes in economic activities as well (Sudarkasa 1973, chs. 5, 6).

Customarily, on occasions such as naming ceremonies for newborn babies, weddings, and funerals, the wives of each man, together with other wives of the compound, collectively carried out specific roles that were traditionally assigned to them. For example, the wives were collectively responsible for some of the preparation and distribution of food that took place. They might also have specific social or ceremonial roles to play. During a traditional wedding, for instance, as the bride and her procession moves through the town, the wives of her father's compound (excluding her own mother and some of the older women) bring up the rear of the group, singing traditional songs of sorrow at the loss of a daughter from their husbands' lineage. In positioning and in demeanor, the wives provide the counterpoint to the brides' attendants who dance and rejoice with her at the head of the procession.[6]

Generally, it might be said that among the Yoruba the wives of a compound collectively constituted a quasi-kin group within the extended family. They were and are referred to as "wives" by both the females and the males of their husbands' lineage. They also refer to each other by terms that mean senior or junior wife. (They are usually *addressed* as "Mother of So-and-So" even though they are referred to and refer to each other as "wives.") During my research, I found that despite some rivalry and competition among wives of the same husband, the relationships among wives of the entire compound were characterized by a considerable degree of camaraderie and cooperation (Sudarkasa 1973:104-109, 146-152).

The cohesion of the polygynous Yoruba family derived in large measure from the explicit rules or codes defining appropriate behavior for all persons in the group. Within the polygynous family, the children are referred to as *Omo Baba* or *Obakan*, i.e., "children of one father." Differential and deferential behavior among children of one father is based on seniority as determined by age, regardless of which wife is the mother. However, the Yoruba also have the concept of *Omo Iya*, meaning "children of the same mother [by the same father]."[7] The concept of *Omo Iya* comes into prominence mainly in matters of inheritance. Certain of a deceased man's properties are divided into as many parts as there are wives with children. Thus, for certain purposes, a mother and her children do constitute a subunit within the family, but they do not constitute a separate unit within the family.

The Yoruba recognize that the emotional bond between the children of the same mother and father *(Omo Iya)* is not necessarily shared by all the children of the same father by different mothers *(Omo Baba)*. However, in day-to-day affairs, all children of the same father are expected to behave toward each other as if there were no differences in maternity. As far as the behavior of the husband/father is concerned, it is considered very reprehensible for him to show favoritism toward any wife other than a new bride during the "honeymoon" period, or to treat the children of one wife differently from the children of the other wives (Sudarkasa 1973, chs. 5, 6).

No institution has been more maligned by observers of African societies than the institution of polygyny (popularly termed polygamy). The anthropological and popular literature abounds with discussions of rivalry and jealousy among co-wives. Even when anthropologists describe the bond between co-wives, they tend to refer back to an underlying conflict between the women (see, e.g., Fortes 1949:126 ff.). When mention is made of the fact that women themselves often encouraged their husbands to take additional wives, it is usually explained solely in terms of the economic or material benefits of polygyny. For example, it is often noted, as I myself did, that the addition of a junior co-wife frees the senior wife from certain domestic chores (Sudarkasa 1973).

It seems, however, that before the spread of western criticism of polygyny, *African women valued the companionship of co-wives.* In fact, in a recent study of Nigerian women it was reported that the majority of women still said they would be "pleased" to have a second wife in the home (Ware 1979). The negative attitudes of some Western-educated African women toward polygyny cannot be taken as representative of the traditional attitudes toward the institution.

After years of studying African social organization I have concluded that *the premium Africans placed on having children led women as well as men to place a high value on a system (namely polygyny) that afforded all women the possibility of motherhood within the context of a family.* According to African values, having a system of co-wives was preferable to having a system where women bore children outside of marriage or where women could live out their lives as childless spinsters. In fact, in traditional Africa, these occurrences would have been perceived as outside the normal and appropriate mode of behavior.

CONJUGALITY AND CONSANGUINITY IN THE AFRICAN EXTENDED FAMILY

Paradoxically, although "the concept of the extended family developed from studies of African peoples" (Aldous 1965:10), the "classical" model of the extended family described by Murdock (1949) missed one of the most distinctive features of these families. Murdock, who appears to have coined the phrase "nuclear family", also put forth the polar concept of the "extended family" as two or more nuclear families linked by the parent-child tie or the sibling tie (Murdock 1949, pp. 2, 23; see Figure 4).

Anxious to confirm his hypothesis concerning the universality of the nuclear family and its centrality in all other types of family groupings, Murdock imposed upon the empirical reality of the extended family an analytical paradigm that emphasized the primacy of the nuclear family. Of course, in some parts of the world there are extended families built upon nuclear families as Murdock's model suggests. However, this model does not fit the reality of African extended families and, as I shall attempt to show, it has obscured some of the important realities of African American families, as well.

The Murdock model of the extended family did not take into account the important contribution to comparative family studies made by Ralph Linton in *The Study of Man* (1936). Linton had proposed a generic division of all families into two types: "conjugal" (built around the marital pair) and "consanguineal" (built around "blood relatives"). Linton and Murdock were each seeking concepts to describe the same empirical realities. Linton defined his types by reference to principles of family formation, whereas Murdock defined his types by reference to presumed

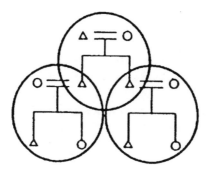

△ Male
○ Female
⌒ Sibling Bond
| Parent-child link
= Marriage

FIGURE 4. The Murdock model of the extended family as a group of inter-realted nuclear families.

basic structural characteristics. Murdock's concepts (i.e., "nuclear" and "extended" families) are the ones that gained general acceptance; hence, I must stress the importance of consanguinity within African extended families rather than refer to them as consanguineal families as Linton had done.

The primacy of the consanguineal core over the conjugal family as the "building block" of the African extended family is evident in a number of ways. First of all, the stability of the family is not dependent upon the stability of conjugal unions. Although (for reasons alluded to earlier in this paper) divorce was relatively rare in most precolonial African societies, nonetheless, when divorces did occur, they did not cause the "dissolution of the family." Spouses could come and go, as it were, but the extended family remained intact. In the patrilineal societies, when a divorce occurred, the wife would return to her natal compound or move to that of her new husband. Her older children would remain behind to be cared for by their paternal grandmother (who resided in the same compound as her husband and sons), by one of their father's other wives or by one of the other women resident in their compound. Conceivably also, one of the children might go to live with the father's sister in the compound of her husband. In a matrilineal situation women often did not change residences at marriage, and when a divorce occurred, they simply remained in their natal compounds with their children and members of their lineages.

A second indicator of the primacy of the consanguineal group over the conjugal group in the African extended family is the contrast in the consequences of the departure of a spouse versus the departure of a member of the lineage core. As I indicated, when a spouse leaves the compound, the stability of the family is not seriously jeopardized. On the other hand, when a member of the lineage core of the extended family decides to make a permanent break away from the compound, this starts a process of fission that could have serious disruptive consequences. For example, in the case of patrilineal groups one brother's departure could trigger the exodus of several other males and their wives and children. Eventually the process could culminate in the formation of a new lineage segment and a new branch of the extended family. Interestingly, in virtually all African societies stories recalling this process of lineage and family segmentation describe it as resulting from a quarrel between brothers (see, e.g., Radcliffe-Brown and Forde 1950).

A third clue to the preeminence of consanguinity in the African extended family is the fact that in various societies, when a member of the core dies or is barren or impotent, his or her procreative functions would be assumed by a brother or sister. Thus, a man might marry his deceased brother's widow or sire a child on behalf of an impotent brother or "cousin" within the lineage. A woman might replace her deceased sister in a marital union or bear a child in her barren sister's stead. These practices are usually discussed in terms of their importance to the maintenance of marriage alliances between lineages or in terms of their contribution to the continuity of the lineage (Radcliffe-Brown 1950:64-65; Marshall 1968). Looked at from the perspective of the present discussion, they demonstrate that within the extended family, the priorities of the consanguineal core group can determine the manner in which the conjugal family's procreative functions will be carried out.

A fourth consideration that negates the primacy of the conjugal family within the African extended family is the fact that two of the important functions that are attributed to families cross-culturally—namely socialization and economic cooperation—are not carried on by separate conjugal families within the extended family but are shared, albeit in varying degrees, by all members of the larger group. For example, all adult members of a Yoruba compound share in the upbringing of children in that compound. Extended family members in other compounds are also called upon to assist in the socialization process (Sudarkasa 1973). Similarly, among the Yoruba and in virtually all other African societies, people are linked into extensive networks of financial obligation and economic cooperation. These networks embrace not only family members who are co-resident in a given compound or a given locality but extend to distant communities and foreign lands (Sudarkasa 1974, 1977, 1979; Eades 1979; Shimkin and Uchendu 1978).

Having shown that the consanguineal core is the building block of African extended families, it is important to reiterate that marriage was expected to be a stable institution in traditional African communities. In fact, most marriages were lifelong unions. It was through marriage that families as well as individuals were joined together, and the linkages formed were valued for their political and economic ramifications as well as for the social and psychological solidarity they fostered.

The point I am making here, then, is not that conjugality was unimportant in African extended families; it was very important. After all, it was only through procreation that the consanguineal kin groups could continue to exist, and most African societies had strong negative sanctions against having children outside of marriage. The point that I am making is that, important though it was, marriage did not have the primacy of place in African kinship that it has in the nuclear family of the West.

THE EXTENDED FAMILY IN AFRICAN COMMUNITIES

The extended family was a unit wherein the basic production and distribution of material goods and services took place.[8] Because of its relatively large size and composition (including both sexes and members of all generations in the society), it was an efficient economic mechanism. The skills that had been accumulated over centuries were harnessed and utilized within the extended family, with the elders providing the know-how based on experience and the younger members providing the labor to get various tasks accomplished. Innovation and change also resulted from the interaction between young and old.

The size of the extended family and the division of labor by gender and age made it possible for all members to contribute to the economic activities that took place outside the domestic unit as well as inside the compound itself. Thus, for example, young married women could engage in productive work outside the home because older women assisted with the childrearing and young unmarried women helped with other domestic chores (*Infra*, chap. 14). Moreover, both males and females could accomplish a variety of complex productive and distributive tasks because the work was done in cooperative groups rather than in isolation.

The responsibilities for socialization and social control that were carried out by the family also involved the cooperation of the entire unit, although some of the tasks were allocated at different times to different segments or persons within the larger unit. Because of the structure of the extended family, it could serve as the society's basic educational facility, imparting both skills and values to the youth. It could also function as an effective agent of social control, because it was the source of much of the satisfaction and many of the "rewards" its members received. By having the power to withdraw sources of emotional support, which might be done, for example, by ostracizing recalcitrant members of the family, the leadership of the extended family was able to serve as a basic law enforcement agency. The strength of the extended family explains in part the absence of elaborate policing mechanisms and penal institutions in precolonial Africa. Moreover, through the use of arbitration and diplomacy, the male and female elders in the extended family were able to settle many disputes without recourse to the courts that did exist.

The extended family provided social security in the form of companionship, counseling, and emotional reinforcement for the society's youth, adults, and aged. Africans did not subscribe to the view that "true" emotional gratification, satisfaction, and support come mainly through groups based on sexuality. In fact, husbands and wives looked to their wider extended family relations as well as to each other (sometimes more than to each other) for companionate, gratifying, and satisfying relationships. The extended family also provided care for the infirm as well as the emotionally or mentally disabled, with the burden of these responsibilities being shared among various members of the unit.

Interpersonal relations within the extended family were guided by a number of ethical principles as well as by the various sanctions that could be brought to bear on members whose behavior was considered too deviant to be tolerated. In this paper I can not attempt to summarize the vast amount of data that exist on patterns of authority, decision-making, and other aspects of interpersonal behavior in African kin groups. I have elsewhere suggested that four principles—respect, restraint, responsibility, and reciprocity—underlie and undergird interpersonal behavior in the family and the wider community in most indigenous African societies (Marshall 1970).

Two of these principles, namely respect and responsibility, are often mentioned in discussions of African kinship. Reciprocity is usually held to be a principle governing economic relations, but as Mauss (1954), Sahlins (1972, ch. 5), and others have shown, it is equally applicable to the broad spectrum of behavior within the family. It is only the principle of restraint that might seem unfamiliar to students of African societies. Any questions about this concept should be dispelled when it is realized that I use it to refer to the impetus that causes individual desires or proclivities to be weighed against and possibly subordinated to the sentiment of the group.

Respect is the cardinal guiding principle for behavior within the family and in the society at large. It not only governs the behavior of family members toward the head of the compound and the other male and female elders, it is expected of siblings and is the key to harmonious relations within the polygamous family. Displayed primarily through patterns of deference and forms of address, children learn to show respect even before they learn to speak. It manifests itself in greetings, bows, curtsies, and other gestures signaling recognition of seniority; it manifests itself in knowing when to be seen and not heard; it requires acknowledgement of and submission to persons in authority.

Restraint is the principle that makes possible communalism within the family and in the wider society. Restraint means that a person cannot "do his or her own thing." The rights of any person must always be balanced against the requirements of the group. In the family restraint is manifest in many ways. It is evident in patterns of consumption, it governs verbal communication, it is necessary in the management of polygamous connubial relations. Restraint is related to the notion of "sacrifice." Parents exercise restraint over their own desires in order to provide for their children, who, in turn, repay the "sacrifice" by putting their parents' needs before their own in many instances.

Responsibility is manifest in every area of family life and is the principle that needs the least elaboration. It is obviously closely related to the foregoing principle of restraint. What needs to be emphasized, perhaps, is that given the size of African families, the lines or chains of responsibility extend much farther than they do in most Western family situations. For Africans, kinship offers a wide network of security, but it also imposes the burden of extensive obligations.

Reciprocity "ties it all together." Without the principle of reciprocity, the other principles would not stand. Traditionally, it is expected that generosity will prevail, especially among relatives, but it is also expected that good deeds will be reciprocated either in the short run or in the distant future. Sometimes obligations are carried over from one generation to the next, but they are eventually reciprocated.

THE TRANSFORMATION OF THE FAMILY FROM AFRICA TO AMERICA

The earliest forms of African family organization re-created in America by enslaved Blacks represented both an amalgamation of specific features from different ethnic groups and an adaptation of these features to the realities and demands of the slave regime. The foregoing description and interpretation of African family organization provide some of the "baseline" data needed to study the *transformation of African family patterns* re-created in America *into African American family patterns* reflecting changes developed over time in the context of different social, economic, and political conditions. Research into the continuities and changes in African-derived family patterns among African

Americans must be undertaken in a historical context and must begin with models of African kinship that accurately depict past realities on that continent.

In this regard, the oft-cited writings of Wade Nobles deserve comment. The "principles" he describes as underlying African family organization ("oneness of being" and "survival of the tribe") are of such a level of generality that they cannot explain recurrent patterns or variations in the behavioral and structural aspects of African family life. Moreover, some of Noble's formulations can be misleading. He states, for example, that "the Black African definition of the family, prior to the intrusion of the European presence on the continent, included every member of the tribe" (Nobles 1974b:15; see also Nobles 1974a, 1978, and King 1976). Only in a strictly metaphorical sense can it be said that all members of a given community or a given "tribe" belonged to one family. When it is realized that many of the "tribes" to which Nobles refers were nations embracing millions of people, it becomes apparent that this part of his description of African kinship cannot be taken literally.

Moreover, while it is true that the idea of a founding ancestor for an entire people was widespread in precolonial Africa, and the idealogy of common descent was used to mobilize some of the so-called segmentary societies,[9] neither of these facts should be construed to mean that Africans considered everyone in their ethnic group or their nation to be members of one family. In precolonial Africa as in other parts of the world, the very notion of kin implied its opposite, namely, non-kin. Thus, some people were defined as relatives and some were not. Those who were non-kin constituted the pool from which spouses were taken.

Turning to the areas that require clarification in the study of the relationship between African and African American family structure, I want to discuss briefly three: (1) the issue of documenting continuities as well as discontinuities between African and African American family patterns; (2) the need to study the operation of the principles of consanguinity and conjugality in African American families without assuming that the conjugally based nuclear family is superior to any other form of the family (*Infra*, chap. 1); and (3) the need to study the temporal and spatial aspects of the adaptation of African-derived family patterns to different American environs, defined in geographic, sociopolitical, and economic terms.

The issues involved in documenting continuities and changes in African family patterns transplanted in America have been the subject of decades of debate (Frazier 1939; Herskovits 1941; Bracey et al. 1970; Shimkin and Uchendu 1978). Without attempting to cite all the parties and positions in this debate, let me outline the situation as I see it, recognizing that not all of my formulations are original or unique.

It is necessary, first of all, to establish that we are seeking to understand the processes by which Africans and African institutions were transplanted and transformed in America. This might seem a simple or obvious point to make, but it is not one which undergirds most of the historical scholarship on Blacks in America. Enslaved Africans are generically referred to as "slaves" and their institutions as "slave" institutions, as if their identity were totally determined by the condition of their oppression. (Note that Israelites enslaved in Egypt for centuries are always referred to as Israelites in a state of bondage or in slavery.) Yet despite mainstream academia's attempt to deny the cultural heritage of early America's enslaved population, their own researchers belie their efforts. Even in the hands of a writer such as Herbert Gutman who is skeptical of "African survivals" (his quotation marks), the data show that most of the patterns of family and kinship (and patterns in other areas outside the purview of this paper) found among enslaved Africans were basically "retention and reinterpretations" of patterns found on the continent of Africa (Woodson 1936; Herskovits 1941).

As a student of continental African societies, it is not surprising to me that contemporary writings on African American history, most notably those of Blassingame (1972), Genovese (1974), and Gutman (1976), reveal the presence of African patterns in African American consanguineal kin groupings ("kin networks"), husband-wife relations, sibling bonds, socialization practices, patterns of exogamy, marriage rules and rituals, naming practices, relationships between alternate generations (i.e., grandparents and grandchildren), patterns of respect and deference, and the extension of kinship terminology to elders throughout the community. As I pointed out in the first section of this paper, in the realm of kinship more than in any other aspect of social organization, there was variation only in details, not in essentials, from one indigenous African society to the next. Furthermore, as has been repeatedly shown, most of the Africans enslaved in America came from contiguous areas in the western part of their mother continent, where there had been a long history of culture contact and a high degree of institutional similarity (see, e.g., Herskovits 1941:1-85).

Lineages, extended families, polygynous conjugal families, large residential units, and other structural features and behavioral patterns described in the preceding sections of this paper were found throughout the area from which the African captives were taken to America. Eyewitness descriptions of late seventeenth-, eighteenth-, and nineteenth-century Africa and ethnographic reconstructions of precolonial social organization provide evidence of the prevalence of the kinship patterns noted.[10] These patterns were found in precolonial states as well as in the so-called stateless or segmentary societies. They were found in the Savanna (or Sahel) as well as along the coast. They cut across almost every type of grouping into which African societies have been divided. Thus, regardless of the "diverse" backgrounds of the Africans enslaved in America (a diversity that is usually greatly exaggerated), there was a commonality in the familial patterns known to them.

It was this shared social organizational "baseline" that enabled the Africans enslaved in America to create recognizably *African* patterns where they lived. Obviously, these captive people had to adapt to the realities of the savage system of slavery in which they existed, but that did not obliterate the fact of their origin. If Israelites enslaved in Egypt for centuries could remain Israelites, if diverse European peoples in the twentieth century can still acknowledge cultural survivals from ancient Greece and Rome, I wonder why it is considered so preposterous that Africans only a few generations removed from their homelands would show evidence of their cultural roots. Unfortunately, in this area of scholarship as in many others we are confronted with persistent and pervasive pseudo-scientific "postulates" about the nature of African people. These so-called theories and the so-called facts adduced to support them do nothing but pervert and prevent the progress of reasonable scholarship.

As an Africanist reading historical writings on the Black family in America, I have to marvel at the refusal of many scholars to make the most obvious interpretations of their data when these data point to the fundamental Africanity of Blacks enslaved in America. One has only to note Gutman's reluctance to attribute the most obvious African patterns to their cultural source. In his speculation over the origin of the marriage ritual of "jumping over the broomstick." he includes the possibility that it was "learned from whites" (1976:277)! In a discussion of "naming practices" described as African in origin by a former enslaved woman, Gutman seemed to think it unusual that the practice survived among people who "had been separated from direct contact with West Africa at least a half century and probably much longer" (1976:193). European peoples are considered to have what might be termed "cultural memories" that span millennia; apparently those of Africans, on the other hand, cannot be expected to last the lifetime of a single person!

Gutman also illustrates another tendency among certain scholars of early African American life, namely the tendency to discount a practice as being African when it becomes fused with some Euro-American elements. Herskovits long ago appropriately referred to such manifestations as "syncretisms" (in the case of certain religious practices) and "reinterpretations" (in more general instances). It is very interesting in this connection that when Gutman labels an institution or custom as African American he seems to assume that the Americanness, as it were, is more significant than the Africanity. This is revealed, for example, in his discussion of the practice of naming babies after siblings who died in infancy. Gutman almost triumphantly labels the practice African American (rather than African) because the names used were Euro-American names (1976, P. 193). It is as if he thought Africans were free to give or use African names whenever they wanted to. One has only to recall the savage beatings that led Kunta Kente to take the name Toby (Haley 1976).

It appears that to most Euro-American and to some African-American scholars, the social science axiom about the tenacity of culture does not apply when describing the experience of Africans transplanted in America. All too often we are confronted with variations of Elkin's view of "the slave":

> Much of his past had been annihilated; nearly every
> prior connection had been severed. Not that he had

> really "forgotten" all these things—his family and kin-
> ship arrangements, his language, the tribal religion,
> the taboos, the name he had once borne, and so on—
> but *none of it any longer carried much meaning.* The
> old values, the sanctions, the standards, already unreal,
> could no longer furnish him guides for conduct, for
> adjusting to the expectations of a complete new life.
> Where then was he to look for new standards, new
> cues—who would furnish them now? He could now
> look to none but his master, the one man upon whose
> will depended his food, his shelter, his sexual connec-
> tions, whatever moral instruction he might be offered,
> whatever "success" was possible within the system, his
> very security—in short, everything. (Elkins 1959:101-
> 102; *emphasis added*)

This statement was born of Elkin's own imagination, not from the
evidence that already existed at the time he wrote and that is
coming more and more to light with each new publication.

The writings of Blassingame, Owens, Genovese, Gutman, and
others suggest that Blacks on the plantations behaved as slaves
toward whites and in relation to matters concerning the "Masters"
or their surrogates. Most of the older literature on slavery would
have us believe that the slave role was all-consuming. The more
recent historical writings point to the fact that in some areas of their
lives, *enslaved Blacks behaved toward each other as Africans,* albeit
Africans whose customs had to be adapted to the context of slavery. The interpreter of early African American life must not be mis-
led by the fact that Blacks on the plantations almost literally ran
away from the label "African" or hid from the "Master" anything
that could be labeled "voodoo." They denied their Africanity
because in so doing they sought to enhance their chances of survival in a situation where to be African was to invite the whip or
worse. But the point is, they lived out much of their lives as
Africans. Their Africanity was manifest in their family and community relations; in their music and their recreation; in their spirituality; and in their rituals and rites of passage (most especially in
the way they mourned their dead). The point is that certain manifestations of Africanity could be tolerated or overlooked ("That's
jes' the way the Niggers is"). It was those aspects of Africanity that

were perceived as dangerous to the survival of the slave regime that were outlawed or forbidden. Thus, African religions, Islam, secret societies, "voodoo," night funerals, and evidences of the recreation of political structures, such as "chieftaincies," were among the practices that were banned. Ironically, neither the "Masters" nor the "slaves" seemed to realize that the most powerful "Africanism" of all was the extended family, which *did* survive, and thereby enabled a people to survive.

One of the most important areas for research is the reassessment of the extent to which and the ways in which the slave status was prevented from intruding upon the daily round of life in the "slave quarters." Many of the recent descriptions of these quarters suggest African-derived communities where the internal behavioral norms were almost as foreign to the whites as would have been customs on the African continent. Gutman's book provides a wealth of data on early African American families, but we have yet to see an ethnohistorical study of enslaved African families and communities. This is a piece of research that is urgently needed.

The second issue that requires clarification in studies of African and African American family structure concerns the principles upon which these families are organized. The implications of the operation of the principle of consanguinity in relation to that of conjugality must be fully explored before the dynamics of African American families can be appreciated and their similarities to African families and differences from Euro-American families fully understood. This point was the main theme of a lecture I presented to the National Medical Association in 1972. At that time, I stated:

> Black families are not necessarily centered around conjugal unions, which are the *sine qua non* of the nuclear family. Among Blacks, households centered around consanguineal relatives have as much legitimacy (and for most people, as much respectability) as family units as do households centered around conjugal unions. When this fact is understood, it becomes clear that the instability of conjugal relations cannot be taken as the sole measure of instability of the family. That Black families exhibit considerable stability over time and space is evidenced by the enduring linkages and bonds

of mutual obligation found among networks of consanguineal kin. (*Infra*, chap. 1, p. 8)

A number of studies that have appeared since 1972, including those by Stack (1974), Ashenbrenner (1975, 1978), Agbasegbe (1976), McAdoo (1978), Shimkin et al. (1978), Martin and Martin (1978), and Kennedy (1980), have provided documentation and amplification of those observations.

The question of the relationship between consanguinity and conjugality in Black families is not to be broached solely in terms of the prevalence of one or the other. We need to study the circumstances and conditions under which one or the other predominates in matters of family and household formation, delegation of authority, maintenance of solidarity and support, and so on. This implies, of course, that we must study the operation of these principles in transresidential family groupings as well as in individual households.

When the study of Black families is approached from this perspective, it becomes apparent that the old debate (joined most recently by Gutman) concerning the historical predominance of one-parent or two-parent families among African Americans requires reformulation. Virtually all of Gutman's extraordinary data should be evaluated from another perspective. He was concerned with proving the antiquity of "the nuclear family" among Blacks; this he considered to have been accomplished by his abundant documentation of the stability of conjugal unions over time. From the data I presented on *African* families, it should be clear that stable conjugal unions are not to be taken as necessary indicators of the prevalence of nuclear families of the Western type. What is critical to investigate are the ways in which and the extent to which the conjugally based groupings described by Gutman were embedded in or articulated with the wider kin networks also described by him.

By now it should be apparent that the old (and unfortunately continuing) debate about the presence or absence of the nuclear family among Blacks rests on the assumption that the nuclear family represents a form of family organization that is superior to all others. As I noted previously:

A survey of the literature on comparative family organization shows that the emphasis on the nuclear family...does not derive from its universality or its structural primacy, but rather from the value placed upon it in Western societies. What European...scholars did was to take the type of family...that existed in their own societies and rationalize its existence elsewhere. Where other types of family existed, they construed these to be "built upon" nuclear families. Moreover, where nuclear families did not exist as the normal or preferable form of family organization, they were promoted through the various propaganda agencies and techniques utilized by European missionaries, political officials, and scholars....

Studies of Black families in the U.S. must be viewed in the general context of the development of comparative family studies. The value premise undergirding these comparative studies asserted (and still asserts) that the conjugally based nuclear family is the "healthy," "normal," "organized," and "stable" form of family whereas families that depart from the nuclear family ideal are "unhealthy," "abnormal," "disorganized," and "unstable." (*Infra*, chap. 1, pp. 6–7)

One would hypothesize that the farther back in time we go in the study of Afro-American families, the more likely we are to find that, barring direct interference from "masters," both two-parent households and one-parent households would be conceptualized by the enslaved Africans as parts of interlocking family networks in which consanguinity played a significant organizing role. This is not to imply that conjugality and the stable conjugal unions documented by Gutman were unimportant. Indeed, given that the constraints of slavery did not permit the replication of African consanguineal kin groups, one would expect that husbands and wives as elders in the family would assume an even greater importance than they did in the original African context of full-fledged lineages and extended families with various elders domiciled in one large compound.

What I am suggesting is that the conjugally-based groupings described by Gutman probably should not be conceptualized as nuclear families, as he is inclined to do, but rather as groups linked to others through ties of consanguinity and affinity which involved the types of obligations and mutual assistance associated with African family organization. A corollary of this interpretation is that it was *after* slavery, when Black American extended family organization was not encumbered by the restraints of the slave regime, that we find the reemergence of kinship groupings that exhibited many of the features of their African antecedents. The data on families in rural and urban Black communities tend to support this interpretation (Agbasegbe 1976; Shimkin et al. 1978; Aschenbrenner 1975; Martin and Martin 1978).

Of course, as many writers have pointed out, these multi-functional, mutual-assistance kin groupings that are Black extended families were vital to the survival and (as Billingsley and McAdoo have shown) to the upward mobility of Blacks in America (Billingsley 1968; Hill 1971; McAdoo 1978). However, it is important to reiterate that these groups did not originate in America in response to the adverse socioeconomic and political circumstances in which Blacks found themselves. The groups originated in Africa, where they had always served many of the same purposes they came to serve in America. The various adaptations of these groups to American conditions, and the changes that occurred in the process thereof, remain to be systematically explored (see Green 1978).

Such a study would involve the third issue I wish to touch upon, namely, the need to identify those factors that account for the evolution or development of different family patterns in different circumstances and different time periods in America. Certain patterns were obviously due to regulations and conditions imposed by the regime of slavery as manifested in different areas. For example, the size and configuration of the living quarters as well as the small size of many of the plantations and farms on which enslaved Blacks lived prevented the replication of African compounds and African extended families. Nevertheless, consanguineal kin networks and stable conjugal unions did persist (Gutman 1976). Other patterns may have been due to other factors—such as the proximity of free Black families to Native American communities. In a manner similar to Jacquelyne Jackson's researches on contemporary Black families (1971), we need to know more about the impact of varying economic conditions and demographic factors, such as sex ratios on Black family and household configurations over time. Studies such as those of Furstenberg et al. (1975) on female-headed households in nineteenth-century Philadelphia are useful in this connection.

Gutman's intriguing data on patterns of exogamy during slavery, i.e., patterns of marriage outside of stipulated kin groups and communities, point to another area that should be studied for evidence of African and African American continuities, as well as changes that occurred as American customs were superimposed on those from Africa. Moreover, the whole question of the disappearance of the lineage principle or its absorption into the concept of extended family requires research. Gutman's data showing that enslaved Blacks named sons after their fathers suggests one mechanism for keeping the lineage principle alive despite the constraints of slavery (see Gutman 1977:188-190, passim).

As we move farther and farther away from Africa in time and as the African American population increases in size, socioeconomic complexity, and geographical diversity, we can expect to see evidence that some patterns of African American family life diverge significantly from those found in Africa. And, of course, in many respects contemporary African American families, extended as well as all other types, differ considerably from those of precolonial and present-day Africa.[11] Interestingly, however, the operation of various factors associated with Westernization and modernization in contemporary Africa are leading to the emergence of family patterns similar to those found among Blacks in the United States. Clearly, a comparative study of changes in the African family, both on the continent and in the American diaspora, would contribute enormously to our understanding of what happens to the structure and functioning of extended families in different socioeconomic environments.

CONCLUSION

In this paper I have outlined the main features of African family organization and indicated some of the issues to be taken into account in relating the African patterns to those that developed among the Africans who were captured and enslaved in America. The task of actually specifying the continuities and discontinuities in African and Afro-American family structure and of analyzing the bases for these is obviously too vast for the present paper. It does seem, however, that such an undertaking would make an important contribution to the ongoing reinterpretation of much of the data on Black families (English 1974; Staples 1978; Allen 1978). Such a study would also provide a synthesis of the various approaches to Black family studies which Staples (1978) describes as "conceptual models" under the headings "Pan-Africanism," "Historical Materialism," and "Domestic Colonialism."

From my perspective, the approach to Black family studies that starts from the premise that African familial patterns were re-created in a modified form in America is not properly termed a "conceptual model," if by that is meant that some other "conception" has equal validity. It is a *fact*, supported by evidence that accumulates with each new historical and sociological study of Black families, that African patterns of family organization survived among enslaved Blacks and continue to be manifest to the present day. This fact is not inconsistent with a view that takes into account economic forces and racial ideologies in studying the changes that have occurred in African-derived family patterns over time and in different geographical and political environments.

As regards the studies that would specifically focus on illuminating the African family patterns that were transplanted and transformed in America, I would reiterate that we should begin to look comparatively at specific behavioral patterns, specific structural features, and specific values rather than continue to generalize about African cosmological views that are said to undergird Black American life (Nobles 1978). Not only is it extremely difficult to substantiate this claim (one has only to study an African society to appreciate how complex a matter this is), but so long as we continue our discussions at such highly abstract levels, we make it possible for those who are doing the concrete historical and sociological studies from Eurocentric perspectives to continue to misinterpret or misrepresent the data they uncover.

NOTES

1. In 1984, Bamidele Agbasegbe Demerson called my attention to a paper by the late Herbert J. Foster entitled "African Patterns in the Afro-American Family" (*Journal of Black Studies,* December 1983, pp. 201-231), in which substantial portions of the present chapter (first published in *The Black Scholar* in 1980) were lifted verbatim without quotation marks. In other instances, Foster used only a slight paraphras-

ing of my words without any attribution whatsoever. This *prima facie* case of plagiarism was brought to the attention of the Editor of the journal (Dr. Molefe Asante), who expressed his regret that "this severe case of misappropriation has occurred." Because of Foster's ill health, I decided not to pursue a case against him, but I call attention to this here, lest someone read my essay in this book and assume that I have plagiarized Foster's work instead of vice versa. Documentation of the corresponding passages from Sudarkasa and Foster is available from the present author (N.S.) and has been filed with Africa World Press.

2. Among the Yoruba of Nigeria, the rule of exogamy prohibits marriage within one's own patrilineage, one's mother's patrilineage, one's father's mother's patrilineage, and one's mother's mother's patrilineage.

3. The reader is reminded that kinship is fundamentally a *social* phenomenon, not merely a biological one. In some societies, certain genetically related persons are defined as marriageable non-kin. For example, one's mother's brother's son or daughter might be so defined. In other societies the same relative might be defined as too close for marriage. Moreover, in all societies there are provisions for making non-kin into kin (adoption is one such process). When we use the term "consanguineal" or "blood" relatives, we are referring to persons so defined by the rules of their society or ethnic group.

4. Here we are excluding the so-called double-descent systems, in which a person belongs to a matrilineage traced through the mother and a patrilineage traced through the father.

5. Colson begins her analysis by terming this the "nuclear group"; later she terms it the "family nucleus" to which "the husband and father is attached." Subsequently, she refers to the mother-child grouping as the "nuclear family" (1962).

6. I observed such weddings during my fieldwork in the Yoruba town of Awe in 1961 and 1962 (*Infra*, chap. 13).

7. Children of the same mother by different fathers are termed *Iyekan*, but inasmuch as they belong to different lineages and normally reside in the compounds of their respective fathers, they do not come under discussion here.

8. For other discussions of the functioning of African extended families, see Tetteh (1967), Okediji (1975a), Shimkin and Uchendu (1978), and Kerri (1979).

9. Sahlins (1961) refers to these as "tribal" societies based upon segmentary lineage systems.

10. The bibliography in Herskovits's *Myth of the Negro Past* cites many of the early accounts of precolonial West Africa. An introduction to the vast ethnographic literature can also be gleaned from that source or from others cited in this paper.

11. In a pilot study measuring extended family interaction among Nigerians,

Black Americans, and white Americans, Okediji (1975b) shows that Nigerians scored highest on his scale of intensity and frequency of such interaction, followed by Black Americans and then white Americans. There was a significant difference between Black and white Americans, but there was an even greater difference between Nigerians and Black Americans

8

Interpreting the African
Heritage in African American
Family Organization*

INTRODUCTION

Many of the debates concerning explanations of Black family
organization are waged around false dichotomies. The experience of slavery in America is juxtaposed to the heritage of Africa
as the explanation of certain aspects of Black family structure.
"Class" versus "culture" becomes the framework for discussing
determinants of household structure and role relationships. Black
families are characterized either as "alternative institutions" or as
groups whose structures reflect their "adaptive strategies," as if the
two viewpoints were mutually exclusive.

Just as surely as Black American family patterns are in part an
outgrowth of the descent into slavery (Frazier 1939), so too are
they partly a reflection of the African institutions and values that
informed and influenced the behavior of those Africans who were
enslaved in America (Herskovits 1941). With respect to "class"
and "culture," it is indeed the case that the variations in historical and contemporary Black family organization cannot be
explained without reference to the socioeconomic contexts in

*The author wishes to thank Tao-Lin Hwang for his assistance with the
research for this chapter and Bamidele Agbasegbe Demerson for his helpful
comments.

which they developed (Allen 1979). But neither can they be explained without reference to the cultural contexts from which they derived (Nobles 1974a, 1974b, 1978). Whereas Black families can be analyzed as groups with strategies for coping with wider societal forces (Stack 1974), they must also be understood as institutions with historical traditions that set them apart as "alternative" formations that are not identical to (or pathological variants of) family structures found among other groups in America (Aschenbrenner 1978).

After more than a decade of rethinking Black family structure (see, for example, Billingsley 1968; Staples 1971, 1978; Aschenbrenner 1973; English 1974; *Infra*, chap. 1; Allen 1978; Shimkin et al. 1978), a holistic theory of past and present Black family organization still remains to be developed. Such a theory or explanation must rest on the premise that political-economic variables are always part of any explanation of family formation and functioning. But the cultural historical derivation of the formations in question helps to explain the nature of their adaptation to particular political-economic contexts.

Obviously, it is beyond the scope of this paper to try to set forth such a holistic explanation of Black family organization. Its more modest aim is to take a step in this direction by laying to rest one of the false dichotomies that stand in the way of such an explanation. This review seeks to show how an understanding of African family structure sheds light on the form and functioning of Black American family structure as it developed in the context of slavery and later periods. It seeks to elucidate African institutional arrangements and values that were manifest in the family organization of Blacks enslaved in America, and suggests that some of these values and institutional arrangements continue to be recognized in contemporary formations.

The relationships of causality, correlation, and constraints that exist between the political-economic sphere and that of the family cannot be dealt with here. What this paper seeks to clarify is why Black familial institutions embrace certain alternatives of behavior and not others. It suggests a cultural historical basis for the fact that Black family organization differs from that of other groups even when political and economic factors are held relatively constant.

Thus, it is suggested that it does not suffice to look to politcal and economic factors to explain, say, the differences between low income Anglo- or Italian-American families and low income African American families. One has to come to grips with the divergent culture histories of the groups concerned. In other words, one is led back to the institutional heritage stemming from Western Europe on the one hand and that from West Africa on the other. Knowledge of the structure and functioning of kinship and the family in these areas helps to explain the structure and functioning of families formed among their descendants in America.

It might appear that this is too obvious a point to be belabored. However, when it comes to the study of Black American families, historically the scholarly community has taken a different view. Whereas it is generally agreed that the history of the family in Europe is pertinent to an understanding of European-derived family organization in America (and throughout the world), many—if not most—scholars studying Black American families have argued or assumed that the African family heritage was all but obliterated by the institution of slavery. This view has retained credence, despite the accumulation of evidence to the contrary, in large measure because E. Franklin Frazier (1939), the most prestigious and prolific student of the Black American family, all but discounted the relevance of Africa in his analyses.

The paper takes its departure from W.E.B. DuBois (1908), Carter G. Woodson (1936), and M.J. Herskovits (1941), all of whom looked to Africa as well as to the legacy of slavery for explanations of African American social institutions. Herskovits is the best-known advocate of the concept of African survivals in African American family life, but DuBois was the first scholar to stress the need to study the Black American family against the background of its African origins. In his 1908 study of the Black family, DuBois prefaced his discussions of marriage, household structure, and economic organization with observations concerning the African antecedents of the patterns developed in America.

> In each case an attempt has been made to connect present conditions with the African past. This is not because Negro-Americans are Africans, or can trace an unbroken social history from Africa, but because there is a distinct nexus between Africa and America which,

> though broken and perverted, is nevertheless not to be
> neglected by the careful student (DuBois 1908:9)

Having documented the persistence of African family patterns in
the Caribbean, and of African derived wedding ceremonies in
Alabama, Du Bois noted:

> Careful research would doubtless reveal many other
> traces of the African family in America. They would,
> however, be traces only, for the effectiveness of the
> slave systems meant the practically complete crushing
> out of the African clan and family life. (p.21)

With the evidence that has accumulated since DuBois wrote, it is
possible to argue that even though the constraints of slavery did
prohibit the replication of African lineage ("clan") and family life
in America, the principles on which these kin groups were based,
and the values underlying them, led to the emergence of variants
of African family life in the form of the extended families which
developed among the enslaved Blacks in America. Evidence of the
Africanity to which DuBois alluded is to be found not only in the
relatively few "traces" of direct *institutional* transfer from Africa
to America, but also in the numerous examples of *institutional
transformation* from Africa to America.

No discussion of the relevance of Africa for understanding
African American family organization can proceed without confronting the issue of the "diversity" of the backgrounds of
"African slaves" (read "enslaved Africans") brought to America.
Obviously for certain purposes, each African community or each
ethnic group can be described in terms of the linguistic, cultural,
and/or social structural features which distinguish it from others.
At the same time, however, these communities or ethnic groups
can be analyzed from the point of view of their similarity to other
groups.

It has long been established that the Africans enslaved in the
United States and the rest of the Americas came from the Western
part of the continent where there had been a long history of tran-
scultural contact and widespread similarities in certain institutions
(Herskovits, 1958: chs. 2 and 3). For example, some features of
kinship organization were almost universal. Lineages, large co-resident domestic groups, and polygynous marriages are among the

recurrent features found in groups speaking different languages, organized into states as well as "segmentary" societies, and living along the coast as well as in the interior (Radcliffe-Brown 1950; Fortes 1953; Onwuejeogwu 1975).

When the concept of "African family structure" is used here, it refers to those organizational principles and patterns which are common to the different ethnic groups whose members were enslaved in America. These features of family organization are known to have existed for centuries on the African continent and are, therefore, legitimately termed a part of the African heritage.

AFRICAN FAMILY STRUCTURE— UNDERSTANDING THE DYNAMICS OF CONSANGUINITY AND CONJUGALITY

African families, like those in other parts of the world, embody two contrasting bases for membership: *consanguinity,* which refers to kinship that is commonly assumed or presumed to be biologically based and rooted in "blood ties," and *affinity,* which refers to kinship created by law and rooted "in-law." *Conjugality* refers specifically to the affinal kinship created between spouses (Marshall 1968). Generally, all kinship entails a dynamic tension between the operation of the contrasting principles of consanguinity and affinity. The comparative study of family organization led Ralph Linton (1936:159-163) to observe that in different societies families tend to be built either around a conjugal core or around a consanguineal core. In either case, the other principle is subordinate.

According to current historical research on the family in Europe, the principle of conjugality appears to have dominated family organization in the Western part of that continent (including Britain) at least since the Middle Ages, when a number of economic and political factors led to the predominance of nuclear and/or stem families built around married couples. Certainly for the past three or four hundred years, the conjugally based family has been the ideal and the norm in Western Europe (Shorter 1975; Stone 1975; Tilly and Scott 1978). Whether or not the European conjugal family was a structural isolate is not the issue here. The point is that European families, whether nuclear or extended (as in the case of stem families), tended to emphasize the conjugal relationship in matters of household formation, decision making, property transmission, and socialization of the young (Goody 1976).

African families, on the other hand, have traditionally been organized around consanguineal cores formed by adult siblings of the same sex or by larger same-sex segments of patri- or matrilineages. The groups which formed around these consanguineally related core members included their spouses and children, and perhaps some of their divorced siblings of the opposite sex. This co-resident *extended family* occupied a group of adjoining or contiguous dwellings known as a compound. Upon marriage, Africans did not normally form new isolated households, but joined a compound in which the extended family of the groom, or that of the bride, was already domiciled (*Infra*, chap. 7: 101–105).

African extended families could be subdivided in two ways. From one perspective, there was the division between the nucleus formed by the consanguineal core group and their children and the "outer group" formed by the in-marrying spouses. In many African languages, in-marrying spouses are collectively referred to as "wives" or "husbands" by both females and males of the core group. Thus, for example, in any compound in a patrilineal society, the in-marrying women may be known as the "wives of the house." They are, of course, also the mothers of the children in the compound. Their collective designation as "wives of the house" stresses the fact that their membership in the compound is rooted in law and can be terminated by law, whereas that of the core group is rooted in descent and is presumed to exist in perpetuity.

African extended families may also be divided into their constituent conjugally-based family units comprised of parents and children. In the traditional African family, these conjugal units did not have the characteristics of the typical "nuclear family" of the West. In the first place, African conjugal families normally involved polygynous marriages at some stage in their development cycle. A number of Western scholars have chosen to characterize the polygynous conjugal family as several distinct nuclear families with one husband/father in common (Rivers 1924:12; Murdock 1949:2; Colson 1962). In the African conception, however, whether a man had one wife and children or many wives and children, his was one family. In the case of polygynous families, both the husband and the senior co-wife played important roles in integrating the entire group (Fortes 1949, chs.3, 4; Sudarkasa 1973, ch.5; Ware 1979). The very existence of the extended family as an "umbrella" group for the conjugal family meant that the latter group differed from the Western nuclear family. Since, for many purposes and on many occasions, all the children of the same generation within the compound regarded themselves as brothers and sisters (rather than dividing into siblings versus "cousins"), and since the adults assumed certain responsibilities toward their "nephews" and "nieces" (whom they term sons and daughters) as well as toward their own offspring, African conjugal families did not have the rigid boundaries characteristic of nuclear families of the West.

The most far-reaching difference between African and European families stems from the different emphasis on consanguinity and conjugality. This difference becomes clear when one considers extended family organization in the two contexts. The most common type of European extended family consisted of two or more nuclear families joined through the parent-child or sibling tie. It was this model of the stem family (or joint family) that was put forth by George P. Murdock (1949:23,33,39-40) as the generic form of the extended family. However, the African data show that on that continent, extended families were built around consanguineal cores and the conjugal components of these larger families differed significantly from the nuclear families of the West.

In Africa, unlike Europe, in many critical areas of family life the consanguineal core group rather than the conjugal pair was paramount. With respect to household formation, I have already indicated that married couples joined existing compounds. It was the lineage core that owned (or had the right of usufruct over) the land and the compound where families lived, farmed, and/or practiced their crafts. The most important properties in African societies—land, titles, and entitlements—were transmitted through the lineages, and spouses did not inherit from each other (Goody 1976).

Within the extended family residing in a single compound, decision making centered in the consanguineal core group. The oldest male in the compound was usually its head, and all the men in his generation constituted the elders of the group. Together they were ultimately responsible for settling internal disputes, including those that could not be settled within the separate conjugal families or those that could not be settled by the female elders among the wives (*Infra*, chap. 14). Male elders also made decisions, such as those involving the allocation of land and other resources, which affected the functioning of the constituent conjugal families.

Given the presence of multiple spouses within the conjugal families, it is not surprising that the decision making within them also differed from the model associated with nuclear family organization. Separate rather than joint decision making was common. In fact, husbands and wives normally had their own distinct purviews and responsibilities within the conjugal family (Sudarkasa 1973; Oppong 1974). Excepting those areas where Islamic traditions overshadowed indigenous African traditions, women had a good deal of control over the fruits of their own labor. Even though husbands typically had ultimate authority over wives, this authority did not extend to control over their wives' properties (Marshall 1964; Oppong 1974; Robertson 1976; *Infra*. chap. 14). Moreover, even though women were subordinate in their roles as wives, yet as mothers and sisters they wielded considerable authority, power, and influence. This distinction in the power attached to women's roles is symbolized by the fact that, in the same society where *wives* knelt before their *husbands, sons* prostrated themselves before their *mothers*, and status among *siblings* was governed by *seniority*, which was determined by age rather than gender (Sudarkasa 1973, *Infra*. chap. 14)).

Socialization of the young involved the entire extended family, not just the separate conjugal families, even though each conjugal family had special responsibility for the children (theirs or their relatives') living with them. It is important to note that the concept of "living with" a conjugal family took on a different meaning in the context of the African compound. In the first place, husbands, wives, and children did not live in a bounded space, apart from other such units. Wives had their own rooms or small dwellings, and husbands had theirs. These were not necessarily adjacent to one another. (In some matrilineal societies, husbands and wives resided in separate compounds.) Children ordinarily slept in their mothers' rooms until they were of a certain age, after which they customarily slept in communal rooms allocated to boys or girls. Children usually ate their meals with their mothers but they might also eat some of these meals with their fathers' co-wives (assuming that no hostility existed between the women concerned) or with their grandmothers. Children of the same compound played together and shared many learning experiences. They were socialized by all the adults to identify themselves collectively as sons and daughters of a particular lineage and compound, which entailed a kinship, based on descent, with all the lineage ancestors and with generations yet unborn (Radcliffe-Brown and Forde 1950; Uchendu 1965; *Infra*, chap. 7).

The stability of the African extended family did not depend on the stability of the marriage(s) of the individual core group members. Although traditional African marriages (particularly those in patrilineal societies) were more stable than those of most contemporary societies, marital dissolution did not have the ramifications it has in nuclear family systems. When divorces did occur, they were usually followed by remarriage. Normally, all adults other than those who held certain ceremonial offices or who were severely mentally or physically handicapped lived in a marital union (though not necessarily the same one) throughout their lives (see, e.g., Lloyd 1968). The children of a divorced couple were usually brought up in their natal compound (or by members of their lineage residing elsewhere), even though the in-marrying parent had left that compound.

Several scholars have remarked on the relative ease of divorce in some traditional African societies, particularly those in which matrilineal descent was the rule (see, e.g., Fortes 1950:283). Jack Goody (1976:64) has even suggested that the rate of divorce in precolonial Africa was higher than in parts of Europe and Asia in comparable periods as a corollary of contrasting patterns of property transmission, contrasting attitudes toward the remarriage of women (especially widows), and contrasting implications of polygyny and monogamy. If indeed there was a higher incidence of divorce in precolonial Africa, this would not be inconsistent with the wide-ranging emphasis on consanguinity in Africa as opposed to conjugality in Europe.

Marriage in Africa was a contractual union which often involved a long-lasting companionate relationship, but it was not expected to be the all-encompassing, exclusive relationship of the Euro-American ideal type. Both men and women relied on their extended families and friends, in addition to their spouses, for emotionally gratifying relationships. Often, too, in the context of polygyny, women as well as men had sexual liaisons with more than one partner. A woman's clandestine affairs did not necessarily lead to divorce because, in the absence of publicized information to the contrary, her husband was considered the father of all her children (Radcliffe-Brown 1950). And in the context of the lineage (especially the patrilineage), all men aspired to have as many children as possible.

Interpersonal relationships within African families were governed by principles and values which I have elsewhere summarized under the concepts of respect, restraint, responsibility, and reciprocity. Common to all these principles was a notion of *commitment to the collectivity*. The family offered a network of security, but it also imposed a burden of obligations (*Infra*, chap. 7). From the foregoing discussion, it should be understandable that, in their material form, these obligations extended first and foremost to consanguineal kin. Excepting the gifts that were exchanged at the time of marriage, the material obligations entailed in the conjugal relationship and the wider affinal relationships created by marriage were of a lesser magnitude than those associated with "blood" ties.

AFRICAN AMERICAN FAMILY STRUCTURE: INTERPRETING THE AFRICAN CONNECTION

Rather than start with the question of what was African about the families established by those Africans who were enslaved in America, it would be more appropriate to ask what was not African about them. Most of the Africans who were captured and brought to America arrived without any members of their families, but they brought with them the societal codes they had learned regarding family life. To argue that the trans-Atlantic voyage and the trauma of enslavement made them forget, or rendered useless their memories of how they has been brought up or how they had lived before their capture, is to argue from premises laden with myths about the Black experience (Elkins 1963:101-102; see also Frazier 1966, ch.1).

Given the African tradition of multilingualism and the widespread use of *lingua francas* (Maquet 1972:18-25)—which in

West Africa would include Hausa, Yoruba, Djoula, and Twi—it is probable that many more of the enslaved Africans could communicate among themselves than is implied by those who remark on the multiplicity of "tribes" represented among the slaves. As Landman (1978:80) has pointed out:

> In many areas of the world, individuals are expected to learn only one language in the ordinary course of their lives. But many Africans have been enculturated in social systems where multiple language or dialect acquisition have been regarded as normal.

The fact that Africans typically spoke three to five languages also makes it understandable why they quickly adopted "pidginized" forms of European languages as *lingua francas* for communicating among themselves and with the captors.

The relationships which the Blacks in America established among themselves would have reflected their own backgrounds and the conditions in which they found themselves. It is as erroneous to try to attribute what developed among them solely to slavery as it is to attribute it solely to African background. Writers such as Herbert Gutman (1976), who emphasize the "adaptive" nature of "slave culture" must ask what it was that was *being* adapted as well as in what context this adaptation took place. Moreover, they must realize that adaptation does not necessarily imply extensive modification of an institution, especially when its structure is already suited (or "preadapted") to survival in the new context. Such an institution was the African extended family, which had served on that continent, in various environments and different political contexts, as a unit of production and distribution; of socialization, education, and social control; and of emotional and material support for the aged and the infirm as well as the hale and hearty (Kerry 1979; Okediji 1975; Shimkin and Uchendu 1978; *Infra*, chap. 10).

The extended family networks that were formed during slavery by Africans and their descendants were based on the institutional heritage which the Africans had brought with them to this continent, and the specific forms they took reflected the influence of European-derived institutions as well as the political and economic circumstances in which the enslaved population found itself.

The picture of Black families during slavery has become clearer over the past decade, particularly as a result of the wealth of data in Gutman's justly heralded study. Individual households normally comprised a conjugal pair, their children, and sometimes their grandchildren, other relatives, or non-kin. Marriage was usually monogamous, but polygynous unions where the wives lived in separate households have also been reported (Gutman 1976: 59, 158; Blassingame 1979:171; Perdue et al. 1980:209).

Probably only in a few localities did female-headed households constitute as much as one-quarter of all households (Gutman 1976, chs. 1-3 *& passim*). The rarity of this household type was in keeping with the African tradition whereby women normally bore children within the context of marriage and lived in monogamous or polygynous conjugal families that were part of the larger extended families. I have tried to show elsewhere why it is inappropriate to apply the term "nuclear family" to the mother-child dyads within African polygynous families (*Infra*, chap. 7) In some African societies—especially in matrilineal ones—a small percentage of previously married women, or married women living apart from their husbands, might head households that were usually attached to larger compounds' heads. However, in my view, on the question of the origin of female-headed households among Blacks in America, Herskovits was wrong, and Frazier was right in attributing this development to conditions that arose during slavery and in the context of urbanization in later periods (Frazier 1966; Herskovitz 1958; Furstenberg et al. 1975).

Gutman's data suggest that enslaved women who had their first children out of wedlock did not normally set up independent households, but rather continued to live with their parents. Most of them subsequently married and set up "neo-local" residence with their husbands. The data also suggest that female-headed households developed mainly in two situations: (1) A woman whose husband died or was sold off the plantation might head a household comprising her children and perhaps her grandchildren born to an unmarried daughter; (2) a woman who did not marry after having one or two children out of wedlock but continued to have children (no doubt often for the "master") might have her own cabin built for her (Gutman 1976, chs. 1-3).

It is very important to distinguish these two types of female-headed households, the first being only a phase in the developmental cycle of a conjugally headed household, and the second being a case of neolocal residence by an unmarried female. The pattern of households headed by widows was definitely not typical of family structure in Africa, where normally a widow married another member of her deceased husband's lineage. *The pattern of neolocal residence by an unmarried woman with children would have been virtually unheard of in Africa. Indeed, it was also relatively rare among enslaved Blacks and in Black communities in later periods.* Before the twentieth-century policy of public assistance for unwed mothers, virtually all young unmarried mothers in Black communities continued to live in households headed by other adults. If in later years they did establish their own households, these tended to be tied into family networks that included several households.

The existence during slavery of long-lasting conjugal unions among Blacks was not a departure from African family tradition. Even with the relative ease of divorce in matrilineal societies, most Africans lived in marital unions that ended only with the death of one of the spouses. In the patrilineal societies from which most American Blacks were taken, a number of factors, including the custom of returning bridewealth payments upon the dissolution of marriage, served to encourage marital stability (Radcliffe-Brown 1950:43-54). Given that the conditions of slavery did not permit the replication of African families, it might be expected that the husband and wife as elders in the household would assume even greater importance than they had in Africa, where the elders within the consanguineal core of the extended family and those among the wives would have had major leadership roles within the compound.

When the distinction is made between family and household—and, following Bender (1967), between the composition of the co-resident group and the domestic functions associated with both households and families—it becomes apparent that the question of who lived with whom during slavery (or later) must be subordinate to the questions of who was doing what for whom and which kinship relationships were maintained over space and time. In any case, decisions concerning residence per se were not always in the hands of the enslaved Blacks themselves, and space alone served as a constraint on the size, and consequently to some extent on the composition, of the "slave" cabins.

That each conjugally based household formed a primary unit for food consumption and production among the enslaved Blacks is consistent with domestic organization within the African compound. However, Gutman's data, and those reported by enslaved Blacks themselves, on the strong bonds of obligation among kinsmen suggest that even within the constraints imposed by the slave regime, trans-residential cooperation—including that between households in different localities—was the rule rather than the exception (Gutman 1976:131-138 *& passim*; Perdue et al. 1980:26, 256, 323 *& passim*). One might hypothesize that on the larger plantations with a number of Black families related through consanguineal and affinal ties, the households of these families might have formed groupings similar to African compounds. Certainly we know that in later times such groupings were found in the South Carolina Islands and other parts of the South (Agbasegbe 1976, 1981; Gutman 1976; Johnson 1934, ch. 2; Powdermaker 1939, ch. 8).

By focusing on extended families (rather than simply on households) among the enslaved Blacks, it becomes apparent that these kin networks had many of the features of continental African extended families. These African American groupings were built around consanguineal kin whose spouses were related to or incorporated into the networks in different degrees. The significance of the consanguineal principle in these networks is indicated by Gutman's statement that "the pull between ties to an immediate family and to an enlarged kin network sometimes strained husbands and wives" (1976:202; see also Frazier 1966, pt. 2).

The literature on Black families during slavery provides a wealth of data on the way in which consanguineal kin assisted each other with child rearing, in life crisis events such as birth and death, in work groups, in efforts to obtain freedom, and so on. They maintained their networks against formidable odds and, after slavery, sought out those parents, siblings, aunts, and uncles from whom they had been torn (Blassingame 1979; Genovese 1974; Gutman 1976; Owens 1976). Relationships within these groups were governed by principles and values stemming from the African background. Respect for elders and reciprocity among kinsmen are noted in all discussions of Black families during slavery. The willingness to assume responsibility for relatives beyond the conjugal family, and selflessness (a form of restraint) in the face of these responsibilities, are also characteristics attributed to the enslaved population.

As would be expected, early African American extended families differed from their African prototypes in ways that reflected the influence of slavery and of Euro-American values, especially their proscriptions and prescriptions regarding mating, marriage, and the family. No doubt, too, the Euro-American emphasis on the primacy of marriage within the family reinforced conjugality among the African Americans even though the "legal" marriage of enslaved Blacks was prohibited. As DuBois noted at the turn of the century, African corporate lineages could not survive intact during slavery. Hence, the consanguineal core groups of African American extended families differed in some ways from those of their African antecedents. It appears that in some of these African American families membership in the core group was traced bilaterally, whereas in others there was a unilineal emphasis without full-fledged lineages.

Interestingly, after slavery, some of the corporate functions of African lineages reemerged in some extended families which became property-owning collectivities. I have suggested elsewhere that "the disappearance of the lineage principle or its absorption into the concept of extended family" is one of the aspects of the transformation of African family organization in America that requires research (*Infra*, chap. 7:127). Among the various other issues that remain to be studied concerning these extended families are: (1) Did members belong by virtue of bilateral or unilineal descent from a common ancestor or because of shared kinship with a living person? (2) How were group boundaries established and maintained? (3) What was the nature and extent of the authority of the elder(s)? (4) How long did the group last and what factors determined its span in time and space?

CONCLUSION

At the outset of this chapter it was suggested that a holistic explanation of Black family organization requires discarding or recasting some of the debates which have framed discussions in the past. I have tried to show why it is time to move beyond the debate over whether it was slavery *or* the African heritage that "determined" Black family organization, to a synthesis which looks at institutional transformation as well as institutional transfer for the interplay between Africa and America in shaping the family structures of African Americans.

Obviously, Black families have changed over time, and today one would expect that the evidence for African "retentions" (Herskovits 1958:xxii-xxiii) in them would be more controvertible than in the past. Nevertheless, the persistence of some features of African family organization among contemporary Black American families has been documented for both rural and urban areas. Although this study cannot attempt a full-scale analysis of these features and the changes they have undergone, it is important to make reference to one of them, precisely because it impacts upon so many other aspects of Black family organization, and because its connection to Africa has not been acknowledged by most contemporary scholars. I refer to the emphasis on consanguinity noted especially among lower-income Black families and those in the rural South. Some writers, including Shimkin and Uchendu (1978), Agbasegbe (1976, 1981), Aschenbrenner (1973, 1975, 1978), Aschenbrenner and Carr (1980), and the present author (*Infra*. chap. 1, 7) have dealt explicitly with this concept in their discussions of Black family organization. However, without labelling it as such, many other scholars have described some aspects of the operation of consanguinity within the Black family in their discussions of "matrifocality" and "female-headed households." Too often, the origin of this consanguineal emphasis in Black families, which can be manifest even in households with both husband and wife present, is left unexplained or is "explained" by labelling it an "adaptive" characteristic.

In my view, historical realities require that the derivation of this aspect of Black family organization be traced to its African antecedents. Such a view does not deny the adaptive significance of consanguineal networks. In fact, it helps to clarify why these networks had the flexibility they had and why they, rather than conjugal relationships, came to be the stabilizing factor in Black families. The significance of this principle of organization is indicated by the list of Black family characteristics derived from it. Scrutiny of the list of Black family characteristics given by Aschenbrenner (1978) shows that 12 of the 18 "separate" features she lists are manifestations of the overall strength and entailments of consanguineal relationships.[1]

Some writers have viewed the consanguineally based extended family as a factor of *instability* in the Black family because it sometimes undermines the conjugal relationships in which its members are involved. I would suggest that historically among Black Americans the concept of "family" meant first and foremost relationships created by "blood" rather than by marriage. (R.T. Smith [1973] has made substantially the same point with respect to West Indian family organization.) Children were socialized to think in terms of obligations to parents (especially mothers), siblings, and others defined as "close kin." Obligations to "outsiders," who would include prospective spouses and in-laws, were definitely less compelling. Once a marriage took place, if the demands of the conjugal relationship came into irreconcilable conflict with consanguineal commitments, the former would often be sacrificed. Instead of interpreting instances of *marital* instability as prima facie evidence of family instability, it should be realized that the fragility of the conjugal relationship could be a consequence or corollary of the *stability* of the consanguineal family network. Historically, such groups survived by nurturing a strong sense of responsibility among members and by fostering a code of reciprocity which could strain relations with persons not bound by it.

Not all Black families exhibit the same emphasis on consanguineal relationships. Various factors, including education, occupational demands, aspirations toward upward mobility, and acceptance of American ideals concerning marriage and the family, have moved some (mainly middle- and upper-class) Black families toward conjugally-focused households and conjugally-centered extended family groupings. Even when such households include relatives other than the nuclear family, those relatives tend to be subordinated to the conjugal pair who form the core of the group. This contrasts with some older type Black families where a senior relative (especially the wife's or the husband's mother) could have a position of authority in the household equal to or greater than that of one or both of the spouses. Children in many contemporary Black homes are not socialized to think in terms of the parent-sibling group as the primary kin group, but rather in terms of their future spouses and families of procreation as the main source of their future emotional and material satisfaction and support. Among these Blacks, the nuclear household tends to be more isolated in terms of instrumental functions, and such extended family networks as exist tend to be clusters of nuclear families conforming to the model put forth by Murdock (1949, chs. 1, 2).

For scholars interested in the heritage of Europe as well as the heritage of Africa in African American family organization, a study of the operation of the principles of conjugality and consanguinity in these families would provide considerable insight into the ways in which these two institutional traditions have been interwoven. By looking at the differential impact of these principles in matters of household formation, delegation of authority, maintenance of solidarity and support, acquisition and transmission of property, financial management, and so on (Sudarkasa 1981), and by examining the political and economic variables which favor the predominance of one or the other principle, we will emerge with questions and formulations that can move us beyond debates over "pathology" and "normalcy" in Black family life.

NOTES

1. Of the following eighteen characteristics of Black extended families listed by Aschenbrenner, numbers 1–12 collectively attest to their overall consanguineal emphasis, as derived from African kinship. The remaining four features also can be directly traced to the African cultural heritage in African American family and community life: (1) the relative strength of parent-child and sibling ties in Black families; (2) a high degree of visiting, contact, and various types of economic and social support among relatives beyond the nuclear family; (3) a bilateral orientation, but with the matrilateral kin often given more weight; (4) extended kin groups existing in a social environment in which primary-type relations are extended into the larger community; (5) a high degree of residential propinquity among related households; (6) a high value placed on children and motherhood; (7) responsibility to children diffused throughout extended families; (8) frequent fosterage of children with relatives or neighbors; (9) care for dependent and highly mobile family members, adult or children; (10) emphasis on respect for elders; (11) dependence of the strength of marital ties on certain conditions, e.g. social support by in-laws and a strong economic interdependence between husband and wife; (12) the possibility of undermining of a marital tie when it conflicts with another kinship loyalty; (13) a 'segregated' husband-wife relationship; (14) the existence of, on the one hand, marital relationships with strong public sanctions and economic bases, and on the other hand, a number of private liaisons between men and

women.

"In addition to these structural characteristics...(15) an emphasis on family occasions and rituals, particularly birthdays and funerals; (16) a religious orientation; (17) a high evaluation of family and individual moral 'strength' as a human quality; and (18) a lack of complete correlation between 'strength,' and respectability and economic achievement" (Aschenbrenner 1978: 187).

9

TIMELESS VALUES FOR TROUBLED TIMES: STRENGTHENING TODAY'S AFRICAN AMERICAN FAMILIES

INTRODUCTION

African American families are changing; there is no question about that. But then, so are families all over America. Today, the American ideal of the nuclear family, comprised of two parents and their children living by themselves, is rapidly disappearing as the predominant type of family grouping occupying a single household. Various permutations of the "step-family," resulting from the marriage of couples who have children from previous marriages, are becoming commonplace. Households comprised of single mothers and their children have increased dramatically in the past 25 years—especially among African Americans. Single parenting by men is also on the rise, as is the incidence of parenting by couples of the same sex. For all the changes in family and household structure in America, however, it is only the *Black* family that is consistently portrayed as being "in crisis." Everybody else's families are simply described as "changing"—or *"in transition."* The Black family, we are told, is "unstable"..."on the brink of collapse"... "pathological."

Without trying to minimize the problems faced by many Black families, particularly those engulfed in poverty, we must not allow ourselves to be deluded about what is pathological in America.

What *is* pathological are the conditions of poverty in which most African American families are forced to exist; conditions that offer little or no alternative employment to drugs and crime; and conditions that cover too many of our communities with a blanket of hopelessness and desperation. What is pathological are the deplorable state of too many schools that our children are obliged to attend, and the policies that force most of them into dead-end tracks and stifling "special" education classrooms.

What families could possibly emerge unscathed from the conditions in which many African Americans are forced to live? One-third of our people live below the poverty line—and those are only the official statistics. The numbers are much higher if one counts the people the Government refuses to count. Official statistics do not include the unemployment and poverty statistics persons who supposedly do not want to work. Leaving aside the question of how officials know which people "are not looking for work" or "do not want to work," I would maintain that a person without food will starve whether he or she is looking for work or not. A person without a job is unemployed whether he is looking for work or not.

In the circumstances in which so many of our families exist, it is no wonder that they are fighting for their very lives. But we do not need this war on or among Black families. We need a genuine war on poverty—one that will provide jobs for all the able-bodied poor people who are out of work, not simply a "poverty program" that benefits a few and basically leaves poverty alone. We need a real war on drugs, that is, a war on drug producers, drug importers, drug controllers—not just a hunting expedition against drug users and drug pushers.

As African Americans, we must not allow ourselves to believe the myth that Black family structure is the root cause of the poverty, drug abuse, and crime spreading through our communities. Problems within Black families are more often the result than the cause of these social ills. Of course, we can and should take steps to strengthen our families. But, as the Reverend Jesse Jackson so often stated, to attack the root causes of social degradation in our communities, we must first create jobs. When men are jobless, on the streets, or in jail, they cannot be expected to play normal roles in their families. When women and their children are hungry, survival—not success in school—is the priority.

Employment provides not only incomes, but a large measure of self-worth. All the evidence we have shows that conditions that are allegedly due to our "pathological family structure" rapidly improve when people in poverty are provided with the skills and opportunities to earn a decent living.

At one level, it is important to establish who "is to blame" for the situation in African American communities. At another level, however, it does not matter who is "at fault," because the Black community itself must take initiatives to alleviate conditions that are causing it to self-destruct. We must not only lobby the Government and major corporations to create jobs, we must also establish and support our own businesses that will create jobs. Not only must we lobby for better schools, and equal opportunities for higher education, we must create our own schools, teach our children through our churches and civic organizations, and support Black colleges which continue to be the primary vehicles of upward mobility for hundreds of thousands of our young people. Finally, we must take it upon ourselves to improve the quality of our family life despite the arsenal of degradation and destruction aimed at our communities.

Toward that end, the National Council of Negro Women, under the leadership of Dr. Dorothy Height, is waging a nationwide campaign to reassert and reaffirm the importance of families in our history—and in our lives today. Their "Black Family Reunions" are held annually in cities across the country and should spark other organizations to take equally concrete steps to support and strengthen familyhood in our communities.

For instance, our sororities, fraternities, churches, and public service groups could host forums to bring together all generations in our communities to talk about and plan for the African American family of the future. Rather than sequester senior citizens in "old folks" homes, we need to encourage the building of housing units that will put single mothers and their children in proximity to older women who might be willing to look after the children whose their mothers are at work. We need to use our financial resources to design and build new types of housing units and housing developments that will accommodate families of varying sizes and configurations, rather than assume that a family unit must be a husband, wife, and two-and-a-half children living alone, unto themselves. We must recognize that the key to the survival of Blacks in America has always been the *flexibility* of our family organization. Our first and most resilient political, economic, and social networks were our extended family networks that incorporated single-parent families as readily as two-parent families. Our task now is to recreate similar kinship and friendship networks that will take us into the twenty-first century.

These new extended family networks should be undergirded by traditional *values* that will strengthen relationships within the family and between families and the wider community. Years ago, from my research in West Africa, I identified four principles that seemed to be universal and essential values guiding traditional African life, namely: respect, responsibility, reciprocity, and restraint. Recently, I have had occasion to reflect on these values and have added three others that have been equally important to African families in the past—reverence, reason, *and* reconciliation. Some of these values were also carried over into African American families of the past and, to a lesser extent, they can be found in our families today. I hope the reader will agree with me that they constitute timeless values that can strengthen the families we are building for the new age.

Respect is the cardinal principle that guided behavior within African families and in the African societies at large. It not only governed the behavior of children toward their parents, but also was extended to all elders in the family and in the community. Respect was required of and toward sisters, brothers, aunts, uncles, and so on throughout the kin group. Respect was shown by forms of address—in all communities older people were referred to by titles or by kinship terms such as "uncle" and "aunt." Respect was also shown by the way younger people treated their elders— through greetings, bows, and courtesies and other gestures that children learned early. Respect manifested itself in knowing when to be seen and not heard. We need to teach our children, once again, to respect others so that they can demand respect for themselves. And we have to do this by example.

Responsibility: Africans had to be their brothers' and sisters' keepers, and indeed African Americans have been noted for the willingness to accept responsibility for their kinfolk. Of course, in all societies, familyhood implies some acceptance of responsibility for others in the group. What is African (as opposed to American) about the principle of responsibility is the fact that it extends to a wider range of kin than is the case where the nuclear family, comprised of a married couple and their children, is conceived of as the boundary of "real" responsibility to kin. Traditionally in African and African American communities, we house our cousins; feed distant relatives who come to the city looking for a job; and help take care of nieces and nephews. If African Americans are to survive and prosper in the twenty-first century, we have to continue to assume responsibility for our extended families, as well as for the close relatives with whom we live.

Reciprocity is the principle that compels us to give back to our families and communities in return for that which we receive. Among African peoples, it is expected that generosity will prevail, especially among relatives, but it is also expected that good deeds will be reciprocated either in the short term or in the distant future. Sometimes obligations even may be carried from one generation to the next, but they should never be shirked. In our communities today, we must continue to reach out, reach down, and reach back to help those less fortunate than ourselves as a way of repaying those who assisted us.

Restraint is probably the value that is hardest to teach and accept in today's highly individualistic and materialistic society. In America, "me and mine" always takes precedence over "thee and thine." Everybody wants to "do his own thing." But within African families, a person has to consider the good of the group when making decisions for and about himself or herself. Restraint was manifest in so many ways—people gave their guests the best they had; a brother sacrificed his own ambitions to send another to college; marriages might be postponed to enable one of the partners to render financial help to a sister or brother. Parents and grandparents sacrificed for their children, who, in turn, reciprocated the sacrifice by helping them in their old age. Such selflessness must be rekindled if we are build strong kinship networks for the future.

Reverence: Africans are traditionally spiritual people and in the past African Americans were no exception. Africans traditionally taught their children to revere the earth and its Creator. They taught reverence for the ancestors as well as for all living things. Today, our children and indeed many parents have no time for spirituality, but—regardless of one's religion—it is important to have reverence for the God who, as James Weldon

Johnson said, has brought us thus far on the way.

Reason: We often portray ourselves as an emotional people; we like to emphasize our spontaneity and our expressiveness. But what impressed me when I first conducted research in Nigeria and Ghana in the 1960s was the fact that, first and foremost, Africans wanted to be thought of as a reasonable people. When a dispute broke out, elders appealed to reason, not to emotion, to settle the matter. Among the Yoruba of Nigeria, where I first conducted anthropological field work in the early 1960s, people did not take many disputes to the formal Government courts. They took them to family and community elders, and these wise men and women took as much time as necessary to persuade the parties concerned to come to reasonable settlements. Sometimes I was amazed at how much people were willing to compromise to reach a reasonable conclusion to a dispute. I often thought that Americans, including Black Americans, would have done far less. We have got to get our people to *know* that they must use their reason and their intellect as much as their emotion and sentiment in approaching the problems we face, within our families and outside.

Reconciliation: When I reflected on what I have seen in the decades that I have been in and out of Africa, I realized that reconciliation was a value that cannot be overstressed in family and community life. People knew that they had to be able to forgive each other and reconcile their differences. The Yoruba have a practice of prostrating or kneeling before another to beg forgiveness, and it is virtually unthinkable for anyone to be so hardhearted as to fail to reconcile himself or herself with a relative or friend, or even with a former adversary, when the elders and the person himself beg to have the matter put to rest.

Respect, responsibility, reciprocity, restraint, reverence, reason, and reconciliation—let these be the seven cardinal values for the African American family of the future. Let us draw on our heritage as a people for whom family has been the greatest source of strength and security, and move forward to reaffirm the value of kinship now and in the new age.

Planning *for* the Family versus "Family Planning"—The Case for National Action in Nigeria

INTRODUCTION

No social scientist would quarrel with the proposition that the family is one of the most basic, if not the most basic, of social institutions. In any given society, it can be demonstrated that the structure and function of the family impinge upon virtually every other aspect of that society. For example, the size and composition of the family have implications for the kinds of domestic dwellings that will be erected in any given community; the values imparted to the young via the family's socialization process are important factors in determining the aspirations and achievements of youth; the family's effectiveness as an agent of social control is often reflected in rates of juvenile crime or delinquency; the quality of the relationships among the adults in the family affect their performances in occupations outside the home; and the overall physical and mental health of the community is in large part a reflection of the family's well-being.

Given the pivotal position of the family in any society, one would expect that its welfare would be of concern to all those who are charged with planning or providing for the overall well-being, development, or advancement of that society. It is surprising, therefore, that when one examines many of the Development

Plans which serve as the blueprints for directed socioeconomic change in contemporary African nations, there is no discussion of the role which the family as an institution plays or should play in the development process; there is no provision for channeling resources to or through the family as an institution; there is no attempt to utilize the family as an institution in the training, mobilization, or deployment of the people who, after all, are the backbone of the development process.

Nigeria's Third National Development Plan (1975–1980) is among those which does not mention the family as an agent in its programs for the advancement of the society. Even in discussions of "social development," education, health, housing,and "town and country planning"—areas directly related to the family—there is no statement of policy as to how the family will be utilized in, or affected by, planning in those areas.

The only place in which one finds mention of the family is in the section of the Nigerian Development Plan devoted to "population policy," and there the focus is not on planning for the family, but rather on birth suppression, which Western sociologists, demographers, and health practitioners have misleadingly labeled "family planning." This is not to say that attention to family size is not important but simply that it is not "family planning." This is a point to which I will return in a later section of this paper.

The point here, however, is that, by and large, Nigeria's Development Plan, like that of most other countries, focuses on almost every institution except the family in devising programs for social advancement. Education and communications media, for example, are apparently viewed as the primary vehicles of socialization, as the institutions which provide the value frame for the society, as the institutions mainly responsible for developing the quality of persons within the society, and the channels through which preparation for earning a livelihood takes place. Yet, any realistic analysis of the social structure of Nigeria and other African countries would reveal that the family still has critical responsibilities in all the areas mentioned above.

I would suggest that the primary reason why there is no focus upon families as basic societal institutions in many Development Plans, including that of Nigeria, derives from the nature of the research and policy recommendations on the family that emanate from those academicians to whom the planners look for guidance on these matters. For the most part, the major research on the family, and the policies, programs, and projects that grow out of this research, are concerned with that aspect of family life which is called "family planning" but which is little more than "birth suppression" or "birth control."

Perhaps another reason for the lack of evidence of concern for the family as an institution lies in the fact that most modern Development Plans rest upon the implicit assumption, rooted in Western philosophical and political notions, that individuals are the agents and instruments of change and should be the recipients of resources designed to promote change. It is Western individualism which undergirds the notion that "human resources" are best conceptualized as disaggregated entities, rather than as persons functioning within the context of families and other social networks.

The present paper reflects upon the problem of planning for the family in programs of national development and considers the role of social research in that planning process. First, by way of background, the paper begins with an overview of the traditional roles of the family in African societies and briefly considers the implications of the changes that resulted in the allocation of many of these roles to other social institutions. Secondly, the paper undertakes a brief review of the research on African families, with emphasis on the problems studied, the theoretical framework into which these studies fall, the policy implications of the research and the projects that have been undertaken as a result of this research. Thirdly, the paper suggests an institutional framework out of which future research on the family might grow. It stresses the need for collaboration among various segments of the society in developing preferred models of family organization and in studying the roles these groups could play in the overall strategies and programs for national development. Finally, the paper suggests some of the broad research concerns that should grow out of this collaboration between policy makers and academics—research that should eventuate in genuine family planning programs rather than in birth-control programs promoted under the label of family planning.

II

Despite what Africa's detractors would have us believe, the continent is well known historically for the richness of her natural endowments. The student of history might conclude that Africa should be even better known for the richness of her social heritage. Were traditional anthropologists not preoccupied with demonstrating the "primitivity" of Africa's precolonial institutions, they would recognize that on this continent were developed some of the most sophisticated and successful social arrangements ever devised to provide for the well-being of all members of the society.

I would daresay that no African institution deserves more attention as an ingenious societal invention than does the traditional African extended family. These families were (and are) large, multi-generational groups of kin, related by descent and by marriage. The network of kin who comprised a single extended family cut across many residential and geographical boundaries. However, the extended family grouping that lived together in one household or group of households (called a "compound") is the focus of this discussion.

Traditionally, in patrilineal societies, such as we find in Nigeria, several generations of male members of a lineage formed the core group in the co-residential extended family. As lineage members, they collectively owned the land on which the compound was built, and many of them had their own houses within the compound. In addition to the males of the compound, the extended family included their wives (who were mothers and grandmothers to the second and third generations in the compound), unmarried adult sisters, and dependent children. The married sisters of the family lived in the compounds of their husbands. The men in each extended family compound were related as fathers, grandfathers, sons, grandsons, uncles, nephews, brothers, and cousins (who were usually referred to as brothers).

The extended family was a unit that provided for the economic, social and emotional well-being of its members. Various clusters within the family cooperated in the production and distribution of food and other material goods and services. Because of its size and its composition (including both sexes and members of all generations in the society), it was an efficient economic mechanism. The skills which had been accumulated over centuries were harnessed and utilized within the extended family, with the elders providing the know-how based on experience, and the younger members providing the manpower (or should I say the man- and woman-power) to get the various tasks accomplished.

The size of the unit and the division of labor by gender and age made it possible for all persons within the extended family to engage in economic activities in the public domain of the society as well as to contribute to the smooth running of the domestic unit. Thus, for example, young married females could engage in productive work outside the home because older females assisted with childrearing and other domestic duties within the home. Both females and males could accomplish a variety of complex productive and distributive activities because the work ethic stressed laboring in cooperating groups rather than in isolation.

The extended family provided social security in the form of companionship, counselling, and emotional reinforcement for the society's youth, adults, and aged. The family also assumed responsibility for the care of the infirm as well as the emotionally disabled, with the burden of these responsibilities being shared among various members of the unit.

The responsibilities for socialization and social control that were carried out by the smaller family sub-groups also involved the cooperation of the entire unit. Because of the structure and composition of the extended family, it could serve as the society's basic educational facility imparting both skills and values to the youth. It could also function as an effective agent of social control because it meted out sanctions, punishments and rewards to its members. Ostracism and "bad-mouthing" were forms of punishment feared by both adults and children. The elders were respected for their spiritual power as well as their secular authority.

One of the most highly developed techniques of social control was that of arbitration. Anyone familiar with African societies knows that the art of arbitration and diplomacy were among the most valued of sociopolitical skills. These skills were utilized within and between families in order to prevent their having to use the courts. In fact, the network of extended families was such an effective law-enforcement agency that there was little need for prisons and other penal institutions.

With the intrusion of Europe onto the African continent, there began a process of cultural, economic, and political domination that is usually termed "modernization." This is not the place to review what actually took place under the guise of "modernization"; however, the impact destroyed or undermined many African institutions, including the extended family (see Rodney:1972 for an overview).

The most direct onslaught against the African Family came from those agents of European dominion who were presented as "defenders of the faith." The noted anthropologist, President Jomo Kenyatta of Kenya, has provided a vivid picture of the way in which the missionary's values undermined the social system of the Kikuyu (Kenyatta 1938), and similar examples can be supplied from all over the continent. Missionaries attacked the structure of the extended family by promoting the view that the nuclear family of the West represented the highest form of family organization achieved to date. The network of relatives which had been so important to the African was represented as a deterrent to "development." Polygyny was also attacked and outlawed without any attention to the fact that it was this system of plural spouses that guaranteed that *all* adults had the opportunity to lead normal lives within the context of a family.

Just as the *structure* of the family was assailed by the European agents for change, so were the *functions* of the family "factored out" to other, imported institutions. For example, schools replaced the family as the primary agency for the socialization and education of those who attended them. I am aware that in most analyses people maintain that whatever else might be said against the missionaries, it is nonetheless to their credit that they introduced schools. It should be remembered, however, that these schools were not intended primarily to educate Africans for self-reliance, but rather to indoctrinate them with Western values that stressed above all else the necessity for "backward Africa" to be dependent on the West. It is my view that Africans succeeded *despite* their education, not because of it. It is to the credit of Africans rather than their imported teachers that those who came through the mission schools could emerge to demand to be allowed to reclaim their destiny.

With the introduction of the European cash economy, and mechanisms such as taxation which insured participation in that economy, much of the society's labor force was disengaged from the family. Males and females started to leave their family bases to migrate to the centers where various occupations provided the incomes (in the form of European currency) that were increasingly necessary to procure goods and services throughout the society (Amin 1974).

This Westernization of the economic, social, and political life of African peoples has had a profound and far-reaching effect on the African family. One way of summarizing this effect is to say that the overall emphasis in the society shifted from social collectivities to atomized individuals, and the benefits that accrued to these individuals did not reverberate or filter throughout the family in the way that such benefits would have in the past.

The ethos of individualism and "modernization," and the realities of the financial burdens created by the relatively high cost of procuring education and other imported commodities and services, had the effect of de-emphasizing sharing and emphasizing personal accumulation. These processes served to restrict overall social and economic benefits to much smaller segments of the society than had been the case in the precolonial past. Moreover, the persons who benefitted were precisely those whose Westernized training made then predisposed to opting for speeding up the de-Africanization of family structure, and predisposed them to viewing the extended family as a constraining factor rather than a potential resource in the modernizing process.

Lest there be some misunderstanding of the intent of the foregoing analysis, let me clearly state that when we look at the state of African societies today, we should realize that the processes we subsume under the label "modernization" served to undermine and eliminate a number of features of African societies that had worked well in the past but were *a priori* defined by Europeans as anachronistic in the "modern" era. These institutions were never given a fair chance to prove their worthiness as instruments of indigenous modernization. *Africa has yet to modernize on its own terms,* drawing on its own inspiration and ingenuity, its own social, economic, and political institutional heritage. After all, in the generic sense, *modernization does not have to be synonymous with "Europeanization."*

III

There is no question but that the nature and findings of research on African families have influenced (and will continue to influence) the thinking of those who are involved in developing policies related to these families. It is therefore extremely important to be aware of the stated or unstated motivations behind the research that is undertaken, and to be aware of the interests that have been or will be served by the policies derived from this research. It appears to me that, to date, most of the research on African families has been generated, ultimately, in intellectual and political circles outside Africa, for the purpose of maintaining control over events in Africa.

In the period before the 1950s, most of the research on African families was anthropological research concerned primarily with describing so-called "primitive" forms of social organization for the members of the profession and for colonial officials who could use the information in controlling the societies under their authority. Included in this genre is *African Systems of Kinship and Marriage* (Radcliffe-Brown and Forde 1950), which is usually proclaimed "an anthropological classic" by practitioners in that field. This study, like its predecessor *African Political Systems* (Fortes and Evans-Pritchard 1949), was aimed not only at "students and educators" but also at "administrators" who had to deal with Africans said to be in transition from "kinbound societies" to "another social world."

During the late 1950s, and particularly in the early 1960s, political events in Africa led to a "run" on the continent by social scientists in fields other than anthropology. With African states becoming independent in "droves," information-gathering about the continent could no longer be left to anthropologists, whose rather esoteric jargon and theories concerning "primitives" were considered by professionals in some other disciplines to be inadequate to deal with the situation of "rapid social and political change" in which the erstwhile "primitives" were involved.

Whereas the study of African social systems had been virtually the exclusive domain of anthropologists, a number of sociologists, economists, geographers, and political scientists began to conduct research in this area. In the specific area of family studies, a number of sociologists and anthropologists turned their attention to two primary areas of study, namely, (1) changing family structures and (2) fertility regulation.

As might be predicted, most of the studies of changing family structure have been carried out among the "Westernized elites." These studies generally document the trend—*toward* the conjugally-based nuclear family and *away* from the extended family—that is evidenced among these "elites." Most of the studies make some attempt to identify the social and economic factors that seem to account for changes in the size and composition of households, and in role behavior (particularly conjugal role behavior) and role expectations within the families of these "Westernized elites."

If one attempts to determine the overall theoretical framework into which these studies fit, it appears than they are the new wave of research that propagates the notion that the conjugally-based nuclear family is the most adaptable and the most preferable form of family organization in the "modernizing context." Studies such as those by the English anthropologist Christine Oppong on Ghana suggest that the "tensions" created by the transition from extended to nuclear families are mitigated in situations where the families most closely approximate the ideal of the nuclear family (see, e.g., Oppong 1974). In other words, these studies suggest that the more discretely bounded the family becomes —i.e., the more insulated it is from the wider network of relatives—the better off it is.

A moment's reflection reveals some of the basic problems raised by a research strategy that focuses on "changing family structure among elites." First of all, it is obvious that the Western-educated members of African societies will be those whose family systems will most closely approximate those of the West. Without studying the changes that are taking place in families that are not built around Western-educated couples as heads of households, we cannot claim to have a realistic picture of family change in contemporary Africa. Moreover, when young adults in Africa, such as those in secondary schools or universities, read study after study reporting the trend toward the nuclear family as the direction of family change in Africa, the impression is created that this is the only possible option, or the most effective option, for dealing with the situation of change. Since information influences behavior, these young people might seek to emulate the behavior of the already established "elites" without acknowledging or appreciating any other options.

It would seem that the majority of the studies that do describe changing family patterns among non-Western-educated segments of African populations concern situations in which families have been fractured as a result of some disrupting processes imposed during the colonial period. Such, for example, is the case of some of the studies from Central and Southern Africa where families have been disrupted for much of this century by the forced migration of males to the mining areas. What is needed are more studies of families that have not been subjected to such obviously disruptive forces of change but are nevertheless having to change in response to what are now normal processes such as relatively rapid urbanization, changing occupational structures, changing patterns of land use, of housing, etc. Such studies, undertaken in rural as well as urban areas, would likely provide a realistic picture of the range of family groupings now existent in Africa and an estimate of the extent to which these groups serve as models of successful adaptation to changing socioeconomic conditions.

At the time of this writing, the greatest emphasis in family studies in Africa for the last fifteen years (1960-75) has been on fertility regulation or "family planning." Throughout the continent, a number of sociologists and others have undertaken and are planning research designed essentially to determine (1) what factors stand as obstacles to the acceptance of various methods of birth control, and (2) what means can be instituted to lessen the resistance to the adoption of such methods. There can be no disputing the fact that the amount and intensity of research on "family planning" and population control is a reflection of concerns in this area that were generated outside of the African continent. Money is literally being poured into research on the problem of curtailing fertility, with the purported justification that overpopulation is one of Africa's major obstacles in the way of development.

A number of scholars from Africa and Asia and a number of scholars of African descent in the U.S.A. have argued that the population problem is not essentially one of numbers, but one of distribution of resources. For example, Benedict Zwane has maintained that whereas Africa can be said to be overpopulated in the sense that existing economic systems do not adequately sustain their countries' populations, the problem is *not* the result of population growth *per se*, but rather of population growth in the context of colonial oppression and continued "exploitative agricultural and industrial relations." He maintains that the solution lies in a restructuring of the patterns of agricultural production and in a redistribution of wealth, rather than in enforced population control (Zwane 1975).

Whether or not one advocates some degree of control over population size as a solution to the problem of inequitable distribution of resources in Africa (and elsewhere), it is obvious that scholars concerned with research on the family in Africa (including Nigeria) have concentrated on the issue of fertility control to the neglect of many other problems. The reasons for this seem to be the fact that research priorities are being defined in too many cases by the overseas Foundations that finance research rather than by a careful assessment of the overall policy needs in the countries concerned. In fact, however, in the absence of a mechanism for an on-going appraisal by a group of scholars, planners, and ordinary citizens of what types of family research are to be undertaken, it is not surprising that the research goals will be determined by what should be extraneous considerations such as what topics outside patrons want to fund.

IV

There appears to be a need for a reorientation of research on the African family. At a time when Western scholars are pointing out the negative effects which nuclear family organization has had in their own societies, and looking to the non-Western world for models of family organization that might be promoted for the future, it would seem obvious that *African scholars should be studying their own indigenous types of family organization for clues as to what variants of family structure might be best suited to indigenous African modernization*. Of course, we cannot expect that family systems of the past are necessarily suitable in their entirety to the demands of the present; however, the different aspects of these families should be held up for scrutiny to determine which of these features should be rescued or promoted and which ones allowed to fade into history.

Research of the type that I am advocating would pave the way for genuine family planning (i.e., planning *for* the family). I would suggest that one of the prerequisites to such planning, or in any

case one of the elements in such planning, should be the establishment of Community Family Councils wherein representatives
of government, of academia, and of the populations whose interests they want to serve can have on-going deliberations as to the
types of family organization that seem most conducive to providing for the well-being of all their members. These Community
Family Councils would generally be charged with recommending
to the government ways to promote and protect the viability and
vitality of the family. To this end, they could make recommendations as to specific research projects that should be undertaken
in order to shed light on situations or problems which they identify as important. Within such contexts, the amount of attention
given to questions concerning fertility regulation and family size
would be dictated only by the demands of African socioeconomic
realities rather than by outsiders who aim to control policy decisions regarding population.

These Councils could also be the conduit through which
research findings on the family could be channelled to community action agencies or directly to the members of the community
who might benefit by these findings. They could also serve as the
umbrella organizations under which scholars and laymen with
different types of expertise and representing different interests
might gather to discuss the impact which any given development
project might have on the structure and/or functioning of the
family. Architects and city planners, for example, might be called
together with sociologists and laypersons from a given community to discuss the possible effect on the family of a proposed
change in housing patterns in that community. Finally, these
Councils might serve as "agencies of accountability" to which
proposed research projects might be submitted for discussion as
to the effect of the projects on family life in the area. Researchers
would therefore be made to be accountable in some specified
ways to the communities in which the research is undertaken.

V

I shall conclude by briefly pointing to what I believe to be some
of the topics for research related to genuine planning for the family. Of necessity, such research would be concerned with the functioning of total family networks rather than focusing solely on the

conjugal dyad and isolated households. It could be concerned, for example, with identifying factors that trigger disruptions of kinship links within the modern versions of the extended family as well as detailing the advantages which accrue to those who actively maintain such links. (The literature abounds with discussions of the *dis*advantages). This genuine type of family-planning research would focus on those factors that seem related to the long-range stability of family networks rather than simply dealing with marital stability or instability.

Genuine family-planning research should be concerned with the relationship between family organization and various other aspects of society, such as education or occupational structure. Differential educational opportunities within families often result in tensions and lack of communication across generations and between the sexes. Family-planning research might be concerned, for example, with devising programs, involving home and school, that would keep such educational disparities to a minimum or at least minimize the possibility of developing widespread "generation gaps" of the sort that exist in the West.

Another concern of family-planning research might be the investigation of the type of government support systems that could help the family maintain its social security functions *vis-a-vis* orphans, *vis-a-vis* the aged, or *vis-a-vis* other members of the family who might otherwise be forced to turn to public facilities. There is certainly abundant evidence that public facilities that care for the aged, for motherless children, for the emotionally disturbed, and so on, are no substitute for the family. Hence, in Africa, where the tradition of family care for such persons is still alive, governments could channel resources into families, to enable families themselves to continue these services, rather than channeling all available funds into the creation of public facilities with no proven track records.

Obviously, one cannot enumerate all the concerns that would occur to those involved in family-planning research, in as much as these concerns would grow out of the specific needs of the communities in question. The main point to be reiterated is that once governments embark on a policy of planning for the welfare of the family rather than planning mainly for the elimination of births within families, families can begin to play their proper roles as contributors to rather than constraints on development.

PART III

AFRICAN WOMEN: PATTERNS OF INDEPENDENCE, RESPONSIBILITY, AND LEADERSHIP IN THEIR FAMILIES AND COMMUNITIES

"In order to understand fully the roles that Black women came to play in America, it is necessary... to understand the tradition of female independence and responsibility within the family and wider kin groups in Africa. It is also necessary to understand the tradition of female productivity and leadership outside the home, in the public domain in African societies."

Niara Sudarkasa, "The Status of Women in African Societies — Implications for the Study of African American Women's Roles" *(Infra, p.183)*

The "Status of Women" in Indigenous African Societies— Implications for the Study of African American Women's Roles

INTRODUCTION

Long before the women's movement ushered in an era of renewed concern with the "status of women" in various societies and cultures, a number of writers had addressed the question of the "status of women" in various African societies (Perlman and Moap 1963). Some writers characterized women in African societies as "jural minors" for most of their lives, falling under the guardianship first of their fathers and then their husbands. Other writers stressed the independence of African women, noting their control over their own lives and resources.

From my own readings on Africa and my research among the Yoruba in Nigeria and other parts of West Africa, it appears that in precolonial times—and except for the highly Islamized societies in Sub-Saharan Africa—in this part of the world more than any other women were conspicuous in high places. They were queen-mothers, queen-sisters, princesses, female chiefs, female holders of other offices in towns and villages, occasional female warriors, and—in one well known case, that of the Lovedu—a female supreme monarch. Furthermore, almost invariably, African women were conspicuous in the economic life of their societies, being involved in farming, trade, or craft production.

The purviews of female and male in African societies were often described as separate and complementary (Paulme 1963:1-16). Yet, whenever most writers compared the lot of women and men in Africa, they ascribed to men a better situation, a higher status. Women were depicted as saddled with home and domesticity; men were portrayed as enjoying the exhilaration of life in the outside world. For me, the pieces of this portrait did not fit. Not only was there an obvious distortion of the ethnographic reality—for, indeed, women were outside the home *as well as* in it—but there was also something inappropriate about the notion that women and men were everywhere related to each other in a hierarchical fashion, as was implied in the most common usage of the concept of status of women.

The *status* of women is often used simultaneously in the two conceptual meanings that it has in social science. On the one hand, the term is used in Ralph Linton's sense to mean the collection of rights and duties that attach to particular positions. According to this usage, status, which refers to a particular position itself, contrasts with role, which refers to the behavior appropriate to a given status (Linton 1936:113-31). On the other hand, the concept of the status of women is also used to refer to the placement of females relative to males in a dual-level hierarchy. In this sense, the term status connotes stratification and invites comparison with other systems of stratification. It was this notion of sexual stratification that seemed inappropriate for describing the relationships between females and males in most of the African societies I had studied.

Martin K. Whyte concludes his cross-cultural survey, *The Status of Women in Preindustrial Societies,* with a similar observation. After discussing the status of women in the hierarchical sense used above, Whyte's first major finding is that there is a general absence of co-variation among the different indicators of status in this hierarchical usage. He notes that one cannot assume "that a favorable position for women in any particular area of social life will be related to favorable positions in other areas."

Similarly, there is no "best indicator" or "key variable" that will yield an overall assessment of the status of women relative to men (Whyte 1978:170).

More to the point of the present argument is Whyte's observation that this lack of covariation in the indicators of the status of women signals a difference between this area and other areas where stratification is a known feature of the social structure. "This lack of association between different measures of the role and status of women relative to men still constitutes something of a puzzle ... In the study of stratification we ordinarily expect indicators of status at the individual level to be positively, although not perfectly, associated with one another." Drawing on Simone de Beauvoir's distinction between the position of women and that of oppressed national or racial groups, Whyte concludes that "powerful factors" in all preindustrial societies lead to the perception by females and males that women's statuses differ from those of men but in a manner that does not imply the hierarchical relationship characteristic of those linking occupational and ethnic groups. Going further, Whyte states that "the lack of association between different aspects of the role and status of women relative to men is due largely to the fact that women as a group (in preindustrial societies) are fundamentally different from status groups and classes" (Whyte 1978:176, 179-80).

This observation by Whyte seems to make sense of the data from most African societies. Although his cross-cultural study dispels a number of treasured notions about "the status of women," it points to a critical research problem that should be pursued, namely, the problem of determining the conditions under which women's relationship to men *does* take on the characteristics of a hierarchical relationship. I should hasten to point out that, conceptually, this is a different problem from that which seeks to ascertain when an egalitarian relationship between the sexes gives way to a subordinate-superordinate relationship. The very concept of an egalitarian relationship between women and men implies that the female and male are unitary categories that are measured, or "sized-up," one against the other in the societies described.

Here, I will attempt to show that there are societies for which such a conceptualization does not accurately reflect the social and ideological reality of the peoples concerned. The data gathered from some African societies suggest a reason for this. *As I will attempt to demonstrate, in parts of Africa, female and male are not so much statuses, in Linton's sense, as they are clusters of statuses, for which gender is only one of the defining characteristics.* Women and men might be hierarchically related to each other in one or more of their reciprocal statuses, but not in others. Because contradiction, as much as congruence, characterized the status-clusters termed female and male, many African societies did not or could not consistently stratify the categories one against the other, but, rather, codified the ambiguities.

The argument put forth in this article suggests that Engels and a number of his adherents may have missed the mark in arguing that private property and production for exchange served to lower the status of women. It also suggests that Karen Sacks' reformulation of Engels (which, in any case, rests on a controversial interpretation of the African data) *also* misses the mark by arguing that the critical, or key, variable in the subordination of women in class societies was their confinement to production within the domestic sphere and their exclusion from "social production for exchange" (Sacks 1974:207-22). I am suggesting here that various conditions, including most probably the development of private property and the market or exchange economy, created conditions where female and male became increasingly defined as unitary statuses that were hierarchically related to one another. Such conditions appear to have been absent in various precolonial African societies,[1] and possibly in other parts of the world as well.

In recent years, the postulation of separate, non-hierarchically related—and, therefore, complementary—domains for women and men has been disputed by anthropologists who argued that women occupied the "domestic domain" and men the "public domain" and that, because power and authority were vested in the public domain, women had *de facto* lower status than men (*Infra*, chap. 14; Marshall 1970). It has always seemed to me that in many African societies a more appropriate conception (and by that I mean one that makes sense of more of the realities of those societies) was to recognize two domains, one occupied by men and another by women—both of which were internally ordered in a hierarchial fashion and both of which provided personnel for domestic and extradomestic (or public) activities. I have already argued elsewhere (*Infra*, chap. 14) that there was considerable overlap between the public and domestic domains in preindustrial African societies .

In the remainder of this paper, I will examine the roles of women in families and descent groups, in the economy, and in the political process in West Africa. Potentially non-hierarchical models of relationships between females and males are indicated and contrasted with ones that are hierarchical. The data are used from stateless societies, such as the Ibo and Tallensi, and from preindustrial state societies, such as the Asante (Ashanti), Nupe, and Yoruba.Before turning to the data, note that there is no disputing the fact that status, in the hierarchical sense, attaches to sex (or gender) in *contemporary* Africa. Ester Boserup is the best known exponent of the view that the forces of modernization and development have denied African women equal access to formal education and have undermined their contribution to the political and economic arenas of their countries (Boserup 1970). Annie M.D. LeBeuf (1963) was one of the first writers to make this point and was the one who demonstrated it most conclusively for the political sphere. Other scholars have taken up and elaborated the same theme (see Mbilinyi 1972; Van Allen 1974; Smock 1977; *Infra*, chaps. 16,17). The fact of the present-day linkage between gender and stratification in West Africa and elsewhere on the continent and the realization that most of the studies from which we have to take our data were carried out after the onset of the colonial period should be borne in mind as the following discussion unfolds.

WOMEN IN AFRICAN KIN GROUPS

In West Africa, as in most parts of the continent, the three basic kin groups to which females and males belong are: (1) corporate unilineal descent groups, which we term lineages; (2) domiciled extended families made up of certain lineage members and their spouses and dependent children; and (3) conjugally-based family units that are subdivisions of the extended family and within which procreation and primary responsibilities for socialization rest (Sudarkasa 1973; Busia 1951; Fortes & Evans-Pritchard 1940; Ratry 1929). Within their lineages, African women have rights and responsibilities toward their kinsmen and kinswomen that are independent of males. As far as their responsibilities are concerned, female members of the lineage are expected to meet certain obligations in the same way that males are. For example, women offer material assistance to their sisters and brothers; they also do their part (that is, they make the appropriate financial or material outlay) at the time of important rites of passage such as naming-ceremonies, marriages, and funerals. Within patrilineages, women, as father's sisters, sisters, and daughters, generally do not hold formal leadership positions. However, they do take part in most discussions of lineage affairs and the more advanced in age they are, the more influence they wield. As mothers, sisters, and daughters within the matrilineage, some women hold leadership positions and exercise authority equivalent to that of men.

In both partilineages and matrilineages, interpersonal relations on a daily basis tend to be regulated by seniority as determined by order of birth rather than gender. Hence, senior sisters outrank junior brothers. Where males prostrate before their elders, they do so for females as well as males.

In the extended family, women occupy roles defined by consanguinity, as well as conjugality. They are mothers and daughters, as well as wives and co-wives. The position of "wife" refers not only to the conjugal relationship to a husband, but also to the affinal (or in-law) relationship to all members—female as well as male—of the husband's compound and lineage. Among the Yoruba, for example, female members of a lineage refer to their brothers' wives as their own "wives," a formulation which signals that certain reciprocal responsibilities and behavior associated with the "spousal" relationship are observed by the women in dealing with each other.

If there is one thing that is conspicuous in discussions of "the status of women" in Africa (and elsewhere in the world), it is the tendency to assess that status only in relation to the conjugal roles of wife or co-wife. Interestingly, in Whyte's cross-cultural study of the status of women in ninety-three societies, of the twenty-seven indicators of status as related to gender and the family, twenty (74 percent) of the variables had to do specifically with behavior or rights within or related to the conjugal (marital) relationship. The focus on the conjugal roles of women to the near exclusion of analyses of their functioning in consanguineal roles derives, as I have tried to show elsewhere, from the obsession of Western scholars with analyses of the nuclear family and the operation of the principle of conjugality in determining kin relations. In other words, the emphasis derives from an attempt to analyze kinship in other societies from the viewpoint of and with paradigms appropriate to Western kin groups. African extended families, which are the normal coresidential form of family in indigenous precolonial African societies, are built around consanguineal relationships. Failure to recognize this has led to misrepresentations of many aspects of African kinship. One consequence of the focus on conjugal families and the concern with breaking down polygynous families into "constituent nuclear families" is the distortion of an understanding of the roles of women as wives, co-wives, and mothers (*Infra*, chaps. 7,8).

Women as wives generally exhibit overt signals of deference to their husbands in patrilineal African societies. In matrilineal societies, the patterns may not be as pronounced, but wives still defer to their husbands. In other kinship roles, especially those of mother and senior consanguineal kinswoman, women are the recipients of deference and the wielders of power and authority.

Western students of African societies have not only focused unduly on the husband-wife relationship in describing African kinship, they have also sought to define that conjugal relationship in terms of parameters found in Western societies. This has led to a misrepresentation of the essence and implications of what is generally called "woman-to-woman" marriage. This complex institution cannot be described at length here, but I would make the following observations: First, the institution of *"woman marriage" signifies most of all that gender is not the sole basis for recruitment to the "husband" role in Africa; hence, the authority that attaches to that role is not gender-specific.* Second, the institution must be understood in the context of the meaning of the concepts of "husband" and "wife" in African societies, not in Western societies. Third, in African societies, the term wife has two basic referents: (1) female married to a given male (or female); and (2) female married into a given compound or lineage. Thus, for example, among the Yoruba, a husband refers to his spouse as "wife"; a woman refers to her co-wife as "wife" or "mate"; and, as noted earlier, female as well as male members of the lineage refer to the in-marrying spouses as their "wives." The term husband refers specifically to a woman's spouse, but also generally to the males (and females) in her husband's lineage. Again, among the Yoruba, a woman refers to her own spouse and (in certain contexts) to his lineage members—including her own children—as indicated by the term "husband."

Given these usages, it is important to recognize that the terms "husband" and "wife" connote certain clusters of affinal relations. And in "woman marriage" the principles concerned emphasize certain jural relations; they do not, as other writers point out, imply a sexual component to the relationship as do heterosexual conjugal unions (Agbasegbe 1975; O'Brien 1977).

If the concept of conjugal relations in Africa were not circumscribed by that common in the West, it would be appreciated that the unifying factor in the various kinds of woman-to-woman marriage is that everywhere it serves a procreative function, either on behalf of the female "husband" herself or on behalf of her male spouse or male kinsmen. Because marriage is the institution and the idiom through which procreation is legitimated in Africa, it must be entered into by women (just as by men) who want to acquire rights over a woman's childbearing capacity (see also LeBeuf 1963). The existence of woman-to-woman marriage in Africa is consistent with a general de-emphasis on gender and an emphasis on seniority and personal standing (usually but not always determined by wealth) in recruitment to positions of authority.

This brief discussion of African families and kin groups is intended to suggest that one can predict that male gender will require deferential behavior only within the conjugal relationship. The role of "husband" simply is the more authoritative of the two conjugal roles; however, the case of woman-to-woman marriage demonstrates that male gender is not a necessary attribute for entry into the "husband" role. And, even though patterns of deference emphasize subordination of the wife's role, the decision-making process and the control over resources within the conjugal relationship in many West African societies (including those of the Yoruba, Ibo, Ashanti, and Nupe) indicate parallel and complementary control by husbands and wives. In the consanguineal aspects of African kinship, as I have indicated, seniority and personal attributes (especially accumulated resources) rather than gender, serve as the primary indicator of status in the hierarchical sense.

WOMEN IN THE POLITICAL PROCESS IN INDIGENOUS AFRICAN SOCIETIES

Any investigation of women in the political process in precolonial Africa should begin with the excellent article by Annie Lebeuf in Denise Paulme's *Women of Tropical Africa* (1963). Here I only want to highlight certain facts that might aid in addressing the question of whether or not the relationship of females and males within the political domain is most appropriately conceptualized as a hierarchical one.

Africa is noted for the presence of women in very high positions in the formal governmental structure (Lebeuf 1963; Rosaldo 1974; Steady 1981). Africa is also noted for having parallel chieftaincies, one line made up of males, the other of females. One way of interpreting these facts has been to dismiss the female chieftaincies as simply women controlling women. (After all, if women are subordinate anyway, of what significance is it that they have chieftaincies or sodalities among themselves?) Likewise, the presence of women at the highest levels of indigenous government has been dismissed as an instance of women distinguishing themselves individually by entering the "public world of men" (Rosaldo 1974). I would suggest that a formulation which makes an *a priori* judgement that any participation of women in the public sphere represents entry into the world of men simply begs the question. For in West Africa, the "public domain" was not conceptualized as "the world of men." Rather, the public domain was one in which both sexes were recognized as having important roles to play (*Infra*, chap. 14).

Indeed, the positing of distinct public and domestic domains does not hold true for precolonial West Africa. The distinction is also not very useful for looking at the rest of the continent. As many writers on African political structure have shown, even in states in which monarchs were elevated to statuses "removed from their kin's groups," the lineage (and the compound) remained important aspects of political organization in all localities where they existed (Fortes & Evans-Pritchard 1940). Compounds were generally the courts of first resort and the bases for mobilizing people for public works and public services; lineages were the units through which the land was allocated and were the repository of titles to offices in many African societies. Women held formal leadership roles in matrilineages and were influential in decision-making in patrilineages. Their participation in the affairs of their affinal compounds, where married women in patrilineal societies lived most of their adult lives, was channeled through an organizational structure in which women were ranked by seniority, according to the order of their marriage into the group.

To answer the question of whether women's participation in the political process should be conceptualized as subordinate to that of men, I would propose that one examine the kind of political decisions and activities in which women were involved and ask from what kind they were excluded. Throughout most of West Africa, women controlled their own worlds. For example, they had trade and craft guilds, and they spoke on matters of taxation and on the maintenance of public facilities (such as markets, roads, wells, and streams). They also testified on their own behalf in any court or hearing. Thus, in internal political affairs, women were generally consulted and had channels through which they were represented. External affairs were largely in the hands of men, but in any crisis, such as war, women were always involved—minimally as suppliers of rations for troops but in some instances as leaders of armies and as financiers of campaigns (Paulme 1963; Awe 1977; Vatendu 1965).

The question then arises: From what political processes were women excluded? They could not participate in the male secret societies that were important in the political process in some Western African States. They were also excluded from certain councils of chiefs, although this was rare. Much more common was representation on the council by one or more of the women who headed the hierarchy of women chiefs. In all cases, however, it seems that women were consulted on most governmental affairs. Their participation through their spokespersons paralleled the participation of males through theirs. And of course in cases in which the chief rulers were female and male (for example, the queen-mother and monarch-son), the complementarity of the relationship between the sexes was symbolized and codified in the highest offices of the land.

THE INVOLVEMENT OF WOMEN IN PRODUCTION AND DISTRIBUTION IN AFRICAN SOCIETIES

It is well known that African women were farmers, traders, and crafts producers in different parts of the continent. It is equally well documented that their economic roles were at once public *and* private. Women worked outside the home in order to meet the responsibilities placed upon them in their roles as mothers, wives, sisters, daughters, members of guilds, chiefs, or citizens (*Infra*, chap. 14). In the economic sphere, more than in any other, it is easy to show that women's activities were complementary to those of men and that women producers and traders were not subordinate to men. In most African societies, as elsewhere, the division of labor along gender lines promoted a reciprocity of effort. If men were farmers, women were food processors and traders. Where women and men were engaged in the same productive activity (such as farming or weaving), they produced different items. Among the Ibo, females and males grew different crops; among the Yoruba, the female and male weavers produced different types of cloth on different types of looms. Where both females and males traded, they usually handled different commodity lines. Normally, too, men predominated in long-distance trade, and women were predominant in local markets. I have never heard of an indigenous African society in which differential value was attached to the labor of women and men working in the same line or in which women and men were differentially rewarded for the products of their labor.

In the management and disposal of their incomes, the activities of African women and men also were separate but coordinated. Within the conjugal family unit, women and men had different responsibilities that were met from the proceeds of their separate economic pursuits. A husband might be primarily responsible for the construction and upkeep of the home and the provision of staple foods, while the wife (or more probably the wives) assumed responsibility for nonstaple foods and the daily needs of her children.

The separate management of "the family purse" definitely appeared to be a response to a situation in which the members of conjugal units had independent obligations to persons outside these groups. However, it was also a way of minimizing the risks involved in the expenditure (of resources) by disbursing [them] among potentially beneficial investment options, as perceived from the vantage point of the different persons concerned. (*Infra*, chap. 14:238)

IMPLICATIONS FOR FUTURE RESEARCH ON AFRICAN/AFRICAN-AMERICAN WOMEN

I have tried to show that a "neutral" complementarity rather than a subordination/superordination more accurately describes the relationship between certain female and male roles in various pre-colonial African societies. In the process, I have argued that the preconceived notion of a unitary status for female and male, respectively, is probably what led many students of African societies to paint such misleading pictures of the status of African women.

The data presented in this brief discussion are only an indication of those that must be considered in any serious research into the issues raised here. I have always been intrigued by what appear to be linguistic clues into the "neutrality" of gender in many African societies. The absence of gender in the pronouns of many African languages and the interchangeability of first names among females and males strike me as possibly related to a societal de-emphasis on gender as a designation for behavior. Many other areas of traditional culture, including personal dress and adornment, religious ceremonials, and intra-gender patterns of comportment, suggest that Africans often de-emphasize gender as compared with seniority and other indicators of status.

Only brief mention can be made of the fact that in contemporary Africa, the relationship between women and men has moved decidedly in the direction of a hierarchical one. In understanding the change in the nature of these relationships from the precolonial, preindustrial context to the present, it is important that we not presume that the change was from an egalitarian relationship to a nonegalitarian one. Rather, it has been suggested that the domains of women and men in many indigenous African societies should not be conceptualized in terms of ranking at all (which is implied in the concept of egalitarianism because each concept entails its opposite). It is suggested that the changes that occurred with the onset of colonialism (and capitalism, its economic correlate) were ones that created hierarchical as opposed to complementary relations between the sexes. It is therefore appropriate in the modern context to investigate causes and characteristics of the status of women in Africa.

This effort to recast the study of the statuses and roles of women in indigenous precolonial African societies has important implications for the study of the roles that the descendants of African women came to play in the American context. Over the past two decades, most historians of Blacks in America have come to accept the premises that in order to understand that history, one must understand the implications of saying it was "enslaved Africans," rather than "slaves," who came to these shores in chains. The former implies that these Africans brought with them many of the non-material aspects of their cultures—i.e., their beliefs and values; varying degrees of knowledge of their political, economic, technological, religious, artistic, recreational, and familial organization; and codes governing interpersonal behavior between such societal groupings as chiefs and citizenry, old and young, and female and male.

In order to understand fully the roles that Black women came to play in America, it is necessary, therefore, to understand the tradition of female independence and responsibility within the family and wider kin groups in Africa. It is also necessary to understand the tradition of female productivity and leadership outside the home, in the public domain in African societies. It is understood, of course, that the context of slavery did not permit the exact replication of African patterns, but the forms of behavior that did emerge had their roots in Africa.

A brief reference to Black American women's roles in three spheres will suffice to indicate the direction which research into the linkage with Africa might take. I refer to women's activities as leaders on the plantations during slavery and in their communities in later periods; as workers helping to provide economic support for their families; and as key figures in the intergenerational kinship units that formed (and still form) the core of many Black families.

Much has been written about the heroism of women such as Harriet Tubman and Sojourner Truth. Precisely because of their extraordinary deeds, they are portrayed as being unique among Black women. It would seem, however, that these are but the most famous of the Black female leaders whose assumption of their roles came out of a tradition in which women were always among the leaders in a community. A reassessment of the roles of the so-called Mammies in the Big House; of the elderly women who looked after children on the plantation while younger people worked in the fields; of women who planned escapes and insurrections; and of female religious leaders should reveal that there was a complementarity and parallelism between the historical roles of African American male and female leaders that bore a clear relationship to what had always existed in Africa.

The roles of African American women in the economic sphere have long been remarked upon, but most of the analyses have presumed that these women worked outside the home because of economic necessity, rather than because of choice or tradition. In other words, the presumption of the literature seems to be that where possible, Black women, like their white counterparts before the era of "women's liberation," would have chosen the role of housewife and mother over that of working wife and mother.

The present analysis suggests that we should take another look at the phenomenon of Black women in the world of work. We need to examine the continuities that this represents with African traditions where women were farmers, craftswomen, and entrepreneurs par excellence. It is noteworthy that in Africa, unlike Europe, women of privileged statuses (such as the kings' or chiefs' wives, daughters, sisters, and mothers) were not removed from the world of work. On the contrary, their rank in society often conferred special access to certain economic activities. For example, among the Yoruba, the kings' wives were the premier long-distance female traders, as was remarked upon by some of the first European visitors to Yoruba kingdoms in the nineteenth century (see Marshall 1964). Given these traditions, one might expect that middle- or upper-class status would not necessarily incline Black women to prefer a life of relative leisure to that of the workday world. In other words, these women would not necessarily choose the relative confinement of the domestic domain over the public world of work. What we know about black women entrepreneurs and professionals in the nineteenth and early twentieth centuries suggests that regardless of socioeconomic status, African-American women were more likely to be employed outside the home than were their Euro-American counterparts.

Finally, I would suggest that a reexamination of the statuses and roles of women and men in African kin groups can help to unravel the antecedents of a number of patterns of African-American kinship that emerged in the context of slavery and evolved into the forms of family organization we see today. For example, the importance of age and seniority in conferring authority on African females, as well as males, helps to explain the authoritative roles of elderly women, as well as elderly men in African American families. The African emphasis on consanguinity, as opposed to conjugality, helps to explain much of Black American kinship, including, for example, the formation of households around two- or three-generational clusters of "blood relatives" (such as a woman and her adult daughters and their children). The consanguineal focus also helps to explain the importance of the trans-residential extended family networks that characterized Black family organization in the past and still remain in some areas today. The special obligations of mutual assistance and support that exist between sisters, regardless of their marital statuses; as well as the tendency, until recently, for unmarried Black women with children to reside with their "blood" relatives rather than on their own, are patterns that have their roots in African family structures and preferred behavior (*Infra*, chaps. 7, 8).

Much work remains to be done before we can confidently trace the multifaceted connections between African and African-American behavioral patterns, including those associated with the roles and statuses of women in their families and communities. The intention of this brief review of some of the possible linkages is to point to areas where research might be fruitfully pursued. I have suggested that many of the activities and attributes that have been taken to be characteristic of Black women in America have their roots in Africa. These characteristics—leadership in the community, as well as in the home; prominence in the world of work;independence and pride in womanhood—are usually pointed to as evidence of the strength of Black American women.

What I have tried to show in this paper is that this strength had its roots in African societies where women were literally expected to "shoulder their own burdens" and where, in many contexts, respect and responsibility, as well as rights and privileges, were accorded without reference to gender.

NOTES

1. Here the term "precolonial" refers to the period before the mid- to late-nineteenth century from which European colonization is conventionally dated. Some information concerning African social life in precolonial times is gleaned from contemporaneous written sources, but most information comes from anthropological re-constructions of "traditional life," using oral history and ethnographic techniques. Due allowance must be made for possible distortion in these ethnographies, but, for the most part, they are all we have to rely on for descriptions of Africa's sociocultural past.

THE CHANGING ROLES OF WOMEN IN CHANGING FAMILY STRUCTURES IN WEST AFRICA: SOME PRELIMINARY OBSERVATIONS

INTRODUCTION

Studies of changing family structure in West Africa are noteworthy in several respects. First, they tend to focus on patterns that have emerged among those who are usually termed the "educated elite." Very few studies examine the changes that are occurring in family structures among those who comprise the vast majority of the population in the countries of West Africa: farmers, traders, service sector workers, or even the white collar and blue collar workers who now find themselves among the masses who populate cities and towns throughout the region. The second noticeable trend, related to the first, is that studies of elite family patterns tend to focus on tensions between elite households centered on the conjugal relationship and their extended families based on consanguineal lineage relationships. These studies implicitly or explicitly promote the view that the conjugally-based family, and more particularly the nuclear family, is the form of family organization that is most adaptive in societies moving toward "modernization." They also support the corollary view that the extended family is a constraint on upward mobility and destined to break down in the face of modernization.

Where studies of family change have focused on patterns among non-elite segments of African populations, attention has often centered on those families that have been fractured as a result of extremely disruptive processes imposed during the colonial era. Such, for example, are the studies of families in Central and Southern Africa where the female-headed families have resulted from the forced migration of males to the mining areas, and in West Africa where migration of Sahelian males to coastal areas have had similar effects. What is needed are studies of families that are changing in response to the more routine processes of urbanization, rural urban migration, changing occupations, new housing patterns, etc.

Not surprisingly, we find that extended families still persist in West Africa and elsewhere on the continent. These groups are important in stimulating and promoting entrepreneurial activities, in providing assistance to migrants entering cities, in providing financial wherewithal for the education of young people, and in facilitating the mobility and independence of women by sharing responsibility for the care of dependent children. These extended families, which constitute the normal type of family arrangement for most people, are themselves undergoing change, and understanding the nature of this change is critical to a realistic assessment of where these groups are headed. Such an understanding is also vital to planning for the family (rather than "family planning"), which involves consideration of ways to utilize indigenous structures and practices in programs for social welfare and development.

In this brief presentation, I want to offer an interpretation of some of the directions of change in extended and conjugal family organization in West Africa as indicated by the published literature as well as by my fieldwork over the past two decades in Nigeria, Ghana, and, most recently in the People's Republic of Benin. Unfortunately, census data which could aid in this presentation are either absent or out of date. Survey data are also not available although there have been some surveys in Nigeria which eventually might be available for review. Much of the data to which I refer in this paper comes from published case studies or from my own field work, and it is for that reason that my discussion is exploratory.

The changes which I describe here are some of those which affect or impact on women's roles in West African families. The changes affect not only "elites" but also "ordinary women" such as market traders, craft workers and entrepreneurs. Some younger women entrepreneurs qualify by income and education to be included among the higher socioeconomic classes, and a number are married to men in government, business, other professions, or academia. However, those with relatively little education and the older ones who often are not literate in European languages, are normally excluded from the category know as the "elite" even though some may be among the "traditional elite".

I want to comment on three trends that seem to be emerging in West African family organization: (1) the tension between nuclear families and wider extended family structure as traditional obligations to consanguineal kin conflict with redefined conjugal rights; (2) the increase in the number of female-headed households as women opt out of the role of wife when that role becomes too restrictive; and (3) the growing re-definition of polygyny as living arrangements or patterns of residence shift from the co-residence of co-wives to a pattern of spatially distinct and separate domiciles. Before discussing these trends, I present a very brief overview of indigenous family organization in West Africa and of the role of women in these families.

INDIGENOUS FAMILIES

The basic property-holding kin group in traditional West Africa was the lineage, a corporate group of relatives who traced their relationship either through the mother or father line, depending on the rule of descent in the society concerned. The basic residential unit was an extended family living in a compound built on land belonging to the lineage, and comprising the lineage core (either males or females) plus their spouses and children. This co-residential extended family was the common and normal form of the family in Africa. Structurally, it could be viewed as divisible into conjugal families, built around polygynous and/or monogamous marriages. From another perspective, it could be divided into the lineal core of relatives on the one hand and the spouses on the other (who were in a sense the "outsiders" in the household).

As wives, mothers, sisters, and daughters, the women had roles to play in their affinal and natal compounds and lineages that were independent of the roles of men in those units. Women's domestic roles took them into the public domain, particularly into the world of work, but also in many instances, into the world of politics and governance. To be a "complete" woman was to be married with children, but also to be a productive member of the community, through farming, trading, or craft production, depending on the society. Where women's work entailed a great deal of mobility, women depended on each other's assistance in the upbringing of children, as in the case of those who traded in the daily and periodic markets that linked West Africa into a unified economic zone in precolonial times.

Over the course of her life, a woman was likely to have had at least one co-wife even if she started marriage as the first wife. Polygyny was therefore normal even if it was not statistically predominant at any given time or in any given place.

CHANGING FAMILY PATTERNS

Now, then, let us look briefly at some of the directions of family change mentioned earlier in the paper. First, with respect to tensions between extended and nuclear families, it should be pointed out that this observation is not original with me, but I think my *interpretation* of what is happening is new, reflecting what I believe to be a neglected African perspective on the changes concerned.

In general, scholars take the position that the economic and social demands of existing extended family networks serve to create tensions and strains within the conjugally-based nuclear family, and contribute to the instability of such units. Given the temporal primacy of the extended family over the nuclear family in Africa, it seems to me more appropriate to analyze the situation from the opposite point of view. In other words, it is the *increasing nucleation* of the family which, in many instances, creates tensions, strains, and difficulties that ramify through the whole network of people who comprise the extended family.

Starting the analysis from this position, one is not led to the usual implicit or explicit conclusion that the solution to family problems in Africa is the achievement of "closure" within the conjugally-based family (i.e., the more or less total insulation of this family from responsibilities toward a wider kin group). Rather, one is led to the conclusion that *increasing nucleation is likely to lead to increasing strains, and a process which seeks to pro-*

*mote or recreate units of an extended type is likely to have a more sta-
bilizing effect on family life in general.*

Christine Oppong's study of *Marriage Among a Matrilineal
Elite* (1974), which is a very informative and important study,
nevertheless illustrates some of the issues I have raised with respect
to the Western perspective that pervades the study of changing
family structure in Africa.

In discussing the conjugally-based nuclear families of a sample of Akan civil servants living and working in Accra, Oppong
reports that some wives view their husbands' mothers, sisters,
brothers, and sisters' children as virtual outsiders whose "undue"
claims on the husbands' resources make for instability in the conjugal relationship. Oppong implies throughout her analysis,
though she does not explicitly state, that the solution to the problems "created" by the wide-ranging group of relatives whom she
seems to view as outside the *real* family, is the achievement of
what she terms "closure" within the conjugally-based family.

A historical view of Akan family organization reveals, first of
all, that members of a matrilineage, which traditionally formed the
core of the extended family, were expected to render material
assistance to one another. Fortes, whose work on Ashanti is extensively cited by Oppong, shows clearly that in the traditional Akan
system, a person's productive capabilities (i.e., his or her capacity
to generate income and other resources) did not belong solely to
him or her, but also to the lineage, and that it was the duty of a
person to share the benefits of that which he or she accumulated
in his or her lifetime, as well as that which was inherited and
improved upon (see, e.g., Fortes 1948; 1949; 1950).

When one views the contemporary situation against the background data which Fortes (and others) provide, it is clear that
from the point of view of the extended family, an attempt by a
member of the lineage core to bring "closure" to his conjugally-
based household can be seen as a move that threatens or undermines the well-being of a group far larger than the nuclear family.
This is especially the case when such a member has control over
resources that should by tradition be shared with others within the
family.

The point, of course, is that Oppong's study, as well and
those of other scholars working on the African family, see change
primarily from the point of view of persons in their roles as hus-

bands and wives. But in order to fully appreciate the problem of family change, one has to recognize that persons have equally legitimate and binding social roles as sisters, brothers, sons, daughters, uncles, aunts, nephews, and nieces. To do justice to the complexities of changing family organization in Africa, one must not only consider resource allocation, decision making, and expectations within the conjugally based unit, one must consider these processes from the perspective of the larger extended family configuration.

After all, the wives who complain about their sisters- or mothers-in-law are themselves sisters if not mothers-in-law, and their behavior in these latter roles should also be analyzed. No doubt, the analysis would reveal a different side of the same story. Sisters who have expections of support from their brothers (as is customary in matrilineages), also have responsibilities toward them. Moreover, the "demands" which the sisters make must be seen in the context of the resources, both non-material and material, which they provide for their brothers. It is instructive in this regard to note that the elites often in fact receive as much or more support from their relatives than they give. Oppong herself states that: "the range of relatives called in to help [with child care, housework, etc.] was seen to be wide in contrast to the range of kin given financial help" (Oppong 1974:152).

While implicitly embracing the value of "closure" within the conjugally-based family, Oppong fails to appreciate that the sharing of resources among a wide range of kin is itself an important mechanism for promoting economic and social development throughout the entire society. From a long range perspective, support for relations, especially that which contributes to their education, assists them in getting jobs, or provides some of the capital to launch a small business, represents *de facto* investments in the social and economic development of the country. This is particularly evident if one realizes that such assistance is reciprocated in the form of help to ever widening circles of kin.

Studies of the evolution of the nuclear family in the West show it to be one of the primary institutions for promoting the values of individualism, competition, and accumulation, as opposed to communalism, cooperation, and sharing, which were traditionally emphasized in African extended families. One of the important areas for study in contemporary Africa is the extent to which people of different social and economic backgrounds would prefer or intentionally choose family and residential patterns that promote values associated with Western families and Western social life in general.

Another important point to be made with respect to Oppong's study is that in many respects it does not do justice to the reality that most of the elites she canvassed are still very much involved with their extended families. Oppong implies that this is often because they feel that they have no choice. However, one member of the Ghana elite, an anthropologist with whom I discussed this question, pointed out to me that Ghanaians (and other Africans) often develop a stereotypic way of discussing family responsibilities—referring to them as "burdens," for example—and that this is particularly evident when they speak to Europeans, or speak English to each other. This, he said, does not necessarily mean that these communications should be taken literally. In fact according to this anthropologist, many members of the Ghanaian elite go out of their way to provide opportunities and resources for their relatives and feel the better for having done so. He suggested that if most Ghanaians, however much they aspired toward material success, were confronted with the choice of living in isolation from their relatives or sharing their resources with them, they would opt for the latter because of the non-material benefits which they derive from their relations with kin.

Let me end this discussion of Oppong's study by stating that the implications of her work for those involved in social planning should not be overlooked. Studies such as hers are taken as basis for formulating social policy, not only by African officials, but especially by those outside Africa who seek to "aid" the continent. It is therefore an extremely serious matter to suggest that the ideal direction for change in family structure in Africa should be toward a form of family organization that would in many ways be inimical to the interests of all but a relatively small segment of the African population.

The second area of change I want to touch upon is that observed during my fieldwork in 1982 in the Republic of Benin (formerly known as Dahomey). It concerns the growing number of female-headed households. Traditionally, in West Africa, women who were divorced or widowed normally remarried. In fact, I was very surprised to find in 1961 and 1962, when I first reviewed divorce proceedings in the courts of Nigeria, that in almost all cases reference was made to the divorcee's moving into the house of her new husband. In essence, it seemed that women often did not get divorced until they had another husband "lined up," or that it was an affair with a prospective husband that led to the breakup of the marriage in the first place.

In the course of my recent studies of the role of Beninoise women in international trade, I found many women who were divorced or widowed heading households in which they lived with various dependent relatives: children, siblings, nieces, nephews, and non-related dependents. What emerged was that these women had built up their businesses until they often rivalled or surpassed their husbands in income, and after conflicts with their husbands led to divorce, they chose not to remarry. Or, when widowed they concentrated on their business rather than remarry. Of course, a woman without children would not opt for this course unless she was well past childbearing age, and therefore, likely as not, she would have reared a number of children belonging to other relatives.

Typically, the female heads of households were mothers who were devoting themselves to their businesses. It is important to note, however, that such women were very much a part of their kin groups. In fact, those who were separated rather than divorced often maintained their affinal role of wife even after their conjugal role of wife had been relinquished. By that I mean that such women continue to function as wife within the context of the lineage and compound of their husband (if they are separated rather than divorced) but their conjugal duties would be performed by those co-wives actually living with the husband. But regardless of whether they played important roles in their affinal kin groups (i.e., those of their husbands), these women were vital parts of their own natal kin groups: so much so, that one might say that their responsibilities as sisters and daughters were almost as demanding as their roles and responsibilities as mothers.

The final area of family change I want to touch upon also relates to changing conjugal patterns, specifically concerning the changing nature of polygyny in West African societies. First of all, it should be noted that the incidence of polygyny has declined for certain classes of women. Whereas in the period before the twentieth century, a woman usually was a part of a polygynous marriage at some point in her domestic cycle; nowadays, there are women among the educated elite for whom this is not the case. Of course, that does not mean that all of their husbands are strictly monogamous—the phenomenon of "outside wives" is well known. But I want to touch briefly on some changes in the institution of polygyny itself, changes evident among Western Africans who are *not* part of that group referred to as the elite.

Both during my fieldwork in 1968-69 (among Nigerians trading in Ghana) and in 1982 (in the Republic of Benin), I noted the pattern of separate domiciles for wives of the same husbands, particularly in cities. Among the Nigerian traders in Ghana, women and their children often occupied small rented rooms in compounds or large rooming houses, and their husbands took turns in residing with each wife. This arrangement was due not only to the cost and availability of housing, but also to the fact that as migrants, men took wives from a more differentiated social and ethnic pool than would have been the case in Nigeria. Therefore, the likelihood of conflict among the wives was much greater than it would have been in the home setting.

In Benin, I found that women traders used separate domiciles to enhance their independence from husbands who wanted to control their activities. Their husbands had access to their residences, but the fact that one wife might reside in Cotonou and the others in Porto Novo, some thirty kilometers away, meant greater freedom for the women concerned. This was particularly the case if the woman's business made her movements somewhat less than predictable.

The changes in residence patterns of co-wives has many implications, the most basic of which is to remove the women from day-to-day interactions guided by a recognized and sanctioned code of behavior. The co-wives live outside the traditional structures which monitored the husband's behavior and checked sources of conflict among wives. As a consequence, polygyny as it existed in precolonial Africa, with its emphasis on respect and reciprocity among co-wives, and responsibility and accountability of husbands, is giving way to the strife-provoking institution which Westerners erroneously characterized it to be in its primal form.

CONCLUSION

In this brief presentation, I have tried to show how some changes in family patterns in contemporary West Africa involve changes in womens' roles and functioning in their extended families as well as in the domestic unit formed by their conjugally-based nuclear families. In all cases, we note the necessity of carefully looking at women in different familial roles, rather than simply concentrating on the role of wife, a tendency among Western analysts of the family whose traditions emphasize the importance of the husband/wife roles in the nuclear family.

In my view, the research on African families can have important implications for those studying women of African descent in the diaspora. First, of course, by clarifying the traditional roles of women on the continent, it is possible to analyze more precisely what I have termed evidence of institutional transfer as well as institutional transformation that occurred when Africans where brought to the Americas. Equally important, these studies of women in African families today provide an approach to the analysis of the familial roles of African American women and others in the diaspora. For example, it is useful to focus on women in their various and often contradictory familial roles—particularly those of mother, sister, and wife—and to examine the way women reconcile their role conflicts.

On a general level, it is important to relate our studies of African families on the continent and in the diaspora to historical contrasts between African and European traditions in their differential emphases on consanguinity and conjugality in family structures. Many of the problems with the interpretation of African and African-American family organization by European or Euro-American scholars stems from the fact that their personal and academic backgrounds predispose them to favor paradigms and analytical perspectives that give primacy to conjugality in family organization. Too often such perspectives miss or misinterpret many salient features of African and African-American family structure that could enrich comparative scholarship in this area.

In a World of Women: Field Work in a Yoruba Community

INTRODUCTION

When I accepted the invitation to contribute to the volume in which this paper first appeared (Golde 1970), I was en route to Ghana, where I went to study the Yoruba community in Kumasi. Left in Ann Arbor were the notes and documents that I collected, the diaries that I kept, and the copies of letters that I wrote during the fifteen months I spent studying Yoruba women in Nigeria. A copy of my dissertation (Marshall 1964) and a few photographs—highly selective embodiments of my "field experience"—were the only recorded data utilized in this re-creation of my stay in Nigeria.

What follows, therefore, might best be described as remembrances of, and reflections upon, my efforts as an anthropologist-in-the-making. These are the encounters, the evaluation, the episodes that are chiseled in memory. As such, they can only begin to represent the totality of my experience in Nigeria. This shortcoming is at least partly redressed by the fact that here is a measure of the experiences that left their personal and professional marks, and that, hopefully, will therefore interest others in the field.

GETTING TO NIGERIA

Ask any anthropologist equipped with camera, tape recorder, typewriter (and spare ribbons), note pads, ball-point pens (a year's supply), *Notes and Queries*, "sensible shoes," and a veritable pharmacy, whence he or she is headed, and the probable response will be: "I'm going into the field."

Toward the end of May 1961 I set out, via ship, from Liverpool bound for Lagos. Although an American linguist in New York on leave from the University of Ibadan had assured me that virtually anything I would need in Nigeria could be bought in Ibadan or Lagos, my baggage included many items that I would later have been embarrassed to admit had been brought from the States. I hasten to say, however, that these did not include sun helmet, bush jacket, sleeping bags, and many other items listed in one reputable handbook as essential field equipment for Nigeria, to be purchased, if possible, *before* arrival in the country.

My traveling companions in the cabin class were mainly secretaries, lawyers, physicians, young businessmen returning from "U.K. training courses," and students of various vintages. In the first class were government ministers, chiefs, financiers, and first ladies. Nearly all the passengers were West Africans making their way back to their homelands.

At night we danced the "high-life"; during the day we played table tennis and engaged in our favorite pastime—serious and mock debate. In such a setting I had the air of a student on holiday. Were it not for the fact that I kept a diary—a task intended to sharpen my powers of observation and recall—I would have forgotten that I was "headed for the field."

We stopped first at Las Palmas. My companions and I were tourists of the first order: buying this and photographing that. In the evening, back aboard ship, with Las Palmas and Europe behind us, we settled down to await our first sighting of the West African coast.

Such was the magnificence of the coastline of Freetown, our first African port of call, that I could hardly wait to see the city. I was to be shown the city by an American Negro family (the designation "Black American" was not in vogue at the time) employed by the American government. It was in the heart of

Freetown that I saw my first West African market and there that I glimpsed life as it is lived in West Africa. Before I could assimilate the experience, however, we were off to lunch in a typical "Europeanized" section of town.

When we arrived at Takoradi, I prepared to disembark for what I thought would be my first real tour of a West African city. To my surprise, I was met on board ship by an old college friend who was in Ghana to prepare the way for the arrival of the first contingent of Peace Corps volunteers. We drove through the town on our way to lunch with an official of one of the shipping companies in Ghana. Soon Takoradi was no more than an enchanting villa overlooking the Atlantic.

When the MV Aureol finally pulled into Apapa wharf at Lagos, the anticipation of a genuine encounter with an African city gave way to anxiety that, Black or not, with the dispersal of my traveling companions and without the presence of old friends, I would be overwhelmed by a foreign land. Mine were the eyes of a stranger as they looked out on a crowd of women, mostly dressed in subtly varying shades of blue, whose movements and shouts of welcome gave them the appearance of a vast evangelical choir.

For me the pier at Apapa was singular confusion. People were greeting each other with laughter and tears; the women kneeling and bowing; the men shaking hands and prostrating before elders; and everyone embracing. For a moment in the commotion my ability to understand Nigerian English seemed to vanish, and I was in a sea of foreign sounds. I pulled myself together and started to respond to directives that, to my relief, began to come through as sounds that were only variants of those in my mother tongue. After a while I could even be amused and disappointed that, despite nearly six months of study in London, I could not understand a single complete sentence of the Yoruba that was being spoken around me.

I had expected to be met at Apapa by a Canadian couple who had flown ahead to Ibadan and whose trunks I had brought by sea. They were not there, and I had no idea how I could get their luggage through customs. Before I could become too distressed by the situation, however, several of my shipmates came to offer assistance with my luggage, transportation to Lagos, and accommodation until I departed for Ibadan.

My cabin mate advised me to clear my suitcases with the customs, and to leave the trunks, including my own, until I had made contact with Ibadan. I was invited to stay at her cousin's home in Yaba, a Lagos suburb, until I could arrange to go to Ibadan. She herself would be staying there for about a week before proceeding to Eastern Nigeria. I gratefully accepted the invitation and, together with my hostess, set off by car to Yaba.

I do not know precisely what we anthropologists refer to when we speak of "culture shock"; nor am I certain at what point in one's travels it is to be experienced. However, if the concept refers to something more than an initial strangeness in a foreign land—or in one's own after an extended absence—then, intuitively, it does not seem an appropriate phrase to describe the impact that the first days in Lagos had upon me. What struck me most was the familiarity of much of what I saw.

Physically Lagos was reminiscent of many towns I had known in southern Florida. Here were bougainvilleas, crotons, mangoes, poinsettias, hibiscus, papaya, and many other types of flora I had known from childhood. Parts of Lagos reminded me of the crowded shanties that were the heart of the ghettos in many southern cities well-known to me. Tin roofs, pastel-painted buildings stained ugly from the rains, dilapidated houses—these were not strange to me. Nor was the architecture and the elegance of the split-level and ranch-type homes in Ikoyi. The Lagos Marina might have been one of a dozen tree-lined boulevards along the Florida coast. Even the frightening rainstorm that greeted me on my first night in Yaba brought back the thrill and terror of a tropical hurricane.

When I first walked out in Lagos on the day following the rain, my first thought was that the muddy red clay, which I found so irksome in northern Florida towns, would ruin my far-from-sensible shoes.

THE FIELD WORK IN PERSPECTIVE

My interest in Yoruba society developed when, as an undergraduate at Oberlin College, I took a seminar with Professor George E. Simpson on Africa and the Caribbean. The researches of M.J. Herskovits, Simpson, and others on "retentions and reinterpretations" of Africanisms in the New World took on a special rele-

vance when I realized the *esus*[1] formed by my grandparents and
other Bahamians in the southern Florida town where I grew up
were institutions brought to the New World by enslaved Africans
of Yoruba origin. From that time on, my interest in West African
peoples centered on the Yoruba and Dahomey, and when I
decided to do graduate work in anthropology rather than in
English, it was with the intention of eventually studying the extent
to which Bahamian religious beliefs and practices, and patterns of
social organization, could be traced to these two societies.

When I communicated my interest in Africanisms in the New
World to Elliott P. Skinner at Columbia University, he suggested
that I might begin to pursue the problem by writing a master's essay
on the historical influences of African and European mutual-aid
associations on the structure and function of benefit societies in the
West Indies (Marshall 1959). It was my close association with
Professor Skinner, whose research interests had turned to West
Africa after a period of field work in the West Indies, that led to my
decision to conduct predoctoral field work in Africa rather than in
the Bahamas. As a logical development of my earlier interests, I
thought of field work in Western Nigeria, and it was Professor
Skinner who suggested that I study Yoruba market women.

In consultation with Professors Skinner, J.H. Greenberg, and
C.M. Arensberg, I conceived of a study that would focus on the
ways in which women's economic activities affected, and were
affected by, the other activities entailed in their various roles, particularly their roles as wives and mothers. The specific problems
to be studied included: (1) the point in their development cycle
at which women begin their trade activities; (2) the ways in which
women combined the management of business activities with
domestic responsibilities toward their husbands, children, and
other kinsmen; (3) the extent to which women depended on their
husbands and relatives for financial and other assistance in their
trade activities; (4) the extent to which the geographical range of
a woman's trade activities, the commodity lines in which she dealt,
and financial scale of her operations depended upon her position
and responsibilities within the family and community; (5) the
ways in which women's economic independence affected patterns
of authority within their immediate families and other kin and
domestic groups; and (6) the relationship between a woman's

success as a trader and her socio-political status in the community. In preparation for my field trip, I had spent nearly six months doing research in various libraries in London and learning the rudiments of the Yoruba language at the School of Oriental and African Studies. In retrospect, the period of language training in London always appeared much less useful than a comparable period of study at the university of Ibadan would have been. However, this was compensated for by the fact that the formulation of my research plans greatly benefitted from discussions with various scholars in London.[2]

My first base in Nigeria was the University of Ibadan, where I spent the Summer of 1961 getting acquainted with Yoruba towns, markets, and market women. Fortunately my initial ventures "into the field" were guided by scholars whose own researches provided essential background for my own. My first on-the-ground introduction to the morphology of Yoruba towns was provided by Peter Lloyd, well-known for his ethnographic and theoretical writings on Yoruba society. I was introduced to the world of the rural market by B.W. Hodder, who had begun to publish the results of his research on location, periodicity, and function of Yoruba markets; and I was introduced to markets in Ibadan by S. Edokpayi of the Western Regional Ministry of Economic Planning. My appreciation of the implications of my research for the overall study of Yoruba settlements and social organization was enhanced as a consequence of my acquaintance with the work of A.L. Mabogunje.

One of the complaints often voiced by anthropologists against "the field situation" concerns their isolation from scholars with whom they can discuss their research. Conducting field work some thirty-five miles from Ibadan was tantamount to doing research as a member of an on-going seminar. The University's faculty and libraries were available for consultation, as were many informed and interested people based in governmental departments. Moreover, on numerous occasions I was visited "in the field" by academicians who wanted to discuss problems of mutual interest to us. It is difficult to imagine how I would have fared in this first research endeavor had I not been able to draw on the expertise and experience of the many scholars and governmental officials I met in the course of my field work.

A PLACE IN THE SCHEME OF THINGS

When I left New York, I had not chosen a town in which to carry out my research. I had read in manuscript one of Hodder's papers on Yoruba markets (Hodder 1962) and had decided that I wanted to be based in a locality that would enable me to study women who traded in both rural and urban markets. The work of Mintz (especially 1955) and Katzin (1959) in the Caribbean also suggested that a base outside a major city would give me a broader picture of the over-all range of movement of women traders than would a base in the city itself.

While in London I had met Isaac Akinjobgin, who was then a graduate student in history and who directed me to various sources of historical information on Yoruba society. In the course of a conversation about my proposed research, I asked if he could suggest a small town near Ibadan or Oyo in which I might conduct the study. He mentioned Awe as an old and important Yoruba town, described its location, told me something of its history, and recommended that I visit the place when I got to Nigeria.

Soon after I arrived in Ibadan, I drove to Awe, a town of about 5,000 inhabitants, situated thirty-three miles north of Ibadan, thirty-six miles south of Ogbomosho, twenty miles west of Iwo, and a mile-and-a-half east of Oyo. The main street through the town is a major road linking Oyo and Iwo.

The view from "Main Street" left the impression that not very much was going on in the town. My picture of small Yoruba towns had been formed by an acquaintance with those between Ibadan and Oyo, where one sees many women selling foodstuffs by the roadside and gets the impression of lively commercial activity. By contrast, Awe seemed dull indeed. I would later learn that being situated astride a less trafficked route than the Ibadan-Oyo road, Awe's commercial and social activity is evidenced in the morning and evening; in midafternoon, when I first saw the place, the town, as it were, takes a siesta.

Although I was disappointed by the quietness of the town, I decided to see more of it before I considered choosing a different town, perhaps one of those on the Ibadan-Oyo road, as my home base. At the University of Ibadan I was introduced to Ojetunji Aboyade, an economist from Awe, who encouraged my interest in the town by telling something about the economic activities of its women.

I finally decided that I would move to Awe, and through Dr. Aboyade I gained an introduction to the town. One Sunday a few of Awe's "sons" in Ibadan took me to the town and introduced me to the Bale (literally "father of the land") and other chiefs, the leaders of the churches and their congregations, the Imam, and some of the town's older women traders. So gracious and friendly was my reception by the townspeople that I was pleased to have given up the notion of living somewhere else.

Like most anthropologists going into the field, my idea was to station myself in the heart of town and "live like the people." My friends from Awe soon convinced me of the impracticality of such a plan—pointing out, among other things, that the compounds in the heart of Awe contained no "apartments," but rather were divided into small rooms that would probably be too ill-lighted, even by day, for me to be able to do any serious reading or paper work; and that in any case I would find it most inconvenient trying "to live like the people."

Just where I would live in Awe was decided by coincidence. Near completion on the western edge of town was a bungalow belonging to an Awe businessman resident in Ibadan. In keeping with the practice of prosperous Yorubas "abroad"—that is, outside their hometowns—my landlord-to-be was building the house in Awe as a tribute to his success. He had planned to use it as a weekend retreat or to rent it to the high school, located across the street. Dr. Aboyade suggested that I might live there, and the owner of the house was contacted about the possibility of my renting it.

I was delighted when I saw the house, and without giving serious consideration to the few alternatives which had been proposed, I agreed to rent it as soon as it was completed. Everyone in the town regarded it as a stroke of good fortune that the house was virtually waiting for me to move in.

My landlord's housewarming, held in late August 1961, was the first social occasion on which I met a large gathering of Awe citizens. I came from Ibadan in the company of the men who had first introduced me to the town. We arrived to find the chiefs and other town officials seated under a canopy erected for the occasion. Hundreds of men, women, and children from the town and many Awe people resident in Lagos, Ibadan, and Ogbomosho were present to celebrate the opening of the new house. The clothes were elegant; the food and drink abundant; the drumming and dancing continuous.

The drummers came to greet us as we got out of the car. They beat out the praise-names associated with the lineages to which my companions belonged, and the men, in gestures of appreciation, placed coins and pound notes on the foreheads of the musicians.

I was outfitted Yoruba-style for the occasion, and many people expressed surprise and pleasure at my "being able to wear" their national dress. The women were particularly impressed with the way I had tied the gele (the long head scarf); some of the elderly ones danced before me, spreading the hems of their skirts in a playful sign of deference. They addressed me as "Adukenke," an affectionate diminutive of Aduke, a pet name for women. I thought this an auspicious social introduction to the town, and I returned to Ibadan in anticipation of my move to Awe.

When I returned to Awe from Ibadan, I found myself cast in the role of the town's guest. In Yoruba society a stranger, whether from another town or another country, is always a guest. A community, a household, an individual, all make a special effort to be generous and considerate toward strangers. The people of Awe, who seemed to feel a special sense of responsibility for my well-being, made me feel like an unusually pampered and privileged guest. I attributed this to the fact that I was a young unmarried woman who also happened to be Black.

I was informed upon my arrival in Awe by the Chairman of the Town Council that the Council considered it unsafe for me to live alone in a house at the edge of town. Although the Council realized that I would have an interpreter in the house with me, and a steward living in the quarters behind the bungalow, they had decided to hire a nightwatchman for me. He was engaged, at the Council's expense, for the duration of my stay in Awe.

I had been in Awe about a week when the captain of the Awe soccer team informed me that the team would play a match in my honor against a team from the neighboring town of Akinmorin. The match was held at the Awe high-school stadium and attended by hundreds of people from the rival towns. As guest of honor, I was asked to make a speech, to kick out the first ball, and to present the trophy to the winning team. A professional photographer was on hand to take pictures, copies of which were later presented to me. My friends from Ibadan, whom I had invited for the occasion, were as surprised as I was that the young men of Awe had thought of welcoming me in this fashion.

During the first month or so of my stay in Awe and, to a lesser extent, throughout the year I lived there, many people brought me or sent me presents—yams, corn, okra, tomatoes, bananas, oranges, and the like—and sent their children to perform various chores or run errands for me.

My landlord took a special interest in my welfare. Although the house was furnished when I moved in, certain items, including a large oil cooker and a kerosene refrigerator, were added, I was told, especially for me. It was my landlord's custom to visit his relatives in Awe every few weeks, and each time he came, he brought me bread or other provisions from Ibadan.

Not long after I moved to Awe, I went to Ibadan for a few days. On my return, one of the women told me that people had missed seeing me in the town and that she had sent her daughter to see if I was all right. When I told her that I had been to Ibadan, she replied that I should have let them know that I intended to travel. After that, as a matter of routine, I informed certain people in the town whenever I planned to be away for more than a day.

Being "looked after" by the town did not always work to my advantage. Before I moved to Awe, I had told some of the townspeople of my intention to hire a young woman to act as my translator and assistant. On one of my visits to the town, a young woman, born in Awe but resident in Lagos, was introduced to me as someone who "would be suitable" for my purposes. I was told that her father had agreed to let her live with me in Ibadan so that she might begin to learn what would be expected of her. Although my misgivings about her suitability developed during our first conversation, in my desire not to offend the townspeople, I agreed to take her on. The young woman had not been working with me for more than a week when I felt certain she was not the person I wanted as an interpreter and assistant. Her comprehension of English did not enable her to give accurate translations of my speech nor to accurately convey what was being said to me. Although I tried to train her as a translator, it was obvious that she could not cope, and my impatience became apparent.

Soon after we moved to Awe, the pastor of one of the churches accompanied us on a survey of some of the compounds in the town, during which time I was able to appreciate just how inefficient an interpreter the girl would make. The pastor had to correct most of her translations into Yoruba and to elaborate on those rendered in English. By this time I was near the point of total exasperation, and I resolved to get a new translator. The young woman stayed with me for another few weeks, during which time our relationship became very strained, and both of us wanted it to end. Finally she asked for and received my permission to visit her father in Lagos. Shortly afterward her father came to say that she could not continue to work for me without a raise in salary; I said that I could not afford the raise, we both expressed perfunctory feelings of regret that his daughter could not continue to work for me, and that was that. When I informed the pastor and a few others that my translator had left, they assured me that no one would be offended; when I brought a new interpreter from Ibadan, the people of Awe welcomed her as if she were one of their own townspeople.

Before I went to Awe, the only Americans known to most of the townspeople were white Southern Baptist missionaries. Although some of the old people eventually related to me stories they had heard from their parents concerning the slave trade, even some of these old people did not know that there were Blacks in America. (This was in the days before Muhammad Ali and "soul music" became household words in every West African village.)

People were very interested in learning about Blacks in America. They wanted to know how we lived, whether we spoke any language other than English, whether we ever planned to return to Africa to live, and so on. As regards myself, they especially wanted to know if I could trace my genealogy to any particular part of West Africa. When I said I could not, they invariably claimed that I was undoubtedly a Yoruba, and added, jokingly, that my forefathers probably came from Awe. (In Ghana, the Ashantis I met said I must be Ashanti.)

My having grown up in a predominantly Bahamian environment seemed to add credibility to the belief that I was "truly an

Omowale ("a child who has come home"). People were fascinated to hear that I had known about *esus* from my childhood. They were surprised that I could plait my interpreter's hair in styles similar to those worn by Yorubas. When people referred to a market held at eight-day intervals as markets that met "every ninth day," I sometimes told them of my exasperation when, as a child, my grandmother insisted that "from Sunday to Sunday is eight days." Now, I would tell my listeners, I can appreciate that she was using your system of reckoning: one in which the calculation of intervals includes both the first and last day.

Being regarded as an Omowale was one factor that contributed to the transformation of my status from that of a privileged guest to that of an adopted "Omo Awe" (literally, "child or descendant of Awe"). The second, and perhaps more important, factor was my conscious adjustment of some aspects of my behavior to conform to that which I observed around me.

Months before I even saw Awe, I had come to realize that by calling attention to seniority as a determinant of status in Yoruba society, Bascom (1942) had singled out the most important regulator of interpersonal behavior.[3] Age, sex (or gender), office, and what might be termed "priority of claim" are the variables that interact to determine seniority. Degree of formal education is not a determinant of seniority: however, because it enters into the assessment of status, it can affect the patterns of deference displayed in particular situations. In some circumstances the determination of seniority can be a delicate and complex affair, and ambiguity may be a necessary attribute of both the display and interpretation of deferential behavior. Generally speaking, however, men outrank women, and greater age confers seniority. In appropriate circumstances, however, both age and sex may be overridden by office and "priority of claim" as determinants of seniority.

The senior man in a compound is he who holds the position of Bale.[4] He is usually, but not necessarily, the oldest man in the lineage and compound. The ranking of wives according to the order in which they enter—that is, marry into—a compound illustrates that priority of claim may override age as a determinant of seniority.

Some of the signs of deference toward seniors are obvious: men prostrate, genuflect, or bow before their seniors; women kneel, curtsy, or bow before theirs. Normally the plural form of the second person pronoun is used in addressing a senior, and the plural form of the third person pronoun is used in referring to one. These signs of deference may also be used to show mutual respect or social distance between two individuals. Other signs of deference, particularly verbal ones, are more subtle. For example, a subordinate does not normally take the initiative in conversation with his senior, as is evidenced even in the exchange of greetings. It is the senior who inquires, "How are you?" *(se alafia ni?)*, who asks most of the questions about the health of family members, and so on.

One of the first decisions I had to make in Awe was whether I would make an attempt to act in accordance with the general rules governing subordinate/superordinate relationships or whether, as an outsider, I would for the most part ignore them. This is not to say that I considered that I had a choice in the matter. However, the people of Awe, by their expressions of surprise and approval at the fact that I was beginning to "behave like a Yoruba," indicated that I could have chosen otherwise.

In my speech and in other aspects of my public behavior I conducted myself more or less like a Yoruba because, consciously or not, in greeting situations, peopled behaved toward me as if I were one. In such circumstances the fact that I was Black seemed more important than my nationality in determining their responses to me. Young women and men—who undoubtedly would have greeted a white woman by shaking hands—knelt, curtsied, or bowed when greeting me. When children did not greet me in the Yoruba fashion, the parents told them to do so. Old men and women talked to me the same way as they talked to other young women in the town. It seemed that the only thing to do was to adjust my verbal and nonverbal behavior accordingly.

I made many embarrassing, and some hilarious, mistakes in my efforts to speak Yoruba, a tonal language in which, to my ear, too many words sounded alike (I usually asked women about their hoes when I meant their husbands). However, I never made the mistake, as European-speakers of Yoruba often did, of using the familiar mode of address when speaking to adults. My respondents could choose to reciprocate the deferential or respectful mode of address, or, if they considered it appropriate, they could use the familiar mode. When speaking with people older than myself, I followed the Yoruba practice of interspersing my conversation with "Sir" or "Madam."

In a community where most people, even educated ones, spoke Yoruba most of the time, and where they used all the other signs of deference and respect, it seemed to me highly inappropriate that I should try to speak the language and refrain from behaving with respect toward my seniors. Therefore I curtsied, bowed, and sometimes knelt, as I did before the Bale (the Head of the town), as a sign of deference. Yorubas are very fond of discussing people's "characters." I was often told that the townspeople approved of my character; that despite my education and my having grown up in "the European's country," I displayed the humility and respect they so greatly admired.

In retrospect, it seems that one event that also contributed to my becoming a member of the Awe community rather than a guest was the fact that after the incident of the ill-chosen interpreter, I made a point of being candid in my dealings with the people of Awe and less cautious about the "image" I presented to the town. At the same time that I was adopting some of the behavioral attributes of the people around me, I also began to show them more of "myself."

It was a custom in Awe, as it is in many small towns and in most of West Africa, for people to pay visits without notice. I let it be known that the townspeople were welcome to "drop in" on me whenever they chose. However, if people came when I was very busy or had prior commitments, I would apologize for the fact that the visit must be brief and would ask them to come again. After a while people got to know that in the mornings and early afternoons I was usually occupied with some aspect of the research, and they visited me in the late afternoons, or on Sundays, the days when I did not normally attend markets. This habit allowed me plenty of time to visit compounds in the town, to write up my field notes, and to rest.

As soon as I had the opportunity, I began to let people in Awe know what my food preferences were. Since I had been introduced to Yoruba cooking in London and in Ibadan, by the time I moved to Awe, I knew which of the standard dishes I liked and which I did not like. No one expected me to be able to eat stews as peppery as those preferred by most of the townspeople, but in fact it was much easier for me to increase my tolerance for pepper (many West Indian dishes are highly spiced) than it was for me to learn to eat some of the starchy dishes. When I was offered something which I did not like, I simply said, as a Yoruba would, "Thank you, but I don't know how to eat that." My taste in Yoruba food often surprised people in Awe. They could not understand, for example, how anyone could prefer *eba* (a cooked form of cassava meal) to *iyan* (pounded yam) or *amala* (made from yam flour). All the same, when people knew that I would be present for a meal, they prepared what I liked.

My candor about food was reciprocated by those who visited my house. If they came around meal time and I invited them to eat, they would ask , "What could we eat?" and go on to say, "we can't eat European food." It was only when I cooked Bahamian-style that a few of my friends would join me in a meal. Even so, the Bahamian version of okra stew was sufficiently different from that prepared by the Yoruba for one of my guests to remark that West Indians must be Yorubas who had lost their culinary skills.

I served orange squash (orange concentrate mixed with water) to two old women who called on me about two weeks after I moved to the town. Both women gingerly took sips from their glasses and made such frowns as they did so that I burst out laughing. They too laughed and asked if that was the sort of thing I always drank. When I said it was one of the drinks I liked, the women shook their heads. Then I inquired what drinks the women of the town liked, and was told that they "could drink" *krola*, a soft drink that I loathed. Thereafter, I kept a supply of *krola* in the house.

To most people in Awe I was known only in the role of researcher. They saw me in the markets, at funerals, weddings, and other celebrations and on the streets of the town. Such people often referred to me, particularly when we met in markets outside the town, as *arabinrin wa* ("our townswoman" or "our female relative"), and they addressed me by the nondescript, though kinship-derived, terms *"SiSi"* or *"Aunti."* However, my relationship with them never extended beyond an exchange of greetings or an interview situation.

A relatively small group of women, ranging in age from about twenty-five to forty, became my friends. We used the term *"Ore"* (literally, "friend") as one would use a personal name. Each of them referred to me, and addressed me, by that name, and I used the same name for each of them. When I wanted to distinguish among them, I spoke of *Ore* from such-and-such a compound. This was the group of women with whom I often exchanged visits and presents, for whom I did special favors (such as driving them to distant towns or lending them money), with whom I gossiped, to whom I went for advice, and who gave me all kinds of assistance and information relating to my research.

About a dozen old women and a few old men in Awe "adopted" me as their daughter. They called me *"Aduke"* or *"Anke"* (both pet names) or addressed me as *Omo mi* ("my child"). It was generally known in the town that I was particularly close to three of the women and one of the men. They, and one of the women whom I called *"Ore,"* were the ones to whom I reported most of my movements, and whenever I was away from the town, it was from them that people made inquiries about my whereabouts.

These four old people and my special *Ore* were the only ones in town who regularly called me aside to give me advice on personal matters. One might say: "You know, Yorubas are difficult. I don't think you should do too much for So-and-So because other people might be jealous." Or: "You know that little boy who has been visiting you every day—I think his parents might be planning to ask you to take him on as a ward. If you are not prepared to do so, you can just thank him for coming, tell him that you have nothing for him to do, give him a sixpence, and send him home."

If I wanted straightforward information on anything going on in the town, I went to one of my four "parents" or to my special friend. Whenever anything happened about which they thought I had not heard, they would send someone to inform me. If someone died, if a ceremony was being planned, if a dispute or a fight broke out, and the like, these people were usually the first to notify me.

My private social life was quite distinct from my life in Awe. There was almost no social event in the town that I did not attend, but most of the social activities in which I participated took place outside Awe. I was very friendly with a number of people in Oyo, and in the evenings I often went to play cards or drink beer at one of the clubs there. On a Friday or Saturday night I might go to a nightclub in Ibadan.

No doubt one reason why I did not become a part of the social group formed by some of the teachers at the high school was that to a great extent my circle of personal friends was formed before I left Ibadan. My closest friend in Oyo, for example, was an old classmate of a friend of mine who lived in Ibadan, and it was through this friend's classmate that I met most of the people I knew in Oyo.

My regular escort during the time I was in Nigeria was well-known to the people of Awe: he accompanied me to various convivial and ceremonial events in town, and he sometimes joined me on visits to my friends. Unmarried women in Awe did not "date" various men, as American women do. Young men and women of marriageable age had ample opportunity to meet and get acquainted through friends and relatives, at ceremonies, in the churches, in the evening market, and so on. When a young woman started "moving with" a particular man, it was understood that he would become her husband. A female anthropologist of marriageable age who was usually seen in the company of the same man was regarded as behaving in a normal and appropriate fashion; one who "dated" various men would have been suspected of being loose and licentious.

Americans who visited me in Awe often remarked that I had "become a Yoruba." The people of Awe would not have made that statement. I often dressed like a Yoruba; when my hair grew long enough, I sometimes had it plaited like a Yoruba; I took on some of the Yoruba mannerisms. I knew how to greet people in Yoruba, and, to an American listener, my simple Yoruba sentences made it appear that I could speak the language. To the people of Awe I was a foreigner, albeit one for whom they had an affinity, who had acquired some of the manifestations of what is entailed in "being a Yoruba." But to the people of Awe there was no mistaking the difference.

FIELDWORK IN AWE

In Awe I was immediately struck by the separateness of the world of women and the world of men.

At all major ceremonies in the town, women "did their part"; men theirs. At the feasting that accompanied all celebrations— naming ceremonies, weddings, funerals, and the like—the men ate in one place, the women in another. In the churches, no less than in the mosques, women were grouped apart from men. Women usually sat on the lefthand side of the churches, men on the right. The center section was usually occupied by young people, but here too men normally sat in groups, apart from the women. In the compounds men relaxed in their parlors; women sat around on the verandas. Husbands and wives managed their business affairs separately, kept separate purses, and contributed separately, though in cooperation, to the maintenance of the household (see Marshall 1964).

Everyone was aware that my main purpose in coming to Awe was to study the activities of women, and it was taken for granted that, like other women, I would have relatively little to do with the world of men. It was known that I wanted to interview men about their trade and farm activities, but it always seemed to come as a surprise that I wanted to find out some things about men that could not be directly related to Awe history or indirectly to the world of women. This was particularly evident when I made inquiries into the details of men's political activities in the town and when I tried to find out about men's associations and their leisure-time activities.

I was never expected to enter into, and never did see, certain aspects of the life of men in the town. I never witnessed any ceremonies that were barred to women. Whenever I visited compounds, I sat with the women while the men gathered in the parlors or in front of the compounds. At such times, if there was something I wanted to know from the men, I would go to them or they would be called to speak to me, and afterward they went back to their own business. I never entered any of the places where men sat around to drink beer or palm wine and to chat.

Whenever I attended a ceremony, I could observe and record what women were doing, but I often had to rely on the men's report of what they did. There were many times when I wished I had a husband or a male co-worker in the field, to study the life of men while I studied the women. On some occasions, I asked a friend of mine from Ibadan to come to Awe in order to take notes on the male side of something going on in town. At other times I received similar assistance from the son of one of my "mothers" in the town.

I once kept detailed records of the forty-day funeral ceremonies of an old woman who had died in the town. These records included accounts of the expenditures of the woman's daughters and of several of her female relatives who were "doing their part" of the obsequies. I recorded the amount of food distributed, the persons to whom it was distributed, the amount of money paid to drummers who performed for various festivities, the amount of the contributions received by the celebrants, and so on. Although I thought I knew all that was going on in connection with the funeral, it was not until late in the period of mourning that I learned of several celebrations that had been held by male relatives of the deceased. For example, one of the grandsons had celebrated the funeral by providing food and drinks for his age mates. Although this young man knew that I was keeping a record of the funeral expenses, he thought I was only concerned with what his mother and the other women were doing. It had not occurred to him to ask me to witness, or to give me information about, his own part in the funeral rites.

I attended almost all of the weddings held while I lived in Awe, and I kept a detailed record of that of a daughter of the old man who was my special "father" in the town. I observed the preparations (of food, dress, and the like) made by the daughters and wives of the bride's and the groom's compounds, and I noted their roles in the wedding ceremony itself. I had to rely on my "father," however, to supply me with the details of the activities of the men at the various states of the engagement and marriage.

Being a woman, I was naturally able to see aspects of the marriage ceremony that men do not witness. I followed the bride through every step of the marriage ceremony, including her brief seclusion in the room where she changed her dress just before entering her husband's house. There women from her father's house advised her to take care of her husband, to avoid disputes with and to show respect toward him and the other members of his compound, and so forth. It was a time of weeping; the tears were an expression of the genuine sadness with which the women parted and an indication of the joy they felt as the bride prepared to assume her role as a fully adult woman.

It was much easier for me to learn about men's activities from elderly men, who regarded me more or less as a daughter to whom they could explain things, than it was for me to get information from men who were about my own age. I could and did interview some of them concerning their trade and other occupations, but I never felt free to talk to them about "men in general" or to query them too closely about their personal lives. They always seemed a bit uneasy in the presence of the woman whose status put her "out of their class" but whose age made her their peer. It was only from a few young men that I collected detailed information on their domestic affairs, whereas I collected such information from almost all the women I interviewed. The result was that most of my information about men came from old men and from women.

Being in Ghana in a field-work situation as I write this essay, I am aware that my relative insulation from the world of Yoruba men in Awe resulted partly from the way I presented my research interests to the town. In Kumasi as in Awe, the world of Yoruba women is in many ways distinct from the world of men. However, I made it clear from the time I arrived here that I came to study the Yoruba community and to learn as much as possible about the history of Yorubas in Ghana. In Kumasi I have been moving relatively freely in the world of men: I attend their meetings, interview them on various subjects, and receive their fullest cooperation in the research. In many cases I have had to make a point of telling them that I also want to be introduced to, and to interview, the women. Being keenly aware of the contrast between my field experience in Awe and that in Kumasi, I have tried to pinpoint the factors, other than my presentation of the research problem, that contributed to the difference between the two situations. The most important seems to be the fact that here all my assistants are men. (Of course, I am also seven years older and have a four-year-old son.)

I usually interviewed Awe women in their shops and other places of work and in their compounds. Rarely did I conduct interviews in my own house: I regarded people's visit to my house primarily as social occasions, rather than as "research situations." I always tried to be at the places where women worked when I interviewed them about their occupations, and I seldom queried them about domestic matters when they were at these places of business. Women at work, particularly traders, were always impatient with questions that distracted them from the business at hand. It was in their homes that they were prepared to discuss marital histories, genealogical trees, relations with their husbands and relatives, child-rearing practices and so on.

The fact that I was unmarried did not seem to affect my ability to elicit any type of information from the townswomen. Details of practices surrounding conception, contraception, birth, and the like, were freely discussed with me. I never witnessed a birth in Awe, but that was because I was not around at an opportune time.

On days when I did not attend markets outside the town, I usually spent the mornings interviewing traders and other people in the town or collecting information at the sites where women made pottery, palm oil *(epo pupa)*, palm- kernel oil *(adin)*, or soap. At these work sites I sometimes joined the women in some of their tasks. Although women were always amused at my ineptness at handling the long heavy stick that served as a pestle, I was particularly fond of "helping" them with their pounding operations. On one occasion, after watching me struggle with a pestle for about ten minutes, one of the women said: "*Ore*, please sit down. You are pounding the *ekuro* [palm kernels] as if you were handling a pencil."

In general I was much more of an observer of, rather than a participant in, the life of women in Awe. My participation in activities in the town was usually confined to ceremonial occasions. I never joined the women in the work of preparing food for a ceremony, but I made financial contributions toward the expenses, and sometimes I bought and wore the *aso ebi* ("family dress") chosen for the occasion. I was a particularly enthusiastic participant in the dancing at such celebrations. After I had attended a few ceremonies in Awe, the town drummers "composed" a special set of rhythms that was my summons to dance. The townspeople expressed surprise that I was so quick to learn many of the Yoruba body movements, and they were always amused by the Afro-American variations I introduced into my imitation of their dances.

What surprised me most about field work in Awe was the scarcity of topics that people seemed unwilling to talk to me about or, excepting events barred to women, to have me witness. There were a number of aspects of people's personal lives about which I did not choose to ask, and there were some things, such as religious cults, that were so peripheral to my research problem that I did not try to study them. In general, however, by the end of my stay in Awe I felt that I knew as much about what I had come to study as could possibly be known after only a year of research.

In the course of field work one always learns that some questions are likely to be answered honestly, whereas some are not. Early in my stay in Awe I gave up asking straightforward questions about the number of children people had, about how long a woman had been pregnant, and about the amount of a man's contribution to the routine expenses of his household. Answers to these and a few other questions had to be obtained through interrogational subterfuge.

As a matter of course some types of information are kept from any stranger in a Yoruba community. Once I was thoroughly frightened as a result of my ignorance of something that was known to everyone else in the town. One day one of the women with whom I often chatted, and whom I had recently interviewed, confronted me on the street, eyes blazing, and started shouting threats and abuses at me. She accused me of having killed her children, and she vowed to take revenge. My first reaction was to ask what had happened to her children, but before I could finish the question, she lunged at me and had to be restrained by people in the crowd that had quickly gathered. I was shaking with fear. Within minutes I was being sent home in the company of some of my friends. After that day no one ever mentioned the woman or the incident. When I inquired about what had happened to her, I was told that she had been sent to the farm. The emotionally or mentally disturbed were not exposed to outsiders; in many cases they were hidden from everyone outside the family.

THE WORLD OF THE MARKET

By 6 A.M. my assistant and I would be preparing for our trip to the market. About this time an old woman who sold firewood usually passed my house, her load on her head, en route to Oyo. She always called out in a humorous, almost mocking, tone: *"Oyinbo dudu, Oyinbo dudu, e k'aro o!"* ("Black European, Black European, good morning, o!") I would exchange greetings with her from my bedroom window or from the front porch. The day began.

After breakfast we drove to the center of town, where Awe's morning market at Bode was in full swing. Here was a consumer's market: pepper, okra, onions, and tomatoes were displayed in small piles; beans, *gari* (cassava meal), and maize were sold by the panful; smoked and dried fish occupied one section of the unshed-ded marketplace, canned and packaged provisions (groceries) occupied another. The sellers of cooked foods (most of which were made from beans or maize) carried on a brisk business with men, women, and children who were buying their breakfasts before going to the farms, to other markets, or to school. The nonconsumer items sold in the market were leaves, which traders used for wrapping various foods, and firewood, which was bought mainly by women who manufactured soap and oils in various parts of the town.

The town had awakened long before we arrived, and if we lingered at Bode until 8:00 or 8:30 A.M., we would see the beginning of the dispersal of the morning market in Awe. On most days, however, we did not stop long at Bode but proceeded to one of the rural markets in which most Awe women traded.

The rural markets we attended were held at intervals of four days or eight days, and most of them were within twenty miles of the town. Occasionally we might drive to a more distant market that had been described to us by Awe women or that was frequented by "informants" from other towns, whom we had met in rural markets near Awe itself.

During the dry season getting to the markets was not a problem. During the rains, however, it might take as long as forty-five minutes to make our way over gutted laterite roads to a market no more than twelve miles from the town. Our aim was always to reach the market by 7:00 or 7:30 A.M. If we slept late, if the roads were particularly bad, or if we stopped to give someone a lift to a nearby place, we might not arrive until 8:00 or 8:30.

Town met countryside in the rural markets. Some traders from the towns came to buy foodstuffs for resale in the urban markets; others came to sell to the rural population. Men and women from the farms brought yams, maize, *gari, lafun* (dried pieces of cassava), *elubo* (dried yam slices), pepper, plantain, tomatoes, bananas, oranges, green vegetables, and so on, for sale to the buyers who came by lorry and by foot from the towns. The sellers from the towns brought canned and packaged provisions, hardware, ready-made clothing, imported and locally manufactured cloth, patent medicines, cosmetics, and so forth. Alongside the traders in the market were barbers, tailors, hairdressers, tattooers, and men who repaired bicycles and other machines.

From about 7 to 10 A.M. the market was a mass in motion,

the pace being set by the women from towns such as Awe, Oyo, and Ibadan who came to buy foodstuffs from the farmers and their wives. These foodstuff buyers were never stationary: they were busy locating their "customers" (those from whom they bought goods), concluding purchases, and finding new sources of supply.

A farmer spotted along the road with a basket on his head would be met by three, four, five such women, each imploring him to sell to her. Unperturbed, the farmer would move into the market, unload his goods, and state his price. Then began the bargaining, the pleading, the calling of others to witness that a fair price had been offered. Through scores of similar encounters the town-based buyers collected whatever they could afford to buy that day.

There was no possibility of interviewing foodstuff buyers and sellers during the peak hours of the morning. If my assistant and I were in a market that we regularly attended, we would make our routine tour: counting sellers; noting items offered for sale; comparing prices with those collected at other times; looking for our "key informants" (those women whose activities we regularly recorded) and noting their purchases for the day; interviewing market officials; noting the number of trucks in attendance, their capacities, the towns from which they had come, the number of trips they had made; stopping to take notes on the bargaining for this or the gossip about that.

By approximately 10:30 A.M. my assistant and I could begin to approach traders for the individual interviews. Sometimes the interviews could begin earlier—as, for example, when we were interviewing relatively stationary traders such as those dealing in dried fish, hardware, or provisions, who could talk to us in between waiting on their customers.

We interviewed both people from Awe and traders from other towns and villages. The Awe traders whom we interviewed in these rural markets were usually those who sold there. Our notes on the Awe women who came to buy in the rural markets were usually restricted to records of the quantity, variety, and cost of the foodstuffs they purchased. When we returned to Awe, we would interview them regarding the over-all patterns of their trade (see Marshall, 1963). Though most of the foodstuffs buyers from Awe were interviewed only once, there were about ten

214

women (our "key informants") whose activities we followed throughout the year I stayed in Awe. At least once a week we questioned these women about their current trading activities.

Traders from towns other than Awe were interviewed in order to provide the broadest possible picture of the commercial traffic between rural and urban areas. Interviews with these traders provided supplementary and comparative data on the variations in the scale of traders' activities, the levels at which they entered the distributive network, the geographical range of their activities, the sources of supply and destination of their goods, and the array of personnel and facilities utilized in financial and operational aspects of their trade.

I did not interview non-Awe traders at random. My aim was to interview at least two or three traders for each major commodity. If I found that the patterns of trade were highly variable among people dealing in the same goods, I sought out individuals whose activities were representative of the various trade patterns.

It was sometimes very difficult to get non-Awe traders to permit me to interview them. This was especially the case in markets where there were no well-known Awe women or men to make the necessary introductions. People were suspicious of the woman with the notebook, the more so because she did not look like the American student she claimed to be. When I tried to interview people whom I had not met before, I often found that my first task was to convince them that I was not a Yoruba collecting information for the government.

Within the first month of my move to Awe, I discovered that Western-style dresses were very inconvenient for the type of positions I had to assume when conducting interviews in the town and in the markets: I often had to sit on stools about a foot high. Given that my field work predated the era of the miniskirt, it is understandable that both I and my respondents were embarrassed when, thus seated, my legs were more exposed than covered. I opted for the long wrap-around skirts worn by most young women in Nigeria. The result was that although I did not look like a market woman—most of them wore the more traditional type of Yoruba attire—I did look suspiciously like most young Yoruba women seen in the towns.

The fact that I was accompanied by an interpreter was not sufficient to allay suspicions. If people heard me utter a few Yoruba greetings or ask the price of something in the market (the only instances when my Yoruba could possibly be mistaken for that of a native speaker of the language), they became convinced that the use of an interpreter was merely a ploy to throw them off guard. At one market some women sent a group of children to follow me around to see whether or not I understood Yoruba. The children made a number of rude remarks about me, and I had to pretend that I did not understand a word they said.

I was so often "accused" of being a Yoruba that when I went to a market in which I was not certain I would find a friend to identify me, I made a point of speaking only American-sounding English (for the benefit of the English speakers there) and of dressing "like an American." On my first trip to such a market, I even abandoned my sandals in favor of moderately high heels and put on make-up, including lipstick. After the market elders got to know me, and after the "regulars" among the traders had seen me in the market a few times, I would then appear in the more convenient and comfortable long wrap-around skirt and blouse (an outfit referred to as an "up and down").

Even after I became known in a market, I seldom found non-Awe traders who were willing to answer the full range of questions I asked, but at least I could not blame their reluctance on the fact that they thought I was a Nigerian.

Once I had made sure that there were some people whom I could call, when necessary, to introduce me to anyone I wanted to interview, I often found it quite convenient to "pass for a Yoruba" in the market. If I hid my notebook, I was wholly inconspicuous in a crowd. I could listen in on conversations, disputes, and the like, without people being conscious of a strange presence in their midst. I often went around bargaining for those items on whose price fluctuations we kept check. I would then compare the prices quoted me with those given me by other retail buyers. In this way I got an idea of the mark-up that almost inevitably resulted when a seller confronted an *akowe* (literally, "clerk"; colloquially, any educated person) rather than a trader or a woman from the farms.

Although I concentrated on the activities of women traders, I also interviewed men, and I was constantly amazed at the differences in the responses of men and women toward me and my questions. To interview a strange woman was a most difficult task, and the closer she was to my own age, the more reluctant she was to talk. Old women were more expansive, more willing to enlighten me concerning the ways of the market, but even they were often not as cooperative as the male traders. I was queried less frequently by men than by women concerning the purposes to which I would put the information I collected. Men were less reticent about disclosing the details of their financial operations and about discussing their domestic affairs. Many times I had to rely on male traders in the market to convince their female counterparts that they should cooperate with me. Whereas in Awe, where I was known, I had better rapport with the women than with the men, in the markets where I was not known, the situation was completely reversed.

I think this situation reflects the fact that, generally speaking, men "take the lead" in dealing with the public, including dealing with strangers. Anyone who has lived in a Yoruba town knows that when it comes to matters affecting their interests, women will not take a back seat to or allow themselves to be bullied by their men. All the same, in this patrilineal society, the men normally are called upon to act as spokesmen for their families, their compounds, and their communities. It was my impression that women in the markets often felt that if there was any information to be given concerning trade activities, it was the men who should give it.

CONCLUSION

Who can ever say all there is to be said about a first "venture into the field"? Here I have tried to convey something of the atmosphere within which my field work was conducted; to provide a glimpse of those dimensions of the field situation that would not appear in my technical descriptions and analyses of the results of fifteen months of research in Western Nigeria. Each of the experiences I have related reminded me of scores of others left untold. Some of these occurred in Awe; others in Oyo, Ibadan, and the other cities, towns, and villages in which some of my data were collected. Many of these experiences were similar to those recounted by various anthropologists, male and female alike.

There were tragic and comic events to which I could not remain emotionally indifferent. A well-known and highly regarded Awe chief died unexpectedly, and I mourned with the rest of the town. An old man told me about a woman who was so unnat-tractive that after the death of her husband not one of the men in his compound wanted to inherit the widow. The onomato-poetic Yoruba words the old man used in describing the widow wwew so funny that I laughed, with tears streaming down my face, for almost half an hour.

People I met by chance became great friends or went out of their way to assist me with my research. At the end of a meeting I attended shortly after my arrival in Ibadan in 1961, a stately old woman came up to tell me that an uncle of hers, one Oluigbo, had been sold into slavery and to ask if I had ever heard of a family in America bearing that name. This innocent and touching inquiry led to my friendship with Mrs. H. T. Soares, now deceased, who was the Otun Iyalode (second-ranking female chief) of Ibadan. Her subsequent assistance with my research in Ibadan was truly invaluable. More important, however, was the fact that she became my first and most beloved "mother" in Nigeria. Her kindness and affection made me realize that I would actually cherish some of the relationships I would form in the course of my excursion into the world of Yoruba women.

There were incidents and conversations that, like meteors, cast unexpected light on a particular research problem or suddenly revealed new directions the research should take. On one of my strolls around Awe, I stopped at *Ile Eleyiele* (the "House of the Keepers of Birds") to admire a magnificent bird cage that one of the men had made. In the course of our conversation about bird cages, the man remarked that Awe's *Bale* was an *"Omo Ile Eleiyele"* (a descendant of their house). When I expressed surprise that the *Bale* was not a member of the lineage associated with the *Bale's* compound, I was told that the chief had established a right of claim to the title through his mother, who was a daughter of the *Bale's* house. It was this conversation that led me to re-examine some of the generally accepted statements about compound and lineage membership and about the role of women in the inheri-tance of lineage properties in the patrilineal Yoruda areas (see Marshall 1964, ch. 2).

The practical difficulties that came up in the process of col-lecting and recording data were also similar to those reported by many anthropologists. One example will indicate the nature of these problems. Acting on the advice of some social scientists in

Ibadan, I did not use a mimeographed questionnaire in the collection of data on trade and markets. The questions were written in a small notebook, and the responses were recorded on a pad the size of that used by stenographers. I never found this a satisfactory procedure. It was not always possible to ask questions in the order they appeared in my notebook, and without a questionnaire, I could not quickly discern gaps in the information given by a particular respondent. Often it was only after I had typed and reorganized an interview that I realized that some of the important questions had been left unanswered. I could easily collect supplementary information from residents of Awe, but it was often difficult to hold second interviews with people I met in markets outside the town. As a consequence, I found that the amount of quantifiable data on market trade was disappointingly small.

By omitting a full-scale discussion of the technical problems that confronted me in the course of my research, I have neglected some of the most trying aspects of my field experience. However, it is precisely because these problems are those likely to be encountered by any social scientist in the field that I have left them out of this essay. I have tried to present a measure of the experiences and problems that derived primarily from the fact of my being a Black female anthropologist working in Africa.

My experiences in this regard were not the stereotyped ones that usually find their way into discussions of the Black American's encounter with Africa. No doubt my training as an anthropologist partly accounted for the enthusiasm with which I tried to understand, to accept, and to adjust to life in Yoruba society. There is also no question that my response to the life around me was a factor in determining the nature of my reception by the people I met and those with whom I lived. Nevertheless, throughout my stay in Nigeria I was made to feel that the relative ease with which I moved among the Yoruba was due in large part to their interest in, and their eagerness to welcome and to help, a "relation from across the seas."

NOTES

1. My knowledge of the origin of *esu* (an elision of *esusu*) came through the writings of M.H. Herskovits. It was later that I read Bascom (1952).
2. Professor Raymond Firth and Dr. Alice Dewey were particularly helpful

on the question of studying markets and economic behavior, and Dr. William Shack, who had recently returned from field work in Ethiopia, gave me much valuable advice on field work techniques.

3. My use of the term "seniority" differs from Bascom's usage—he limits the meaning of the term to what I call "priority of claim." Bascom juxtaposes seniority to age and sex as a all determinant of status. I am suggesting that age, sex, and "priority of claim" are determinants of seniority.

4. The word *Bale* is a contraction of *Baba Ile* ("father of the lineage"). *Bale* (which is pronounced *Bah-leh*) is a short form of *Baba Ile* ("father of the town").

FEMALE EMPLOYMENT AND FAMILY ORGANIZATION IN WEST AFRICA

INTRODUCTION

Wherever and whenever women work extensively "outside the home," there must be supporting structural arrangements to enable them to combine their domestic roles with their extra-domestic occupational roles. We know from oral and written historical sources that for centuries in West Africa women have been extensively involved in farming, trading, and other economic activities, while at the same time taking care of their responsibilities as wives and mothers. Moreover, during the precolonial period in many West African societies, women had important political and religious roles that entailed their working extensively "outside the home." In contemporary West Africa, virtually all adult females are engaged in some type of money-making activity that involves them in the "public" as well as the "domestic" arena.

In this paper I want to discuss the relationship between the economic roles of West African women and their overall position in the kinship and residential groupings to which they belong. The paper will highlight some of the domestic patterns that facilitate the involvement of women in money-making pursuits. The discussion is prefaced by a comment on the involvement of women in the "domestic" and "public" spheres of traditional West African societies, inasmuch as an appreciation of the roles of women in the traditional societies is essential to an understanding of the widespread participation of contemporary West African women in employment "outside the home."

THE ROLE OF WOMEN IN THE "PUBLIC" AND "DOMESTIC" SPHERES IN TRADITIONAL WEST AFRICA

The distinction between the activities and responsibilities of women "in the home" and "outside the home" underlies many of the current cross-cultural comparisons of the status and roles of women. One of the recurring themes in the articles that comprise the book *Woman, Culture, and Society* (Rosaldo & Lamphere 1974), is the proposition that most societies distinguish between the domestic and the public sphere of activity, and that this distinction is critical to any discussion of the status of women in a given society or in different societies. Michelle Rosaldo draws the distinction between the two spheres as follows:

> "Domestic," as used here, refers to those minimal institutions and modes of activity that are organized immediately around one or more mothers and their children; "public" refers to activities, institutions, and forms of association that link, rank, organize, or subsume particular mother-child groups. (1974:23)

Peggy Sanday, a contributing author to the same work, states:

> The domestic domain includes activities performed within the realm of the localized family unit. The public domain includes political and economic activities that take place or have impact beyond the localized family unit and that relate to control of persons or control of things. (1974:190)

All the contributors to the volume *Woman, Culture, and Society* seem to agree with Rosaldo (1974:17-42) that the nature and extent of authority (and, secondarily, power)[1] wielded by women in the public sphere is the key measure of their overall status in any given society and across societies. Rosaldo suggests that the status of women is lowest in those societies which "firmly" differentiate between the public and domestic spheres and confine women to domestic activities, cutting them off from other women and from the public sphere dominated by men (1974:36, 41). She suggests further that women's statuses are "raised" in societies where they either "enter the men's world" or "create a public world of their own" (1974:36). Both Rosaldo (1974:36) and Louise Lamphere (1974:12) characterize "the most egalitarian of societies" as those in which the public and domestic spheres are only weakly differentiated, and males and females share authority in both.

The few references made to West African societies in Rosaldo's article indicate that she interprets them as societies in which public and domestic spheres and male and female roles are "firmly differentiated." However, in her view women in that part of the world were able to "achieve considerable status and power" by (a) manipulating men and influencing their decisions, (b) by creating a public world of their own in which they exercised authority and power, and (c) taking on "men roles" such as that of chief or monarch (1974:37-38).

It is not my intention in the present paper to undertake a full scale discussion of the utility of the various suggestions and hypotheses put forth by Rosaldo, Lamphere, and their colleagues for an understanding of the status and roles of women in West Africa. This is being done in another essay. Here I simply want to pursue the question of the separation of the public and domestic spheres in traditional West African societies, pointing out in particular the relation between women's roles in their domestic groups and their overall participation in the "public" arena of the societies in which they live.

A factor which must be kept in mind in any discussion of the separation of the domestic and public spheres in West Africa (and indeed throughout the world) is that this separation has been greatly heightened in the late nineteenth and the twentieth centuries. With the spread of the nation-state as the predominant form of political organization and of capitalism as the predominant form of economic organization, much of the "traditional" overlap between the domestic and public spheres was eroded. The state arrogated to its bureaucracy many of the political functions that had been carried out by domestic units. The capitalist (i.e., "market") economic system redefined "labor" so as to make it virtually synonymous with work for which cash or other forms of remuneration was paid.

Whereas in traditional economies in West Africa (and elsewhere) all productive work was recognized as such, under the capitalist economic system productive activities carried on "within the home" by females who received no pay (and to some extent by males and by children as well) came to be regarded as something other than strictly "economic" activities. In short, the growth of the contemporary nation-state and of the "market economy" accentuated and accelerated the divergence of the public and domestic spheres in societies throughout the world. Thus, even though from the perspective of the twentieth century the pubic sphere of a society can be defined, as Sanday has done, in terms of political and economic activities that extend "beyond the localized family unit," when one looks at the pre-industrial, pre-capitalist, and precolonial world, it becomes obvious that many such political and economic activities were in fact embedded, albeit not exclusively, in domestic units.

In considering the issue of the separation of the domestic and public spheres in traditional West African societies, it is convenient to divide the discussion into two parts—looking first at the relation between the domestic sphere and the political realm of the public sphere, and secondly, at the relation between the domestic sphere and the economic realm of the public sphere.

When one examines the political or governmental realm of these societies it can be demonstrated that in both precolonial state societies (such as the Yoruba and the Asante) and in precolonial non-state societies (such as the Ibo [Igbo]) the "domestic sphere" was an integral part of the "public sphere." Power, authority, and influence within the "domestic sphere" was de facto power, authority and influence at certain levels within the "public sphere." This is not to say that the two spheres were coterminous but rather that there was considerable overlap between them.

To understand this point it is only necessary to recall that in precolonial West Africa and in the more traditional areas of contemporary West Africa, domestic groups were (and are) extended families built around segments of matri- or patri-lineages. The predominant type of domestic grouping consisted of an extended family comprising male members of a lineage and their wives and children (see, e.g., Sudarkasa 1973:97-116). These groups resided in dwellings normally referred to as compounds.

Within compounds, which range in size from about twenty

or thirty persons to several hundred persons, both males and females have roles of authority. Members of the compound are usually ranked according to seniority, with order of birth being the usual determinant of seniority within the lineage core of the compound and order of marriage into the compound being the determinant of seniority among the wives of the male members of the lineage (Bascomb 1942; Marshall 1964; Oppong 1974:28-34; Uchendu 1965:39-41, 84-87). Within each polygynous subdivision of the extended family (i.e., within the group comprised of one man and his wives and children), wives are also ranked according to the same principle of seniority. There is normally an official male head of the compound and a female counterpart whose primary responsibility is the safeguarding of the welfare of the women of the house.

This latter point notwithstanding, it would be misrepresentation of the dynamics of compound organization to say that males have authority over adult males and females, whereas females have authority only over other females. Because of the importance of seniority in ordering relationships within the compound male and female elders have authority over junior members of both sexes. The relationship between males and females of approximately the same age is not usually one of superordination/subordination, but rather one of complementarity of functions, one of purview.[2]

In traditional West Africa the compound was usually the minimal unit of political organization, and decisions within the compound had implications for the wider political units, whether this was a village or a town. Thus wives, mothers, sisters or daughters could exert direct political influence over males or they themselves could play important political roles by virtue of their positions of authority, power or influence in their natal and/or affinal compounds.

Traditionally, senior members of the compound constituted the "court of the first instance" for the settlement of many issues that have come to be defined by the nation-state as falling within the jurisdiction of the "public domain." These issues were extra-domestic as well as domestic in their scope and implications. The settlement of disputes, the investigation of charges of theft, adultery, "witchcraft" or other offenses involving members of the same compound was usually carried out in the first instance by the elders of that compound. When members of different compounds were involved these matters were normally handled first by the elders or leaders of the compounds in question. Only when such matters could not be settled at the compound level would they be referred to higher authorities. The involvement of women in the various matters that came before the compound leadership represented de facto involvement in the "public sphere."

The overlap between the public and domestic spheres in traditional West African societies is demonstrated by an examination of the function of lineages as well as the function of compounds. Lineages around which compounds were (and usually are) organized were corporate groups which normally controlled the use of land, provided access to various political and religious offices, regulated marriages, and performed a wide range of political and economic functions which fell within the "public sphere." For example they often controlled access to certain occupational groups within the society (see, e.g., Lloyd 1953). It was common for women to have important roles within patrilineages as well as within matrilineages in West Africa and, in their roles as sisters and daughters of the lineage, they often exercised de facto authority and/or power within the "public sphere" (Fortes 1950:256-57; Lloyd 1955; Sudarkasa 1973:111).

When one looks at the realm of economics, one also finds that there was considerable overlap between the domestic and public spheres in traditional West African societies. In fact there was no clear-cut differentiation in most instances between "domestic" economic roles and "public" economic roles.

In most societies it was usual for females as well as males to be engaged in activities——such as farming, trading, craft production or food-processing-—which involved them in their society's "wider economy." Yet most of the economic activities which females (and males) performed were as much part of their "domestic" roles as they were separate "occupational" roles. To be a good husband and father, a male not only had to support his family (by means of an occupation that took him into the "public sphere"), but he also had to fulfill specific domestic obligations such as participating in the socialization of children and attending to the upkeep of the physical dwellings in which the family resided. To be a good wife and mother, a woman not only had to cook and attend to her husband and children, but she also had to farm, trade, or otherwise contribute to her household's livelihood.

The general point here is that the important economic roles of women in traditional West Africa were part and parcel of the overall domestic roles of wife, mother, sister, and daughter, around which the lives of most females were ordered. At the same time, through their economic roles, women played an important part in the "public sphere." Not only were they physically prominent in the public world of the market, they were also vital contributors to the economy in their roles as farmers, food processors, weavers, potters, etc. Moreover through their trade and craft associations and through what might be termed the economic chieftancies which some females held, women actually played a significant role in the regulation of the economy in many societies (see, e.g., Nadel 1942:147-56; Sudarkasa 1973:57-64).

When the overall political and economic roles of the majority of West African women operating within their domestic and kinship groups are understood, it becomes apparent that the existence of female chiefs and of other female leaders in the public sphere should not be interpreted as evidence of their achieving status by "entering the world of men." This formulation misses the essential point that the "public sphere" in most West African societies was not conceptualized as "the world of men." Rather it was one in which both sexes were recognized as having important roles to play.[3]

FEMALE EMPLOYMENT AND DOMESTIC ROLES IN CONTEMPORARY WEST AFRICA

Over the past century the specific economic roles of women in West Africa have changed but the general pattern of female involvement in the "public" as well as in the "domestic" economic sphere has continued. Throughout West Africa most women regularly work at some occupation which directly or indirectly involves them in the "cash economy." Even women in seclusion in Muslim areas carry on a variety of trade activities from which they earn cash incomes (Hill 1969; 1971). The majority of working women in West Africa are self-employed (i.e., they work "on their own account" as farmers, food processors, traders, crafts-producers, seamstresses, purveyors of cooked foods, hairdressers etc.). Females are also employed as wage earners in clerical and professional occupations such as typists, office receptionists, teachers, civil servants, nurses, lawyers, physicians, and university lecturers. A small percentage of salaried females are employed in the factories that are beginning to be a feature of the West African economic landscape.

Most women who are not self-employed or salaried workers should not be considered "housewives" in the sense that that term is used in America, although in recent years the term has come into vogue in West Africa as a label for married females who do not work for cash remuneration. Usually, however, these females work with relatives or with their husbands in small businesses or in other trading enterprises. Some women who engage in food processing on a small scale (e.g., some of those who make *gari* [cassava meal]) or who work on the farm for part of the year may also be referred to as "housewives" in censuses and in other statistical compilations. The point, however, is that virtually all these women are engaged in pursuits that would, in America, be termed "work outside the home."

The working women of West Africa are as ubiquitous in the urban areas as they are in the rural areas. They are also represented in every socio-economic station in that part of the world. Even the wives of high-salaried males and of wealthy businessmen are usually "working women." In fact many of these females are wealthy businesswomen in their own right or they are professionals who themselves fall into the group of elites by virtue of their own occupations and earnings.

Generally speaking, self-employed women manage their own business affairs, with little or no input from males other than from those men whom the women specifically ask for advice or men whom they employ. Of course, the scale of business operations of the vast majority of self-employed women (most of whom are petty traders with operating capital of less than $100) does not enable them to have employees, although they normally have dependent female or male children working with them. Nevertheless, throughout West Africa there are well-to-do businesswomen with annual incomes in the thousands of dollars, who have male and female employees working under them. A number of the wealthy females who are not literate in English hire male clerks or managers to keep their accounts and to deal with the

European firms with which they often have business connections.

Women in West Africa do not work to get away from their "domestic" situations; they work because it is considered an integral part of their domestic responsibilities. In fact, West African women do not draw the sharp distinction, made in America, between "domestic duties" and a "world outside the home." Females regard employment in money-making occupations as necessary components of their roles as wives, mothers, sisters, and daughters. It is by earning money that women help to fulfill the responsibilities they have not only toward the immediate polygynous or monogamous family into which they are born or into which they marry, but also toward members of the extended networks formed by their consanguineal ("blood") and affinal (in-law) kin.

For the most part, women in West Africa still function within the context of families that transcend the conjugally-based nuclear family. Women are born into lineages and most of them still grow up in compounds. When they marry, they move into compounds or otherwise join families that include many significant actors other than their husbands. Women develop special ties not only to their husbands' lineage members, but also in some instances to other wives of their husbands' compounds. (In most patrilineal societies, women married into the same compound, i.e., to males of the same lineage, are collectively referred to as "wives of the house.") Thus, a woman in the role of "wife" occupies a position with many more dimensions and facets than is the case in the West.

In all their kinship roles, women have placed upon them obligations that are independent of those placed upon their husbands, brothers, fathers, or sons. In other words, within the lineage, and within the compound, women quite literally "pull their own loads." This is both a reflection of the relatively high status of women in West Africa, and a response to the reality that in the past as in the present, women, like men, have had independent resources as a result of their roles in the production and distribution networks in their economies.

In the modern context, the obligations that fall to women include bearing some of the financial responsibility for the upbringing of their children, and, where they can afford it, the children of less fortunate relatives. The most substantial cash outlays in this regard are usually the fees required to pay for formal education or training which children receive in schools, or as apprentices to skilled craftsmen. Women also contribute substantially to their immediate family's requirements of food, clothing and shelter. In no cases of which I am aware, however, do women pool their resources with those of their husbands. Rather a husband "does his part" and each wife does hers. On all ceremonial occasions, such as those associated with the marriage or death of relatives or friends, or the birth of children, women make substantial financial contributions to the costs of the events, and/or take time off from their work to help with the preparations that are made for the entertainment of the crowds that assemble for the occasions.

The various kin groups to which women belong provide the most important structural supports for the involvement of women in economic endeavors. There are elaborate child-rearing networks that operate among women in most West African societies as a result, for the most part, of the involvement of women in employment outside the home. The number of children a woman has living with her, or for whom she is financially responsible at any given time, is seldom a reflection merely of the number of children to whom she has given birth. Older women assist their daughters, sisters, or daughters-in-law in caring for their children when these women's occupations do not permit them to care for their own children. It is very common to find women looking after the children of relatives while some or all of their own children are being looked after by others. Childless women often rear children who have been placed in their care by relatives or by friends.

These situations arise because women take in or disperse children depending on the point at which they are in their own domestic and occupational life cycles and depending on the responsibilities which they feel toward their kinsmen and close associates. A woman's age, education, place of residence, marital status, financial status, and that of her relatives with children are all variables which operate in determining the number, ages, and relationship of the dependent children for whom she is responsible.

In turn women are assisted in their work by the children for whom they take financial responsibility. When these dependents are not in school they are usually busy working with their mothers or guardians.

In addition to assistance from kinsmen, there are at least two other important types of social structural support for the involvement of West African women in employment outside the home. First of all, relatively inexpensive household help is still available in most areas. Women who do not have enough dependents to help them with their day-to-day housework usually have "houseboys" or "housegirls" who are paid by them or by their husbands to help with cooking, washing, ironing, house cleaning and child care. Secondly in all West African countries, there are a number of males and females who make their living from service occupations (such as laundering) that allow others the freedom to pursue their "extra-domestic" occupations. Perhaps the most important of the specialists in service occupations are the women who prepare inexpensive meals for sale in various locations throughout the towns (and villages) of West Africa (see, e.g., Hill 1971:303-304; Marshall 1964:158–163). It is common for working men and women and school children to buy one or more of their daily meals from these cooked-food sellers. Some of these women specialize in making staple dietary items which take a relatively long time to prepare and they sell them to other women who add the stews, vegetables, and other items that make up the main family meal for the day.

The interplay between West African women's domestic and economic roles cannot be concluded without mention of the implications of women's employment for the decision-making process "in the home." I have already intimated that the phrase "in the home" must be divested of its Western implications. The West African wife is actively involved in a number of decision-making domestic and kinship networks, only one of which is the immediate conjugal unit comprised of herself, her husband and, in some instances, her co-wives. Although it cannot be undertaken here, a full discussion of West African women's decision-making role in their "domestic situations" must take into consideration their power, influence, and authority within their natal compounds, their affinal compounds and, in some cases, within the domiciles established and headed by the women themselves. As Christine Oppong's informative study of marriage among Ghanaian civil servants abundantly documents, even the process of decision-making within the immediate conjugal unit itself is intricately tied to the roles which husbands and wives play within their wider kinship networks (Oppong 1974).

If there is a single generalization that can be made concerning the decision-making process within West African conjugal units, it is that husbands and wives often make independent decisions concerning the allocation of their resources. In fact, outside the relatively small circle of "elite" families whose households tend toward the Western nuclear-family ideal, day-to-day joint decision-making by husbands and wives concerning household affairs seems to be the exception rather than the rule.[4] It appears rather that from the onset of most West African marriages, the husbands assume responsibility for certain domains within the household and the wife or wives assume responsibility for others.

I noted among families of traders and farmers in Nigeria, for example, that husbands and wives did not normally consult each other concerning the day-to-day expenditure of their respective incomes (Marshall 1964; Sudarkasa 1973:117-132). However they usually discussed the major responsibilities (such as paying for the education of a child or building a house) that either one was about to undertake at any time. There would of course be consultation on all projects that required the resources of both. The separate management of what some Westerners would regard as a common "family purse" resulted partly from the fact that husbands and wives had independent obligations to persons outside their immediate conjugal unit. However, the practice of controlling one's own income also related to the fact that men and women needed to be able to make independent financial judgments in their separate business activities. By separating their purses, they spread their risks over various investment options in a situation where even the smallest profits could make a big difference in a trader's life (see Marshall 1964; Sudarkasa 1973).

CONCLUSION

This brief overview of the relationship between women's familial and economic roles in West Africa began with a comment on the overall position of women in the "domestic" and "public" spheres in traditional West African societies. The discusssion emphasizes the continuity in the roles of women in so far as their participation in the economic realm of the public sphere is concerned. It has also emphasized the continuity in the way in which women's familial roles have reflected and been affected by their involvement in economic activities outside the home.

It must be emphasized in conclusion that the other side of the picture, namely the discussion of the changes in women's occupational and familial roles that have resulted from overall changes in the economic political and demographic patterns in West Africa, must be analyzed in order to understand the variations in domestic structures and in patterns of domestic behavior evident in West Africa today (see, e.g., Okediji & Okediji 1966; Oppong 1974). This task was beyond the scope of the present paper; however, three important points that shed light on the nature and direction of changes in women's domestic and occupational roles should be noted.

1) Women are being employed in increasing numbers in salaried occupations that are much more disruptive of established domestic patterns than is work in the market place or on the farms. To cite one example: traditionally the first two or three years of a Yoruba child's life was spent in very close proximity to its mother. Yoruba women normally took their young children with them on their backs to the market, to the places where they processed foodstuffs, and to their craft worksites. Today most women traders maintain the tradition of taking their young children with them to the market; however women in salaried positions in the "modern" business or governmental sector of the society must make arrangemenis for the care of their infants in their homes or elsewhere.

2) Traditional compound-based living patterns are being undermined by the increasing migration of men and women to cities within their countries of origin and to urban and rural areas in other countries where economic opportunities are available. A high percentage of male migrants and their wives live in modern derivatives of compounds (i.e., large rooming houses) wherein reside persons from different lineages, different towns, and in many cases different ethnic groups. Moreover, in a number of instances, particularly where the migrants live outside their regions or countries of origins, husbands with more than one wife find rooms for their spouses in a number of different compounds or rooming houses (*Infra*, chaps. 12, 15). These changes in patterns of domicile along with other changes that are also present, are having far-reaching implications for husband-wife relationships, co-wife relationships, child-rearing patterns, and relationships of spouses to their wider kin networks.

3) More and more young women and men are being exposed to Western education, Western values, and Western life styles via the media, academia, and other sources which tend to identify "modernization" with Westernization. This exposure is buttressed by the fact that in many places Westernization is perceived to be the primary path to social mobility. This, in turn, is changing the very nature of what are considered to be suitable occupations for the modern age. It is also undermining the traditional value placed upon maintaining the lineage and extended family ties that were the traditional bases of personal identity and social security throughout West Africa.

NOTES

1. The contributors utilize M.G. Smith's observation that authority is "the right to make a particular decision and to command obedience " whereas power is "the ability to act effectively on persons or things" regardless of whether this ability is legitimized by the society or some segment thereof. Authority "entails a hierarchical chain of command and control," but "the exercise of power has no positive sanctions, only rules that specify the conditions of illegality of its operation" (Rosaldo 1974:21).

2. The question of the relative rank of males and females within the lineage and compound is a complex one which cannot be adequately handled in a few sentences. It can be noted that Fortes observed "a high degree of equality between male and female members of the lineage" among the matrilineal Asante [Ashanti] of Ghana [Fortes 1950:256-57). Among the patrilineal Yoruba, a person's sex and relative seniority are among the factors which determine relative rank in any given situation (Marshall 1964). Nevertheless, the ideology of the Yoruba holds that in general males out-rank females; and in general females do show deference toward males of their own age and older by kneeling or curtsying in their presence. It is misleading, however, to attempt to assess the overall status of females in any West African society on the basis of the deference behavior they display toward males. Thus Rosaldo is mistaken in implying that Yoruba females have low status because they traditionally kneel before their husbands (Rosaldo 1974:20). Her reference to the "bowing and scraping of the Yoruba wife" (1974:22) is a particularly misleading statement. Just as females kneel before their husbands, so do males prostrate themselves before their mothers, older sisters, and other females whose age or position demand that they do so.

3. Moreover, the fact that females organized their own political, economic, and convivial associations did not mean that their statuses rested primarily on their "creation of a public world of their own." These associations

234

separated females from males but they did not insulate females from a "public world of men." Female associations, like male associations, were vehicles through which a pattern of complementarity of action, rooted in domestic groupings, was continued in the wider public arena. Of course the notion of "complementarity of action" implies recognition of difference, and it is clear that males and females in West African societies conceptualized their roles— and in many situations, their interests and objectives—as being different from one another. It is also true that through their associations, females sometimes collectively pursued objectives and interests that brought them into temporary conflict with males. However, it is misleading to focus, as many writers do, on the instances when women used their associations as "weapons" in conflicts with men, rather than to recognize that for the most part these associations were used as vehicles for cooperation or collaboration with the males of the society.

4. This is not to imply that all "elite" families tend toward the nuclear-type household, nor that joint decision-making is prevalent among all of those households that are modeled after nuclear families. First of all, most "elite" families include on or more dependents other than children of the couples who head them. Secondly, in some "elite" households many major decisions regarding allocation of resources and/or household tasks and responsibilities are made independently by husbands and wives, or they are made primarily by the husbands (see, e.g., Oppong 1974).

WOMEN AND MIGRATION IN
CONTEMPORARY WEST AFRICA

INTRODUCTION

For the past three quarters of a century, intranational and international migration has been an especially prominent feature of socio-
cultural change on the African continent.[1] Given the
overwhelming predominance of males in this process in the early
part of the century, it is not surprising that most of the studies of
migrants in Africa in general, and in West Africa in particular,
have focused on men. One result has been the relative paucity of
detailed information based on systematic research about women.
Despite the virtual absence of full-fledged studies of female migration in West Africa, Caldwell's research on rural-urban migration
in Ghana and census data from different countries confirm the
scattered observations of various scholars and other writers that
there is a substantial female migrant population in most West
African towns and cities (Caldwell 1968 & 1969).

In the past twenty-five years, younger women have become a
steadily increasing proportion of those migrating to the cities. In
some areas it even appears that "the female propensity for rural-
urban migration is rising faster than the male" (Caldwell
1968:369). This "propensity" is, of course, a predictable response
to actual and perceived opportunities for employment, education, and/or marriage in the cities. West African women have
been primarily involved in internal migration within their home

countries. However, since early in this century, many of them, particularly traders, have been among the migrants who left their countries of origin to live and work in other West African nations (Hill 1970; Mabogunje 1972; Sudarkasa 1974, 1975).

The present paper outlines the major patterns of female involvement in contemporary West African migration. It indicates some of the effects on the lives of women of their own migration and that of men. It notes the role of female migrants as innovators in the process of contemporary socioeconomic change and raises some questions as to the relationship this bears to the process of development. Much of the illustrative data come from my studies of Yoruba migrants in Ghana, undertaken from a base in Kumasi over a one-year period in 1968-69.

WOMEN AND THE MIGRATORY PROCESS IN TWENTIETH-CENTURY WEST AFRICA

Fundamentally, the reasons for vast twentieth-century West African migrations are to be found in the overall redirection, in colonial times, of economic activity *away from* the precolonial production and trade centers in the interior *toward* the coastal administrative, production, and commercial centers established or promoted by the colonial regimes (Rouch 1956; Sinner 1960; Kuper 1965; Amin 1974; Sudarkasa 1974). By the imposition of taxes, the introduction of various goods and services that had to be purchased with European currencies, and the passage of compulsory labor laws, colonial governments virtually and literally forced people to move away from those areas which could not provide them with adequate cash incomes.

For most of West Africa, with the exception of Nigeria, the inland areas became virtual labor reserves for the coast (Amin 1974). Something of the magnitude of the resultant population shifts is indicated by Samir Amin's estimate that between 1920 and 1970 there was a net population transfer (including migrants and their offspring) of at least 4.8 million persons from the interior to the coast. This number represented about 21 percent of the coastal population and 26 percent of the inland population of West Africa in 1970 (Amin 1974). In Nigeria in the period between 1920 and 1970, millions of people migrated westward (to the Yoruba cities and towns), northward (to the Hausa towns and surrounds), and southward (to Lagos, Port Harcourt, and other coastal cities).

To fully appreciate the magnitude of West African migration, one must add to the numbers of more or less permanent migrants the hundreds of thousands of seasonal migrants (mostly men), who primarily came from Upper Volta (Burkina Faso), Mali, Guinea, and other parts of the Sahel. These men were involved in annual or biennial circulatory patterns of migration from their homelands to work on plantations, in mines, and as unskilled laborers in various rural and urban areas in the coastal states.

In the late 1960s and early 1970s, the flow of international migration within Africa was reduced, though by no means totally eliminated, by legal and economic moves taken against African aliens in various West African states (Gould 1974; Piel 1971 and 1974). The Ghanaian Aliens Compliance Order was particularly hard-hitting because of the large numbers of persons who were repatriated in its wake (Piel 1971 & 1974; Adomako-Sarfoh 1974; Sudarkasa 1975, 1979). Yet in 1972, Amin could estimate an annual flow of 300,000 migrants through the West Africa region (Amin 1974). It is still too early to judge the impact the fledgling Economic Community of West African States (ECOWAS) will have on the patterns of migration. However, one of its objectives is the free movement of persons among member states, and the success of the organization could lead to a new, substantial increase in international movement in the region (West Africa 1975).

International labor migration in West Africa has been predominantly a male phenomenon. One survey of between 400,000 and 500,000 migrants to Ghana and the Ivory Coast in 1958-59 revealed that approximately 92 percent of the migrants were men (Mabogunje 1972). Data from the 1960 census of Ghana, the country that received most of the migrants from the Sahel, also attest to the small size of the female component. These data show that there were four times as many adult males as adult females in the population of the Mossi, who were the largest group of migrant laborers in Ghana, having come there mainly from the Upper Volta. The Mossi population totaled 106,140 persons, of whom 79,910 were classified for the census purposes as "adults" aged fifteen and over (Gil et al. 1964).

Although the Mossi women and other women from the

"labor supplying" areas of West Africa were involved in the migration process, they themselves were *not labor* migrants. Wage-earning opportunities, even in unskilled occupations, were generally not available to women. Hence, the female migrants who accompanied their laborer husbands or mates to Ghana, had, of necessity, to look to self-employment as a source of income, if they were to have an income at all. Those among them who worked outside the home did so on their own account in farming, trade, crafts, and the service occupations. The 1960 Ghana census showed that 78 percent of the 15,720 Mossi women in Ghana did not engage in any type of income-earning activity. Of those earning incomes, 44 percent were engaged in agriculture (mainly as share-croppers rather than as wage laborers), 42 percent were traders, 11 percent prepared and sold cooked foods, millet beer, and so on, and three percent worked in other service occupations (Gill et al. 1964).

In addition to labor migration, an older and equally significant migratory process is one that I have termed *"commercial migration,"* involving traders and independent craftspeople, who also tend to refer to themselves as traders. Whereas labor migration has characteristically flowed from the interior to the coast, commercial migration has tended to be multidirectional, with streams going north as well as south, criss-crossing the Sahel and the coast, and taking in rural as well as urban areas. Typically, commercial migration has involved much more long-term sojourns abroad than has labor migration. In Ghana in 1968-69, I found that in a sample population of Yoruba traders, of whom 62 percent were under forty-five years of age, 92 percent had lived in Ghana five years or more; 89 percent of this population had lived there ten years or more; and 43 percent of these traders had been there twenty years or more. The tendency was for males and females to migrate to Ghana in their teens or early twenties and to remain there for most or their lives.

In both the precolonial period and contemporary times, commercial migration in West Africa has been dominated by a relatively small number of ethnic groups. The Hausa, Djoula, and Yoruba seem to have the longest histories of involvement in trans-West African trade. They are also probably the most widely dispersed of the contemporary commercial migrants (Mabogunje 1972:58-65; Sudarkasa 1974, 1975; Cohen 1969, 1971; Hill

1970; Meillassosux 1971). The Igbo (Ibo) who had well-developed trading networks in precolonial times but were not prominent in *trans-West African* trade, exemplify the groups who gained prominence as commercial migrants in the twentieth century (Sudarkasa 1975; 1979; 1985).

Women are conspicuous among the commercial migrants of West Africa. In the different migrant trading groups, however, there is considerable variation in the relative size of the male and female trading populations. Among Yoruba migrants, for example, women traders usually equal or outnumber male traders in terms of absolute numbers and in terms of percentage of their respective working populations. In Ghana in 1960, Yoruba women traders outnumbered their male counterparts by over 2,000. They also constituted a relatively greater proportion of the female working population than did male traders within the working male population. At the time of the census, 70 percent of the adult Yoruba female population was reported as being employed. Of these, 91 percent were traders and another seven percent were self-employed in crafts and service occupations. By comparison, 48 percent of the working Yoruba males were traders and another 27 percent were employed "on their own account" in other occupations.[2]

On the other hand, among the Hausa, males are the internationally known traders. In Ghana at the time of the 1960 census, Hausa male traders and other self-employed workers outnumbered their female counterparts by three to one. In fact, most Hausa women, kept in seclusion in accordance with Muslim tradition, were not recorded in the census as being income-generating.[3] It is possible, however, that they carried on in-house trade in a manner similar to that described by Hill for Hausa women in Nigeria (Hill 1971). Less than half (43 percent) of the adult Hausa women in Ghana in 1960 were recorded as being employed. Of those who were, 86 percent were traders and another 13 percent were self-employed in other occupations (Gil et al. 1964).

In comparing the Yoruba and Hausa migrants groups, it is noteworthy that in terms of both absolute members and the ratio of females to males, Yoruba women outnumbered Hausa women in Ghana. This indicates the greater mobility of the Yoruba female population. Yoruba women constituted 44 percent of the adult

Yoruba population in Ghana, Hausa women only 33 percent of their adult population. Other mobile female trading populations, as shown by my research on migrant populations in Ghana, include the Ewe of Togo, the Igbo of Nigeria, and various other ethnic groups from Southern Nigeria. In fact, Southern Nigerian women, including the Yoruba and the Igbo, appear to have been the largest group of female international migrants in West Africa.

Most of the millions of women involved in internal migration *within* the various countries would fall under the category of commercial migrants. The vast majority of women move from the rural areas to the cities. However, Mabogunje has demonstrated the importance of urban-to-rural migration (what he terms "the colonization of the rural areas") as a process of mobility in Nigeria before 1950 (Mabogunje 1970). Because women who migrate from rural to urban areas do not have the formal educational qualifications required for the types of wage employment open to women, many of them have had to enter market trade or similar occupations. In the past two decades, however, more and more young women with some degree of formal education have been moving to the cities in the hope of obtaining jobs in the "modern sector." As often as not, these young women do not find the clerical, industrial, or technical jobs they seek, and they, too, have to turn to trading on their own account or with female relatives in order to eke out a living.

Various writers have made much of the incidence of prostitution among female urban migrants. As Gugler (1968) says, "they have attracted a disproportionate amount of attention and curiosity." Kenneth Little's influential writings on women and the urbanizing process have been notable in creating the stereotypic image of female migrants as actual or potential prostitutes (Little 1965; for a critique of Little, see Sanjek 1976). Although female prostitution is one correlate of the large-scale migration of single or unattached males to the urban areas of West Africa, the existing discussion of prostitution simply underscores the need for better data on this subject. It was my observation that only a small minority of female and local women in Kumasi, where I lived while studying migrants in Ghana, relied on the sale of their sexual services as sources of income.

SELECTIVITY FACTORS IN FEMALE MIGRATION

Throughout this century most women involved in international West African migration left their homes after marriage rather than as single youths. This contrasts with the pattern of first migrations for males, who usually undertake their first migration as unmarried youths in their twenties. I found this pattern to hold for Yoruba males who migrated to Ghana to trade. However, Yoruba women migrants, like the Mossi women described by Skinner, normally came with their husbands or were sent for by their husbands (Skinner 1965; Sudarkasa 1974). Those who did not follow this pattern usually came as unmarried girls with their parents or other relatives.

Moreover, nearly all the women in the first generation of migrants were the first wives or the only wives of their husbands, or they were divorcees who had been first wives when they came to Ghana. Whereas nearly all Yoruba men born in Nigeria returned home for their first marriages or brought their first wives with them, those who married polygynously tended to take their second and subsequent wives from among the Yoruba divorcees or widows resident in Ghana or from among Yoruba women who were born in Ghana. Obviously the expense involved in marrying in Nigeria (either in person or by proxy) and bringing a wife to Ghana was the major reason why men did not usually go through that process more than once.

Within the pool of potential female migrants in the home town or village, previously unmarried women stood the best chance of migrating because they stood the best chance of becoming first wives. In addition, women who were junior wives of a potential migrant stood less of a chance of migrating with him than did his first wife. This seemed particularly to be the case when the first wife was still relatively young and of childbearing age. I knew a number of men who had left one wife behind in Nigeria while another traveled with them. In some cases, the wives left in Nigeria joined the family in Ghana; in other cases, these women divorced their absent husbands and married other men. The pattern of female migration after marriage seems to be characteristic of internal as well as international migration. Caldwell's data on Ghana suggest that most women moving to the cities were young brides or brides-to-be who were joining their fiances. Moreover, half of the married male migrants in Caldwell's urban sample reported having been accompanied by their wives at the time of their migration, and two-thirds of the remainder later sent for their wives to join them (Caldwell 1968, 1969).

One reason why the pattern of female internal migration is more complex than that of international migration is that where the distances involved are relatively short, young girls are often taken to the city by relatives with whom they live and work until they reach marriageable age. In the period up to the 1960s, many of these young women then returned to their villages to get married, and often remained there at least until they had one or two children. Next, depending on their husbands' occupational trajectories, they might move back to an urban area or remain in the rural area.[4] However, in the last decade or so, it has become increasingly common for young women who are brought to the city as girls to remain there up to and after marriage. It is my impression, based on observations in Nigeria in recent years, that these young women are marrying at a later age than their counterparts who used to return to the villages. These young female migrants, brought up in the cities, along with the young female school leavers migrating from tile rural areas, are equalizing the sex ratio among single migrants under the age of twenty-five.

Caldwell's point—that formal education is one of the most reliable determinants of migration from the rural areas to the city—holds true for females as well as males (Caldwell 1968). Increasingly, young women who are literate in the European language of their country and who have attended school, look to the intermediate-size towns or the large cities for employment opportunities. More and more of these young women regard themselves as overqualified academically and underqualified experientially for the types of work that women do in the rural areas.

Some young women (and young men) in the rural areas migrate to urban areas to serve as domestic help in the homes of relatives. In return, the relatives provide them with room and board and spending money. Usually they also pay for the young person's apprenticeship with a skilled craftsperson or arrange for their ward to attend some type of technical school. This type of migration from the rural areas is superficially reminiscent of the migration of young female domestic labor common in some Latin

American countries (Jelen 1977). However, in many respects the processes are different. In the first place, since the young African women go to live with relatives, they conceive of their move as one for the purpose of receiving an education, rather than as one for the purpose of working as a domestic . Moreover, since in many cases there is salaried domestic help (often male) in the same homes with the young women (or men) from the rural areas, they can justify the view that they are relatives "lending a hand" rather than serving as domestics. Finally, if they do return to their villages, they do not normally go back with cash savings to turn over to their parents but rather with a skill (such as dress-making) that they can use to earn a living.

When men and women are compared as to their ages at the time of their first migration, the findings are the same. Both sexes tend to move between the ages of fifteen and thirty, or they tend to be juveniles traveling with their parents or guardians. The main difference between male and female migrants in this respect is that most of the males in the fifteen-to-thirty age group are single, whereas most of the females in that category are married. In many areas, women still tend to be much younger than their husbands (Caldwell 1968:368). As I have indicated, this situation is chang-ing as females gain parity with males in terms of education and occupational opportunities.

Of the women who migrate on their own, my research sug-gests that they are usually nearing fifty, widowed or divorced, with previous experience as a head of household. Gugler has observed that barren women often migrate on their own because "without children they are in a weak economic and social posi-tion (Gugler 1968:467). Years ago, Nadel also noted that child-less women often took up long-distance trade and, with it, prostitution. He described some Nupe female migrants in Ibadan as well-known traders and equally well-known prostitutes (Nadel 1942).[5]

Given that women (and men) of various ethnic groups were differentially represented in migratory processes, the question might arise whether ethnicity *per se* operated as a selective factor. The data suggest that the differential participation of various eth-nic groups in certain patterns of migration was primarily a func-tion of the ways in which the colonial economic strategies affected their communities. A careful study of Yoruba commercial migration reveals, for example, a difference in the magnitude of migration from various towns and villages, depending on whether or not the particular localities fell outside the mainstream of colonial "development" in Nigeria (Sudarkasa 1975). Of course, the fact that Yoruba migrants chose to trade rather than to work as laborers, and the fact that Yoruba women were able to maintain relatively successful trading operations in a number of foreign environments, reflect their long experience in trade. However, cultural historical factors rather than ethnicity explain the patterns in question. Where ethnicity did play a role was in the organization of the migrant communities and, in the case of commercial migrants, in the establishment and maintenance of what Cohen has termed "trading diasporas" (Cohen 1971).

MIGRATION AND SOCIAL CHANGE

If one theme recurs in the literature on migration in contemporary Africa, it is that population mobility has been a catalyst as well as a consequence of social change. Scattered throughout the literature are discussions, for example, of the ways in which migration affects the husband-wife relationship, patterns of authority within the home communities, agricultural production cycles, and the host communities in which migrants form "stranger communities". I want to illustrate the impact of migration on domestic patterns by citing one example from the data on Yoruba migrants in Ghana.

In their homelands Yoruba women usually carry on their trade independently of their husbands (Marshall 1963). When I conducted fieldwork in Nigeria in 1961 and 1962 I did not encounter a single case of a woman who traded jointly with her husband. Such cases undoubtedly existed but they were exceptional. In Ghana, however, a number of males and females whom I interviewed reported that they were then engaged in, or had previously been engaged in, joint trading ventures with their spouses. This seemed to me to be directly related to the generally increased *interdependence* of spouses that resulted from their situations as migrants. Such interdependence developed because of (1) the way Yoruba women arrived in Ghana and (2) the conditions under which most Yorubas lived in Ghana.

As I have pointed out, almost all the Yoruba women who

migrated to Ghana as adults came with their husbands or to join their husbands. Usually the man who was married polygynously brought only one of his wives to Ghana with him. Most migrants, even those who were polygynous, tended t o live a *de facto* monogamous domestic life for years at a time. The economics of survival in Ghana was the major factor in limiting the number of women a migrant would marry and the number of wives he would bring with him to Ghana. The fact of living a *de facto* monogamous life would not necessarily have led to major changes in conjugal behavior had the couples been living in Nigeria in a traditional Yoruba compound. There husbands and wives had separate rooms and interacted on a day-to-day basis with the members of their respective genders living in the compounds as much as with each other. In Ghanaian towns and villages, however, Yorubas usually rented rooms in compounds and many husbands and wives (and their dependents) shared the same room. The physical living arrangements had the effect of involving spouses in virtually every aspect of each other's lives.

Moreover, having migrated together and having to face life in a new society, those couples who did not have parents, siblings, or other *close* relatives in Ghana (almost everyone had *some* relatives there) turned almost exclusively to each other as confidants. In this situation, husbands and wives had much more detailed knowledge of their respective financial situations than they necessarily would have had in Nigeria. Most domestic and business decisions were joint decisions. Furthermore, because in Ghana very few migrants had a wide range of persons to turn to for assistance in raising trading capital, husbands and wives who were in serious financial straits often had no option but to pool their resources and work together. Interestingly, when such partnerships proved successful, very often the husband would give his wife a substantial sum of money to resume (or begin) trading on her own. They might even continue to deal in the same line of goods, but with the husband in his market stall and the wife in hers.[6]

The comparative data on Yoruba conjugal behavior in Nigeria and Ghana indicate that joint decision making and consultation and cooperation in the use of conjugal resources within African marriages are not always indicative of "Westernization" or elite status, as Oppong suggests might be the case (Oppong 1974). These characteristics can emerge among non-Western-educated, lower-income, otherwise "traditional" marriage partners whose life-styles have been altered by the demands of existence in a new social environment.

FEMALE MIGRATION AND INNOVATION IN WEST AFRICA

Even though one can debate the question of whether it is appropriate to apply the term "development" to the socioeconomic changes that have taken place in West Africa (and other parts of the continent) in this century, the fact of the female migrant's contribution to these changes is undisputable. Through their occupational activities and their interpersonal relationships, female migrants have been one of the groups that have most consistently served to diffuse innovations throughout the West African region (Mabogunje 1974).

The most obvious arena through which female migrants have contributed to change is the world of "the marketplace." They have been responsible for most of the small-scale distribution of the overseas-manufactured goods imported into some parts of West Africa. They have also been instrumental in moving commodities from one West African country to another, into rural as well as urban areas, thereby making foodstuffs, textiles, housewares, medicinals, etc., available to consumers who would not otherwise have access to them. In many instances, female commercial migrants have also helped to introduce new types of machinery such as pepper-grinding machines and flour mills, and promoted new techniques for getting traditional tasks accomplished (Sudarkasa 1975; 1985).

As important as their role in diffusing material innovations is the fact that female migrants have often been style-setters and social interpreters for their Sisters in rural areas. In their persons, female migrants have been perceived as the embodiment of the material and cultural offerings of the city or the foreign land. Like their male counterparts, returning female migrants often became objects for emulation by the young and sources of information for the old. For women in the rural areas, female migrants have been their eyes in the cities, and it is often as a result of their descriptions of city life that other women become enamored of the prospect of migration.

NOTES

1. For a selected bibliography on migration in West Africa in particular and Africa in general, see the references cited in Niara Sudarkasa, "Commercial Migration in West Africa, with Special Reference to the Yoruba in Ghana" in Migrants and Strangers in Africa, ed. Niara Sudarkasa, African Urban Notes, series B. no.1 (East Lansing: African Studies Center, Michigan State University, 1974).

2. The Yoruba population in Ghana in 1960 numbered 100,560. Adult Yoruba females numbered 25,110; adult Yoruba males numbered 32,000. There were 61,730 Hausa in Ghana in 1960, of whom 28,720 were adult males and 14,420 were adult females, according to Gil et al.

3. Approximately two-thirds of the Yoruba in Ghana in the 1960s were Muslims, but there was no tradition of wife seclusion among them.

4. This was a phenomenon which I observed, for example, when I was conducting research in a small Yoruba town in Nigeria in the early 1960s (Marshall 1964).

5. I have no doubt that this picture I have suggested of the independent female migrant is likely to be drastically revised with the publication of the findings of some of the studies of female migrants recently completed or now in progress. I have in mind particularly the data from K. Okonjo's study of female migrants in Nigeria and from the very comprehensive study of migration in Nigeria undertaken under the direction of F. O. Okediji, in collaboration with J. Harrington and I. Osayimwese. Unfortunately, neither of these studies was available to me at the time of this writing.

6. By separating the trading ventures, the husband and wife are in effect distributing the risk of failure (which is high in the type of market situation in which they operate). Should one of the businesses "go under," they would hopefully still had the other one to turn to.

THE EFFECTS OF TWENTIETH-CENTURY SOCIAL CHANGE, ESPECIALLY MIGRATION, ON WOMEN OF WEST AFRICA

INTRODUCTION

I should like to highlight some of the changes in the economic roles of women in West Africa in the twentieth century, and to focus briefly on the role of women in migration, which is at once an important consequence and a catalyst of socioeconomic change in contemporary West Africa. By way of introduction, I would note the following three points. *First*, in many ways the economic position of women in West Africa during the precolonial period was undermined by economic patterns and practices established early in the colonial period, around the turn of the century. *Second*, migration, which was a key element in maintaining colonial economies, and which continued to be an important feature of the post-colonial economies of the 1960s, has differentially involved and impacted upon males and females. *Third*, the effect of migration on selected aspects of women's lives is an area in which research is needed if we are to comprehend fully the role of female migrants in socioeconomic change in contemporary West Africa.

THE TRANSFORMATION OF PRE-COLONIAL ECONOMIC ROLES OF WEST AFRICAN WOMEN

In pre-colonial West African societies women had substantial responsibilities in the economic sphere. They performed in a number of different capacities, including those of agricultural producers, food processors, traders, craftswomen, medical practitioners (e. g., midwives, herbalists, medical diviners), and service workers (e. g., hair dressers or cooked-food sellers). In fact, so prominent were women in the production and distribution of goods and services in West Africa that many writers have erroneously portrayed them as virtual beasts of burden. However, as Ida Rousseau (1975:41-43) points out in a recently published article on African women:

> The reasoning that has been used to perpetuate the beast of burden myth is based on an idea of work that is non- African.... Economic organization is in family units.... Work is sex-specific and to a lesser extent age-specific. The role of women in traditional African societies can best be understood...in terms of the African woman's traditional integrity within a separate but not subordinate female community. It can be conceived of in terms of the mutually interdependent relationship between the male and female communities.

Given the interdependence and relative parity of male and female economic roles in most West African societies,[1] it seems no more appropriate to label women who tended the fields or carried heavy loads as beasts of burden than it would be to apply that label to the men who built houses or felled trees to clear the land for farming.

The roles which women played in the economy of pre-colonial societies were at once "domestic" *and* "public"; their economic activities were undertaken as part of their duties as wives, mothers, sisters or daughters. At the same time, however, these economic activities were contributions to the public domain, and women, like men, were remunerated for that which they contributed (*Infra*, chap. 14). Women in pre-colonial West Africa were able to play significant roles in the economy because they had access to skills through apprenticeship training just as males did. In fact, occupational training was universal for all normally functioning members of society in pre-colonial West Africa.

The complementarity of male and female economic roles manifest in pre-colonial societies began to break down with the imposition of colonial rule and the spread of the market economic system. With the introduction of European currencies as the standard of value, mode of payment, and medium of exchange in virtually all transactions, and with the virtual exclusion of women from occupations that earned the highest incomes in European currencies, women were placed in an economically disadvantaged position. This discrimination against women reverberated throughout other aspects of social life, and it was not surprising that outside observers and some of the women themselves came to characterize the position of women as analogous to that of beasts of burden.

Ester Boserup (1970), Achola Pala (1974), Judith Van Allen (1974), and Marjorie Mbilinyi (1972) are among the various scholars who have pointed to the different ways in which "modernization" and "development" in Africa have served to undermine actual and potential contributions of women to the economic and political spheres of their societies, and increased their dependency on men. It has been noted, for example, that in the area of agricultural production, women characteristically are excluded from programs designed to upgrade farming skills and increase productivity (Pala 1974). They usually are not trained to use new farm equipment or new types of fertilizer. Nor are they the target population for innovative patterns of land use. Large scale cash-cropping is also an activity from which women typically have been excluded.

A critical factor in what might be termed the process of "underdeveloping" women in the modern era has been their relative exclusion from many educational opportunities, which are prerequisites to entry into many modern occupations. Moreover, where West African women *have* been afforded Western-type training, they tend to be channelled into occupations stereotypically conceived as appropriate for women by the Westerners who designed contemporary African education: teaching in primary schools, nursing, and domestic science rather than the more prestigious professional, managerial, or administrative positions. Of course, throughout West Africa women *are* in the ranks of physicians, lawyers, and academicians, but they are greatly outnumbered by their male counterparts. The magnitude of discrimination against women in educational and professional arenas is indicated by the fact that as recently as 1971-1972 women constituted only 12.3 percent of the 3,794 students who graduated from Nigerian universities during that academic year (Awosika 1976). In 1972 only 5.1 percent of the senior administrative, executive and professional federal civil service officers in Nigeria were women (Awosika 1976).

The observation of a general trend toward excluding women from the most lucrative and prestigious occupations in West African societies is valid despite the fact that women are highly visible and active in the distributive sector of most West African economies. Throughout the colonial period African commercial activities generally were subordinate to those of European and Levantine immigrants (Bauer 1954). Within the African trader population it was usually, although not exclusively, men rather than women who occupied higher positions in distributive networks (Katzin 1964; Sudarkasa 1973:66-67). Today, even though there are some conspicuously well-to-do women traders in West Africa, among the Yoruba, Igbo and Ashanti, to name just three groups in which substantial numbers of males and females are involved in commerce, there are more males than females who can be classed as large-scale wholesalers of indigenously produced and imported commodities. Most women and, of course, many men in West Africa are "petty traders" whose positions are more analogous to that of low-paid laborers than they are to middlemen entrepreneurs (Sudarkasa 1974:94-95).

The discrimination, albeit unofficial, against West African women in the economic sphere has had a corollary in their decreased participation in decision-making positions within the political sphere. Even though women made vital contributions to nationalist movements in colonial West Africa, by and large, they did not and do not occupy official positions commensurate with those that women occupied in pre-colonial times. In modern governmental structures there are no counterparts to the offices of Queen Mother, Queen Sister or any of a number of other positions of authority reserved for women in pre-colonial West Africa.[2] Pre-colonial West African societies had female leaders who officially spoke for women, and in some instances there were chieftaincy hierarchies that paralleled those of men. Nowadays, women are primarily on the fringes of officialdom in West Africa. This is not to say that women do not still have some power, but clearly they have been stripped of much of their authority.[3]

THE RATIONALE FOR THE WIDESPREAD PARTICIPATION OF WOMEN IN MARKET TRADE IN WEST AFRICA

Even though the overall economic position of West African women *vis-a-vis* men can be said to have been weakened by colonial regimes, women nevertheless occupy vital positions in the marketing process in most countries of West Africa. Their widespread participation in market trade represents both a continuation of an economic pattern that had its origin in the pre-colonial period and a response to the specific demands of the colonial economic system.

Basic agricultural subsistence patterns in most West African societies were altered substantially by the colonial presence. Food was still grown on relatively small farms. That food which was not consumed by the producers and their families was distributed through a series of daily and periodic markets. Throughout this century, trade in locally consumed foodstuffs has been almost exclusively In the hands of women. In some cases, such as that of the Yoruba, women traders were continuing an economic function which they had performed for centuries, albeit on an expanded scale (Sudarkasa 1973). In other cases, such as some groups of Igbo and Ashanti, women were changing their roles from that of farmer to that of trader (Ottenberg 1959; McCall 1956). Population increases and the expansion of interregional trade in foodstuffs brought about by improved transportation networks, made it possible to absorb millions of women into market trade in staple goods.

Involving women in commerce was also promoted by the demands of the externally oriented sector of the colonial economies. Basically, two types of workers were needed to assure the production of cash crops, to collect raw materials for export, and to facilitate the distribution of imported manufactured goods. First, there was need for wage-labor manpower for plantations, mines, construction and transportation industries; and for lower-level service and maintenance jobs in the colonial administrative bureaucracy. Second, there was the need for intermediaries to buy from expatriate importers for resale in small quantities to the low-income consumers who were the majority of the African population. Intermediaries were also needed to do the bulking of those export items grown or manufactured by small-scale producers scattered throughout any given country.

When the colonial economy demanded wage laborers, the call was almost exclusively for males. The assumption by colonialists and indigenous people alike was that women were not suited for the jobs involved and, in addition, it was usually males who were given the training required for the various jobs that were considered appropriate for either men or women.4 It was also males, for the most part, who were recruited as "produce buyers," i. e., as intermediaries who bought and bulked the cash crops that ultimately were exported by European firms in the early colonial period and by government-run marketing boards in the later period (Sudarkasa 1973:66-67).

Where there was a need in the colonial economy for small-scale intermediaries to act as retailers of imported textiles, canned foods or utensils, there was both an historical precedent and a necessity for utilizing the skills of women. Most of the males were occupied in farming, as wage laborers, as craftsmen or as traders in other, more profitable items. Some women who entered trade in imported goods remained in or near their homelands. Others migrated to various parts of West Africa, usually with their husbands, in search of greater opportunities to trade.

WOMEN'S INVOLVEMENT IN COMMERCIAL MIGRATION

Maintaining the colonial economic system in West Africa and in other parts of the continent necessitated both temporary and permanent relocation of millions of persons—a process which continued although on a somewhat reduced scale into the post-colonial period (Rouch 1956; Kuper 1965; Mabogunje 1972; Amin 1974). Most of the literature describing these migratory processes deals with the migration of laborers, i. e., persons who leave their homelands in search of wage employment. However, in recent years there has been growing interest in what I have termed "commercial migration," i. e., the migration of traders, craftsmen, and others who leave their places of origin to enhance their opportunities for self-employment (Hill 1963, 1970; Cohen 1969, 1971; Mabogunje 1972, 1974; Sudarkasa 1974).

Samir Amin (1974) recently has reminded us that with the exception of internal migrations in Nigeria, the history of *labor* migration in West Africa has been primarily a history of the movement of males from the arid lands in the region now designated as the Sahel toward the agricultural, administrative, and commercial centers created by colonial governments along the West African coast.

The migration of males from the Sahel usually involved a circulatory movement southward or westward from their homelands to spend several months or a few years "abroad" (i e., in another African country) before returning to their places of origin. For example, Mossi males from Upper Volta (Burkina Faso) migrated to Ghana, the Ivory Coast, and Senegal to work as farm laborers on plantations or in craft and menial service occupations in the cities (Skinner 1960, 1965). After one or two seasons abroad, they usually returned to their villages to work there until the need for cash necessitated another exodus.

Only scanty information is available concerning the impact of Sahelian migrations on women, whether in the home or host areas. Skinner (1965) does indicate that among the Mossi, women who were left behind in home villages, and men who did not migrate, had to assume an increased share of work on the farms. Moreover, these women openly expressed their resentment at having to work harder than the relatively small number of women who accompanied their husbands or lovers to the cities abroad (Skinner 1965:66, 73-75). However, I must say, parenthetically, that I did not find justification in the literature on the Mossi or any other West African people for Ester Boserup's statement that "migration from village to town entails for African women the exchange of a life of toil for a life of leisure" (Boserup 1970:191).

Skinner also noted that Mossi male migration did create for women what I would term a few "petty" job opportunities in the countryside. For example, some were able to earn meager livelihoods selling cooked foods to migrants in and around lorry stops. Of course, the migration of laborers created income-producing opportunities for women in the host countries. These males constituted a large consumer population for goods and services which women offered for sale in markets and the neighborhoods where the migrants resided.

I hasten to add that far too many writers, including Kenneth Little (1973), focus almost exclusively on the sexual services offered for sale to male migrants by female migrants and women from the host country. Male migrants, particularly those in the cities, are described as if they consume little other than sex, and female migrants are described as if most of them are actual or potential prostitutes.[5] That this is a very misleading picture should be obvious to anyone familiar with the patterns of employment of West African female migrants and non-migrants in towns (see discussion below).

Although I have pointed out that it is mainly men who have been involved in labor migration in West Africa, I do not want to give the impression that women are involved in this process only as wives or companions. A number of young women with some degree of formal education migrate from their hometowns or villages in hope of securing wage employment in the "modern sector." Usually, these young women do not migrate on their own but rather accompany relatives or they go to join relatives who assume the responsibility of looking after them and helping them find work. If these young women do not find the clerical, industrial or professional jobs they seek, they have to turn to trading by themselves or with their mothers or other female relatives.

When we turn to an examination of commercial migration in West Africa, we find that women are represented in much greater numbers than in labor migration. We also have more data from which to comment on the impact of these migrations on the lives of women. In most cases, female commercial migrants come from those ethnic groups in which men are also engaged in trade outside their homelands. In fact, most women traders migrate with their husbands, parents or other relatives. The Djoula, Yoruba, and Igbo are groups noted for having formed what Abner Cohen (1971) has termed "trading diasporas" across West Africa. In all these groups, *women* as well as men are involved in market trade. In contrast, among the Hausa, who are perhaps the most famous of all West African traders, it is the men who comprise the vast majority of those involved in commerce. Most Hausa women are kept in seclusion in accordance with Islamic tradition and therefore do not participate in the public world of the market. Polly Hill (1969, 1971) has shown, however, that Hausa women in Nigeria carry on vigorous in-house trading systems, which she termed the "honeycomb market system," where grain and other commodities are bought and sold through a network of children and old women who are not in seclusion.

My own research among Yoruba traders in Nigeria and Ghana provides considerable insight into the activities and mobility patterns of female commercial migrants.

The modern migration of Yoruba males to various areas of commerce and production outside Nigeria began during the first decade of the twentieth century. By the 1920s, the pattern of out-migration by Yoruba males began to be less circulatory and more permanent. By that time, too, large numbers of women had joined the move toward key commercial cities and towns in Nigeria and other West African countries. For women, *international* migration patterns were the same as *intra-national* ones. Married women tended to migrate with their husbands or to follow their husbands once they had become established in the new areas. Unmarried women migrated either with their parents or guardians or as brides-to-be who had been betrothed in their hometowns to men who were based in other regions or in other countries.

The extent of the involvement of Yoruba women in international migration can be gauged by the number of women in the adult Yoruba population in Ghana. Persons aged 15 and over were defined as "adult" for census purposes. The Yoruba in Ghana numbered 100,560, of whom 57,110 were adults. Forty-four percent of the adult Yoruba population was female. By way of comparison, in the Hausa population of 61,730 adults numbered 43,140, of whom 33 percent were women. Igbos (Ibos) In Ghana in 1960 totalled 14,050, of whom 9,140 were adults. Igbo women made up 31 percent of the adult population. The contrast between the percentage of adult women in the Yoruba population and that of adult women in the Mossi population illustrates the differences between a population of commercial migrants and a population of labor migrants. In the total Mossi population of 106,140 there were 79,910 adults, and of these only 20 percent were women (Gil, *et al*. 1964: 62–67, Tab. 13).

Generally speaking, for most of this century, Yoruba women who became involved in interregional migration within Nigeria or in international migration across West Africa, played a critical role in marketing both imported and indigenously produced commodities (Sudarkasa 1973, 1975). In Ghana, the Ivory Cost, Sierra Leone, and other West African countries, Yoruba women gained a reputation as traders in provisions, sundries, and imported textiles which they bought from European, Lebanese, and Syrian companies. (In recent years, African governments and large-scale African businessmen and women increasingly have become involved in direct import as well as in local import distribution.) Before European-manufactured cloth eroded the market for African-made textiles, Yoruba female and male traders had sold Nigerian-made textiles throughout West Africa's rural and urban areas.

Within Nigeria, the migration of Yoruba women and men resulted in the establishment of Yoruba commercial networks throughout the country. Yoruba women based in Ibadan or Ijebu Ode, for example, were supplied commodities from Kano in the north by Yoruba women and men who had settled there. Commodities such as groundnut (peanut) oil, eggs, pepper, and dried meat were shipped by rail to Ibadan where they were collected for resale throughout the former Western Nigeria. Yoruba traders based in the West sent their orders and payments to Kano by letter, by telegram, by lorry drivers, and by other persons going to that northern city (Sudarkasa 1973:45, 130).

Similar networks of Yoruba traders were formed in other West African countries, including Ghana, Sierra Leone, and the Ivory Coast. In the late 1960s and early 1970s many of these networks were broken up as a result of the economic indigenization laws and anti-alien sentiments that surfaced in Ghana, the Ivory Coast, and other West African countries. For example, the Yoruba trade networks were quite extensive in Ghana until 1969 when most Yorubas and other African "aliens" were expelled from that country (Peil 1971; Sudarkasa 1974:95-98; Sudakarsa 1979). Before that time, a number of Yoruba males owned large wholesale stores which mainly sold to other Yoruba traders. Yoruba women traders, who were also supplied by these wholesalers, had stalls in virtually every market in Ghana (Sudarkasa 1974, 1975).

The involvement of Yoruba women in commercial migration had many effects on various aspects of their lives. Patterns of trade, of family life, of recreation, and of association were all affected by their having moved from their homelands into areas where they were strangers.

One of the most obvious differences in trading patterns between the Yorubas whom I studied in Nigeria and those in Ghana relates to the fact that, although Yoruba women traders in Ghana generally maintained their tradition of economic independence, many more of them were involved in trading ventures with their husbands. This seems to have been primarily due to the fact that each of the spouses had relatively few kinfolk in Ghana to call upon during economic crises. When either spouse was low on trading capital, a woman and her husband might pool resources to invest in whatever line of trade seemed most promising. At some later time, the partnership might dissolve into two separate businesses.

Although all the instances of husband-wife business partnerships known to me could be traced to specific economic considerations, I think that this practice also was related to the fact that there was more *de facto* monogamy among Yorubas in Ghana than among those in Nigeria. Most males, including those who were polygamous, tended to migrate with only one spouse. Even in polygamous unions in Ghana, a man often lived with one wife at a time because his wives resided in different compounds and even in different towns. In such circumstances, pooling resources with any one wife would not cause as much conflict as it would in Nigeria where all the wives were resident in a single compound.

CONCLUSION

In this presentation, I have tried to indicate briefly some ways in which a number of twentieth-century economic changes have impacted upon women of West Africa. Particularly, I have tried to show how migration, which has been both a result and a cause of change, has affected women in that part of the world. I have not used the rubric of "development" in discussing socioeconomic change in contemporary West Africa because it is questionable at best whether most of the changes have improved the quality of life of people in the area (see Rodney 1972).

This paper has also attempted to show that women commercial migrants have been among the most important indigenous change agents in contemporary West Africa as a result of their wide-ranging trade activities.

Although there is obviously a need for more research into the impact these commercial migrants have had on events in their home regions and in the host areas, sufficient data are presently available to show that they have played, and can continue to play, a significant role in the economic integration of West Africa. It would appear that both the females and the males among them constitute a population which can be effectively mobilized for various trans-West Africa trade initiatives such as envisioned under the authority of the Economic Community of West African States (ECOWAS).

NOTES

1. In any discussion of the role of women in pre-colonial West Africa, there is apt to arise the question of whether or not the long Islamic tradition in many parts of that area resulted in the "subjugation of women." This is a debate that I must leave to specialists on the societies concerned. I should point out, however, that Polly Hill's data on in-house trade among Hausa women in Nigeria (1969, 1971) show clearly that even though these women are ostensibly secluded from the "public domain," they play a very powerful role in the economic sector of that "domain." Investigation into their roles in the political realm and within their domestic units might reveal that equally powerful roles are played by women.

2. Of course, many female chieftancies are still in existence in various West African societies, and the holders of these offices usually play some role in the modern governmental structure. The point, however, is that the authority of these offices is completely overshadowed in modern government by that of the offices created by the Western-styled constitutional or military regimes. I also recognize that women do hold offices (such as that of minister or judge) in modern governmental structures. Needless to say, their numbers are infinitesimal. One important difference between traditional female officials and those whose offices were created by modern governments is that the former were and still are considered to be representatives of and responsible to a female constituency, whereas the latter are conceptualized as representing "the people," of whom males are the most powerful. In other words, modern governments have tended to undermine the responsibility of female officials to other women, while at the same time promoting the notion of the responsibility of male and female officials to males in the society.

3. Illustration of this is provided by the fact that in 1975 the Nigerian Military Government appointed an all-male committee of about 100

persons to draft a new constitution for the country. Despite the fact that women from different regions, and representing different occupational groups, protested this act as a serious break with tradition as well as an affront to the many "qualified" women among them, the government did not see fit to add a single woman to the group.

4. Persons familiar with the colonial tradition in Africa will know that the first persons to be trained as clerks, stenographers, secretaries and typists were males, not females. It was only after World War II, and especially in the 1950s and 1960s, that relatively large numbers of women began to be recruited into thes jobs. Even today, the male typist or stenographer is not uncommon in West Africa.

5. It is surprising to find a virtual absence of "hard" data on the incidence of prostitution in West African towns. Social scientists such as Kenneth Little (1973) seem content to rely on works of fiction for the bulk of their data on this subject. An exceptionally informed discussion of prostitution among migrant populations is contained in Abner Cohen's book (1969) on Hausa traders in Ibadan.

GENDER ROLES, EDUCATION, AND DEVELOPMENT IN AFRICA

INTRODUCTION

With three-quarters of the twentieth century behind us, through-out most of the world, gender, race, ethnicity, and/or income are still *de facto* if not *de jure* bases of differential access to opportunities and resources. In the realm of education, gender is characteristically the primary basis of the inequalities that exist in most countries. In the developing nations, educational delivery systems are directed mainly toward males. Women partake of formal and informal education in fewer numbers and for shorter periods of time than do men. At the higher levels of schooling, women and men typically pursue different courses of study.

The differences in the availability of education to women and to men, and the different choices the two genders make as regards the educational opportunities that are open to them, are directly linked to the gender role differences that exist in the societies at large, most especially to differences in occupational roles and expectations. Evidence of a division of labor along gender lines can be found in most countries, but in the non-Western world, this division of labor is often most pronounced and most pervasive. Africa is a prominent case in point. Thus, when we approach a discussion of the future of education in Africa or of education for Africa's future, we must grapple with the question of maintaining a division of labor that utilizes gender as one of its underpinnings.

Some writers have answered this question by advocating what one critic termed the "Western concept of mechanical equality [between] the sexes." Others have been equally critical of notions of occupational preserves (or reserves) for one gender or the other (Boserup 1970). It is the view of the present author that the discussion of gender-role differentiation in education and in occupations must take place within the context of a consideration of the present and projected structure of society in the part(s) of the world under consideration.

In this paper, I examine the question of sex role differentiation in education and occupations against the background of the realities of contemporary Africa and in light of some of the projections that have been of offered for societal transformation in that part of the world. The paper is an exploration of, rather than an exposition on, various issues connected with the future of education as it affects women and gender roles in Africa.

GENDER-ROLE DIFFERENTIATION IN EDUCATION AND OCCUPATIONS IN INDIGENOUS AFRICAN SOCIETIES

The division of labor by gender that exists in contemporary Africa is rooted in the values and customs of the indigenous societies on the continent and in the legacy of gender-role differentiation bequeathed to these societies by the former colonial regimes.

Typically, in indigenous African societies, the occupational roles of women were different from but complementary to the roles of men (*Infra*, chap. 14; Rousseau 1975). The particular occupations of women varied somewhat from society to society but, generally, women worked in agriculture, food processing, marketing, crafts production, as well as in domestic activities located more strictly "in the home." Very often men and women worked in the same occupation (for example, in farming or trading), but the tasks undertaken tended to be gender specific (for example, preparing the land for farming versus tending the crops or trading in one line of goods as opposed to another). There does not seem to be a basis for holding that women's occupations were considered to be "inferior" to those of men, although such occupations were usually thought to be inappropriate for men, just as men's occupations were normally considered inappropriate for women. In other words, the maintenance of separate occupational domains for the two genders did not automatically imply a hierarchical relationship between those two domains (*Infra*, chap. 14). And, of course, not all work was gender specific.

It would also seem inappropriate to view the traditional work of women as "drudgery," if that is meant to imply that men's work was not. Men and women worked in the fields; both genders carried heavy loads, walked long distances in trade, and so on. Women may have spent long hours tending crops, pounding grain, or collecting firewood, but men also spent long hours felling trees and clearing the bush for farming, tending and harvesting crops, building and maintaining dwellings, and the like.

Given the interdependence and relative parity of male and female economic roles in most pre-colonial African societies, if one were to apply the "beast of burden" stereotype to women, one should also apply it to men. The disparities that are evident in the economic roles of men and women in contemporary Africa are for the most part the result of socioeconomic changes that have taken place in the twentieth century.

In light of the foregoing discussion, it should be evident that occupational (or vocational) training in pre-colonial Africa was also differentiated along gender lines. However, this training, which was usually provided through "formal" (i.e., structured) apprenticeship arrangements, was available to women as well as to men. A craftsman (or -woman), health or religious practitioner, *griot,* and so on, each received training of varied duration. Training for some occupations, such as farming or trading, did not usually involve formal apprenticeships; however, the trainee received a "formal education" through years of tutelage (often from a parent) before being sent forth to work on her or his own.

Education in pre-colonial Africa was not limited to specialized vocational training. As the late Jomo Kenyatta, one of Africa's foremost anthropologists, illustrated for the Kikuyu, in African societies, all persons, female and male, were given a general education in addition to training in specific occupational skills (Kenyatta 1965). Even though schooling and literacy were not features of most pre-colonial African societies, education was not only important, it was universal for all freeborn members of these societies.

This is a point worth stressing because many Western scholars and lay persons seem to take the view that there was no tradition of education in indigenous Africa. Perhaps these persons would argue that the process of transmission of knowledge that took place in those societies should be subsumed under the concept of socialization, while reserving the concept of education to refer to the schooling process that developed in the Islamic world (including parts of Africa), in Europe, and elsewhere. This rather narrow view of education underlies Phillips's observation that:

> In Africa, education was extremely limited and associated with the very small numbers who were in contact with Islam over the land routes and later with Europeans in the ports or administrative centers already starting to be set up in those parts of Africa which were colonized. Still basically the continent as a whole was still completely underdeveloped and tribal. African potential, though great, was late in being mobilized. (1975:24)

THE TRANSFORMATION OF OCCUPATIONAL ROLES AND EDUCATIONAL PATTERNS IN TWENTIETH-CENTURY AFRICA

Since the publication of Ester Boserup's *Women's Role in Economic Development* in 1970, a number of scholars writing on Africa have pointed out various ways in which the processes of "modernization" and "development" have served as constraints on women's full participation in the economic and political arenas in their countries.[1] The complementarity and near parity of male and female occupational roles found in many indigenous economies were eroded by the spread of the market economy. Of course, it was not just women's roles that were affected by the expansion of the market economy in Africa. Males as well as females found that much of their "traditional work" was rendered nearly obsolete by the introduction of new goods and/or new technologies. They also found that in most cases they were forced to occupy the lowest levels of the economic pyramid because of the absorption of foreigners, typically Europeans and Asians, at the highest levels of that pyramid.

But in the case of African women, they not only experienced the general displacement caused by the colonial regimes; they also found that their economic status generally deteriorated *vis-a-vis* that of their male countrymen. Where women continued in their traditional occupations, as in the case of traders or farmers, they often found their opportunities circumscribed by the preference that the expatriate business community and/or governmental bureaucracy had for dealing with men. Extensions of sizable amounts of credit typically went to male traders rather than to women; innovative productive techniques were usually introduced to male farmers rather than to their female counterparts (Sudarkasa 1973). The migration of women from the rural areas to the cities often meant that if they did not work as petty traders, food sellers or the like, they could not find work at all. And what had been economically a relatively independent female population found itself increasingly dependent on males for support (*Infra*, chap. 15).

With the demise or near demise of various traditional crafts that had provided a livelihood for large numbers of the female population (crafts such as pottery making, weaving, textile dyeing, and soap manufacturing), women found that if they were to work at all they had to join the ranks of the petty traders, thereby rendering that level of commerce even less remunerative than it had come to be (Sudarkasa 1985).

At the center of the problems facing the mass of twentieth—century African women has been their near exclusion from the wage sector of their economies and their having to face various financial barriers to their movement from the lowest levels of commerce and food production into economic activities dominated by expatriates or African males. In both instances the very fact of being female was often enough to call forth discriminatory treatment. However, one very important factor in the process by which women came to be "underdeveloped" in Africa has been their lack of the educational credentials that would enable them to enter into certain modern occupations or to expand the scale of their commercial or productive activities. Of course being female was a barrier to participation in the educational systems themselves.

When we survey the education of women in contemporary Africa we find ourselves reviewing a familiar pattern. The vast majority of African women have no formal or informal education of the Western type. Taking the average of all African countries, the median educational attainment for women in the age group from 15 to 24 is not up to two years. The median level of education for women aged 35 to 64 is less than one year. Eighty-five percent of all African women are illiterate (Boulding 1976).

It should be noted however that most African women still do receive a traditional form of vocational or occupational training. That is, they are instructed by their mothers or other female relatives with whom they live and work until they marry at which time they usually begin to work on their own. It is my impression that nowadays quite a sizable number of young women (at least those in West Africa) acquire some degree of training in certain skills (of which sewing is the most popular) through small privately run "vocational schools." These "schools" or "institutes," as they are often called, are usually held in a woman's home or in a small shop that she rents. The running of such institutes has become a form of business for a number of women who are themselves small-scale entrepreneurs. Girls enrolling in these vocational institutes would often have had some primary schooling but that is not usually a prerequisite for entry.

United Nations data from 1969 show that in the primary schools, on the average girl students constituted 36 percent of the total enrollment (UNECA 1975). These data also show that girls enrolled in primary school comprise 49.8 percent of all the African girls of primary school age. Some of these female students were undoubtedly older than the official cutoff age for the primary school population; hence the percentage of primary-school-age girls who were actually enrolled in school was less than 49.8 percent. These statistics for sub-Saharan Africa compare with the figure of 100 percent enrollment of all primary-school-age girls in Europe and North America; approximately 57 percent enrollment of all primary-school-age girls in North Africa and the Middle East; approximately 76 percent enrollment of primary-school-age girls in Asia; and an approximate 100 percent enrollment statistic for Latin America (Boulding 1976).

The data on *enrollment in secondary schools* show that in 25 African countries girls constituted between 8 and 28 percent of the student population in 1969. Of the four African countries in which girls constituted between 30 and 40 percent of the secondary school population, two (Zambia and Benin) are "Black African" states. Interestingly, in the southern part of the continent

(Swaziland, Botswana, Lesotho, and Malagasy Republic), girls make up between 42 and 52 percent of those attending secondary school (UNECA 1975). These percentages probably reflect the fact that young men in the three countries bordering South Africa migrate to work in the mines rather than remain at home to attend school. It should be noted that the females enrolled in secondary schools in 1969 comprised only 4.5 percent of all girls of secondary-school age (Boulding 1976). Obviously there is a very high rate of female attrition between the primary and secondary levels of schooling in Africa.

At the university level in 1967 African women constituted between one and ten percent of the student population in eight countries. They were between 10 and 20 percent of the university student population in eleven countries. Only in three North African countries (Tunisia, Algeria and Egypt) did women constitute more than 20 percent of the university student population (UNECA 1975). In 1972 women comprised 16.6 percent of the African students enrolled in universities, teacher training colleges, and technical colleges.

Generally the data on education in Africa show that girls enter schools in smaller numbers than boys and that they leave at an earlier age. Outside of primary school they typically enroll in shorter-cycle courses such as are offered by the small, private vocational training schools. Information on the fields of study that women pursue at the higher levels of formal education show that they have clustered in the areas that the colonial educators first defined as appropriate for women: elementary school teaching, nursing, and other health-related fields such as domestic science or home economics (Boserup 1970). Of the professional fields, law and medicine are the two that attract most women, but the proportion of women in these fields is typically under 20 percent in all countries. Women who pursue academic careers predictably end up in education, the arts, or social sciences.

Overall, then, it can be said that the spread of the market economy in Africa adversely affected the economic status of women, turning gender-*differenti*ation within the economic sphere into gender-*discrimin*ation within that sphere. The spread of Western education also served to increase the economic gap between male and female because on the one hand most women were not allowed to be educated, and on the other hand, most educated women were channeled into occupations that were lower paying and/or less prestigious than those held by educated males.

Of course, higher education has enabled some women to move into positions comparable to those of men and, where this has been the case, such women have often experienced less prejudice and differential treatment than Western women in comparable positions. However, the point being made here is that, on balance, Westernization in the occupational and educational spheres has widened rather than narrowed the gap between males and females. This could and did occur while at the same time the position of a few women was being improved in various ways by their exposure (however limited and in whatever limited numbers) to higher education.[2]

OCCUPATIONAL AND EDUCATIONAL SEX-ROLE DISTINCTIONS AND THE FUTURE SOCIAL ORDER IN AFRICA

Many of the discussions of the future of women's education in Africa include generalities concerning the necessity of providing equal access for women to schooling at all levels and of training women for occupational roles (such as that of engineer) presently dominated by men. It would appear however that a number of considerations should precede any prescriptions, however tentative, concerning the desirable quantity or quality of education for Africa's female population. (Some might want to challenge the legitimacy of speaking at all about education specifically for women, maintaining that we should simply discuss education for people—old and young—in the societies concerned. What is, hopefully, ample justification for the focus on education for women will be provided in the next section of this paper).

Among the broad issues to be considered in discussing women's education and the future of Africa or the future of women's education in Africa are the following:

1. What is to be the nature of the social order for which women are being educated and in which future generations of women will be educated? What are the values undergirding this social order? What are some of the distinctive features of the basic institutions that make up that social order?

2. Is this new order to be achieved through directed social engineering, or is it envisioned as resulting from the cumulation of a somewhat more discrete, less manipulated series of changes?

3. To what extent is education being viewed primarily as a catalyst rather than as a consequence of movement toward this new social order?

4. To what extent must the present realities of life in African societies—most especially (in the present discussion) the realities of the life of women—guide decision-making as to the direction, rate, and/or magnitude of social (including educational) change?

These obviously are questions to be raised for discussion rather than ones for which we have definitive answers.

In relating the first broad question to the discussion of gender-role differentiation in education and occupations, one issue that must be dealt with head-on is the question of whether the future social order envisioned by African peoples (or by their "social engineers") is one in which gender-role distinctions will be virtually obliterated. Is it desirable to move toward the creation of a society in which virtually all roles are androgynous ones? If there is any hesitancy about answering this question in the affirmative, then educational planners must ask to what extent would the obliteration of gender-role distinctions in education and in occupations have negative implications for the preservation of valued institutions or life-styles that have their genesis or their existence rooted in gender distinctiveness?

Analysis of present-day African societies would suggest that advocating the evolution toward androgynous roles would not receive widespread support. African women have consistently maintained that one of their differences with Western women's liberation movements stems from the fact that some of the latter's spokeswomen are "anti-male" or they seek to obliterate distinctions between male and female roles. There are practically no indications that the male population in Africa would support the "androgynization" of roles. The tentative moves toward what Mazrui has termed "androgynous liberation" through the incorporation of women into the ranks of the freedom fighters in Guinea Bissau and in Southern Africa do not appear to have social corollaries in other realms of society (Mazrui 1977).

The family, which is still the most important institution in African societies, is rooted in gender-role differentiation. The

African family is built up around the two principles of conjugal-ity (represented in the husband-wife relationship in polygynous as well as monogamous marriages) and consanguinity (repre-sented by the lineage that forms the core of the compound-based extended family). In both the *conjugally*-based immediate family and *consanguineally*-based extended family, separate contribu-tions are expected of males and females in material as well as non-material realms. Although there is much more gender-role flexibility within the African family than is indicated by stereotypic and misleading interpretations of husband-wife roles (e.g., Rosaldo 1974), with the exception of traditional "female hus-bands" there is no ideology of gender-role interchangeability within these units. Any educational policy decisions that lead in the direction of eliminating gender-role distinctions should be scrutinized for their possible impact on the family. Obviously, African families can and will change. The question, however, is in what direction and to what extent.[3]

Another point to be made in connection with the discussion of the possible elimination of gender-role distinctions concerns the strength of same-gender solidarity in African traditions and in contemporary life. Africa is a continent on which same-gender associations (i.e., sodalities, guilds, age-grades, and the like) have a long history and a thriving existence. Interestingly, *Western women's liberation movements are just now seeking to create the sense of solidarity that can sustain women's associations of the type that have always been a feature of African life*. It would seem that the education of women *away* from those values that have nur-tured and sustained this sense of sisterhood (values that stress the differences between male and female) could have *adverse* politi-cal as well as social implications. It is precisely such all-female associations and movements that have the potential for being highly effective instruments for the attainment of equality and equity in the political and economic realms.

The ideology of women's liberation in Western societies explicitly or implicitly promotes the view that equality of the sexes leads (or should lead) to the *elimination* of gender-role distinc-tions. In The United States the trend is for educational institu-tions, particularly the publicly supported ones, to integrate this viewpoint into their curricula. However, study of the precolonial political and economic structures and of certain linguistic features of a number of African societies suggests that parity or near parity between the sexes in the economic sphere resulted from, or was at least correlated with, the maintenance of essentially separate "domains" for males and females (Lebeuf 1973). Contemporary Africa—where gender-role differentiation still exists, but where near parity of the sexes has been replaced by the subordination of women—faces the challenge of determining whether or not a new social order can be created in which the positive features of same-gender solidarity and of gender-role complementarity can be combined with social justice and political and economic equality for females as well as for males.

It is being suggested, in other words, that as regards the issue of gender-role differentiation in occupations and education, indigenous African models might provide a basis for change in a direction that is both culturally acceptable and socially progressive.

The education of women to fill certain occupational roles (and correspondingly the education of men to fill certain complementary ones) should not be taken as an *a priori* sign of unfair or unequal treatment of women. Societies can determine the remuneration to be given for the various occupational roles within them. There is no *a priori* reason why physicians, for example, should be paid substantially more than nurses (and certainly not on a life-long basis) or why elementary school teachers should earn significantly less than college professors. Similarly the fact that farmers are economically less well off than some other professionals is a function of the type of economic order under which they live rather than of the nature of the work they do. The prestige that attaches to certain occupations and the lack of respect for others are likewise culturally manipulable. As long as discussions of sex-role differentiation in occupations and education presume the continuation of a political and economic order that thrives on inequalities of various sorts (that of the sexes being only one), the "solution" to the problem of the injustices caused by these inequalities will continue to be elusive.

EDUCATING WOMEN FOR AFRICA'S FUTURE

What are the implications for educational development of the realities of the present position of women in sub-Saharan Africa and of the prevailing attitudes toward, and the institutionalization of, gender roles on that continent? In other words, given the existence of gender-role differentiation in various spheres, how do we approach the problem of including both genders in any plan for educational development? It is necessary, first, to accept the premise that

> If all the persons who are involved in the human tasks of survival and creation of a better life are allowed to share the opportunities available to apply scientific knowledge and technological advances, development will be achieved at the most rapid rate possible. Conversely, if some persons are left outside the stream of this knowledge, the pace of development will be slowed down for the whole society. And the latter is particularly true if those left out play a major part in economic production and are at the same time the persons who bear the chief responsibility for the health and well-being of all the people. (UNECA 1975)

If it is accepted that both genders must be included in all plans for development, then we can proceed to ask how this will be achieved. We are aware that according to indicators currently used in the measurement of educational development, African populations generally are "in the worst position of the developing regions" (Phillips 1975:39). In 1970, less than half the children of primary school age were actually enrolled in school. And, as was pointed out in a preceding section of this paper, only about one-third of those enrolled in primary school and less than five percent of those enrolled in secondary school were female.

Moving into the twenty-first century, then, Africa faces the problem of "catching up" with the rest of the world as far as its overall educational development is concerned, and it also faces the problem of closing a rather substantial gap between the educational preparedness of its male and female populations.

Much of the discussion in educational circles today concerns the possibility of providing for all the world's populations a "minimum basic education," that is, "literacy, numeracy, and elementary knowledge of the environment, of health, of civics and of standard moral codes" (Phillips 1975:8). Regardless of the position one takes as to the proportion of the educational budget that should be devoted to this minimal education, it would seem that some form of universal basic education (with the terminability that implies), or of universal primary education, is a necessary goal for all sates concerned with development for the masses rather than just for the few.

The recruitment of girls on a completely equal footing with boys is implied in the concept of universal basic education; however, governments should take special measures to see that female students are not allowed to drop out of these programs in larger percentages than boys. This is a special likelihood in cases where the age of entry into the program is raised to eight or nine years and/or the duration of the program is more than four years. Parents might find it "necessary" to remove girls of about 12 years of age from school in order to be of assistance in the home, on the farms, or elsewhere.

Provision should also be made for females to have equal access to the channels leading from the basic education level to higher levels of education. Realities of life in Africa are such that even with policies of open enrollment, females will probably not move into higher education in as large numbers as males. It will be extremely important, therefore, for there to be a vigorous and imaginative program of nonformal continuing education for women in the places where they work and in the communities at large. In fact, such programs should be planned and funded alongside programs for basic education, because it is through the extra-classroom educational experience that literacy, numeracy, and so on, can be provided for the women (and men) who constitute today's non-literate parent generation.

The reality of differential enrollment rates and attrition rates for males and females (especially beyond the basic level) means also that special supportive services should be provided for women to ensure that as many as possible of those who enter the higher educational levels will in fact complete the courses they start. Given the strong male biases of existing educational institutions, it is likely that if women are not given special supportive counseling and academic services, large numbers of them will not have the motivation nor receive the attention necessary to succeed.

With respect to occupations or career goals, it would seem that all fields should be open to both genders; however, if for various reasons women continue to self-select or be channeled into certain fields, one aim of governmental policy should be to ensure that these fields not become or not remain "second-class" occupation by virtue of the differential rewards attached to them.

In any case, it is unrealistic to assume that in the foreseeable future the masses of African women (most of whom, in any case, will probably be recipients of only the basic level of education) or the masses of African men will be engaged in any occupations other than those of farming, trading, food processing, and the like. As long as the tasks in these areas tend toward gender specificity, then the mass of children will be socialized to think in terms of a gender division of labor. Thus, even if these children have the opportunity to move to higher levels of schooling, they would probably self-select occupations in which members of their own gender predominate.

In Africa today, as in the rest of the world, women will tend to move into or be channeled into lower paying, less prestigious jobs than those occupied by men. The higher up the occupational or educational ladder, the fewer the women to be found there (Committee to Study the Status of Women in Graduate Education and Later Careers 1974). Efforts to remedy this situation by providing equal access for women to the higher rungs of the ladder have failed because (1) the process of change is too slow, so women do not in fact "catch up" and (2) too many actors intervene that prevent *de facto* equality of access from occurring.

Nothing short of changing the structure of these societies and the value system that supports them can accomplish the goal of equality of the sexes in occupations and in other spheres. Work of all types must be valued, and vast differences in compensation for different types of work must be eliminated.

CONCLUSION

Male and female occupational roles were more or less at parity in many of Africa's pre-colonial, pre-industrial and pre-market economies. Following Ester Boserup and a number of other writers, this paper has argued that the economic policies, practices and patterns that emerged as a part of the colonial system devalued women and women's work, and created and/or accentuated inequalities of income and opportunity for males and females. Nowhere were the gender inequalities more obvious than in education, which, I hasten to add, was very limited for Africans in general.

Since the 1960s, when most African countries gained their independence from colonial rule, universal basic education and the closing of the educational gap between women and men have been national priorities. To date, however, the results have been meager. Everyone recognizes the need to do more.

This paper suggests that as Africans continue to pursue educational and occupational equality for women, they should give careful consideration to the overall role of gender and the functioning of gender roles in the social order they envision for the future. Among the questions to be considered is whether African societies wish to move toward the gender-role interchangeability advocated in some Western countries. Stated another way, the question is whether gender equality can (or should) coexist with the traditional separation of gender roles around which so much of Africa's social organization is built. The implications of such questions should be considered now, so that future change may be directed by choice rather than by chance.

NOTES

1. See, e.g., Judith Van Allen, "Women in Africa: Modernization Means More Dependency," Center Magazine [Santa Barbara, Calif.] 7:3(1974):60-67; Marjorie Mbilinyi, "The 'New Woman' and Traditional Norms in Tanzania," Journal of Modern African Studies 10:1(1972):57-72; Achola Pala, "African Women in Rural Development" (Washington, D.C.: Overseas Liason Committee, American Council on Education, 1976).

2. Of course it is relatively commonplace to find that the economic status of one group improves over time without improving vis-a-vis a superordinate group (e.g., the situation of the Black population in the United States vis-a-vis the white population in that country).

3. I am not aware of any research specifically relating to changing conceptions of gender roles within the African family.

Male/Female Disparities in Education and Occupations in Nigeria: Implications for Technological Development

INTRODUCTION

More than one speaker at the plenary session of this Conference on Technological Development in Nigeria has called attention to the absence or underrepresentation of social science perspectives and analyses in our deliberations. The present paper addresses one of the issues that such analyses inevitably lead to, namely, the question of differential access by males and females in Nigeria to certain types of technical training, to employment in certain technical fields, and to involvement in the process of technological innovation.

The issues raised here are not new; they have been addressed very ably by a number of scholars in Nigeria. Indeed, many papers on the general topic of differential access by men and women to various sectors of the Nigerian economy were presented to the National Conference on Nigerian Women and Development at the University of Ibadan in 1976, attended by this writer. This theme also surfaced at the NISER Conference on Social Research and National Development held at Ibadan in 1975, also attended by this writer.

As Dr. Aminu remarked earlier in the current conference, technology is fundamentally a matter of human resourcefulness. No discussion of technological development can ignore the factor of human resources in the development equation. Though there can be many points of departure for a discussion of the role of human resources in technological development, to focus on the relative contributions to be made by males and females is to focus on the most basic of all the possible distinctions within the human population.

OCCUPATIONAL ROLES AND EDUCATIONAL PATTERNS IN TWENTIETH-CENTURY NIGERIA

In the decade since the publication of Ester Boserup's pioneering study *Women's Role in Economic Development* (1970), a number of scholars writing on Africa have pointed out various ways in which the processes of "modernization" and "development" have functioned as constraints on women's full participation in the economic arenas of their countries (e.g., Van Allen 1974; Mbilinyi 1972; Pala 1976). The complementarity and near parity of male and female occupational roles found in many indigenous African economies, including those of Nigerian societies such as the Yoruba and the Igbo, have been eroded by the spread of the market economy. Not only were women's roles affected by the expansion of capitalism in Africa. Males as well as females found that much of their "traditional" work was rendered nearly obsolete by the introduction of new goods and new technologies. They also found that in most cases they were forced to occupy the lowest levels of the economic pyramid because of the absorption of foreigners, typically Europeans and Asians, at the highest levels of that pyramid.

But in the case of African women, including those of Nigeria, there was not only the general economic displacement that defined colonial status, there was also the fact of the deterioration of their economic status vis-a-vis that of their male countrymen. Where women continued in their traditional occupations, as in the case of Yoruba traders or Igbo farmers, they often found their opportunities circumscribed because of the preferential treatment given to men by the expatriate business community and by the governmental bureaucracy. Extensions of sizable amounts of credit (when given to Africans at all) typically went to male traders rather than to their female counterparts; innovations in agricultural technology were usually introduced to male farmers rather than to the females even when the latter traditionally performed the tasks involved with the innovations (Sudarkasa 1973). The migration of women from the rural areas to the cities often necessitated their working as petty traders, food sellers, or the like, if they were to find work at all. In these circumstances, what had been traditionally *relatively* independent, *relatively* self-supporting female populations, were transformed into groups increasingly dependent on males for economic support (*Infra*, chap. 15).

With the near demise of various traditional crafts that had provided a livelihood for large numbers of women (crafts such as pottery making, weaving, dyeing, soap manufacturing, etc.), those females found that the only alternative to unemployment was to join the ranks of the petty traders, and by so doing, they rendered that level of commerce even less remunerative than it had come to be (Sudarkasa 1974).

As Dr. Keziah Awosika of The Nigerian Institute for Social and Economic Research (NISER) has documented, at the center of the problems facing the mass of twentieth-century Nigerian women has been their near exclusion from the wage sector of the economy and their having to overcome financial barriers to advancement from the lowest levels of commerce and food production into economic activities controlled by expatriates and/or African males (Awoska 1976 and 1977). Although the factor of gender itself was the primary basis for the discrimination against women, the second most critical factor in the "underdevelopment" of women has been their lack of formal education. (Of course being female was itself a barrier to the attainment of formal schooling, particularly at the highest levels offered.) Without the necessary educational credentials, women could not hope to enter into certain modern occupations or to expand the scale of their commercial or productive activities.

When we examine the data on the education of women in Nigeria, we find ourselves confronting a familiar pattern of an educational delivery system directed mainly towards males. In Nigeria, as in other parts of Africa, girls enter schools in smaller numbers than boys and they tend to leave at an earlier age. Outside primary school, they typically enroll in shorter-cycle courses such as are offered by private "vocational training" schools. These small, privately-run institutes are not to be confused with the "polytechnics" owned by the State and Federal governments. The "vocational schools" for seamstresses, for example, are often held in the proprietor's home or in a small shop which she rents. Many of the proprietors refer to the running of these institutions as a form of "trading."

The statistics on formal school attendance by Nigerian women show that the higher up the educational ladder one goes, the fewer the women in evidence. In 1970, female students in Nigeria constituted 46 percent of primary-school enrollment, 39 percent of secondary-modern-school enrollment, 38 percent of secondary-grammar-school enrollment, 26 percent of teacher-training college enrollment, and 12 percent of university enrollment (Ogunsheye 1976). The data on female enrollment in the polytechnics and other technical schools were not examined, but it is likely that the percentage of women enrolled would not be much higher than that for university enrollment.

The data on the occupations pursued by Nigerian women and other African women who received an education beyond secondary school show them clustered in fields "earmarked" for women: primary-school teaching, nursing, domestic science, and home economics (Boserup 1970). Of the professional fields, law and medicine are the two that attract the most women, but the proportion of women in those fields is less than 20 percent. Most women who pursue university-level academic careers end up, predictably, in education, library science, English literature, social work, or in one of the social sciences.

WOMEN'S ROLES IN THE TECHNOLOGICAL DEVELOPMENT OF NIGERIA

Given the existing gender differentiation in education and in occupations, how is the problem of including both genders in any plan for technological development to be approached? The importance of this issue has been underscored by the United Nations Economic Commission for Africa (UNECA):

> If all of the persons who are involved in the human tasks of survival and creation of a better life are allowed to share the opportunities available to apply scientific

knowledge and technological advances, development will be achieved at the most rapid rate possible. Conversely, if some persons are left outside the stream of this knowledge, the pace of development will be slowed down for the whole society. And the latter is particularly true if those left out play a major part in economic production and are at the same time the persons who bear the chief responsibility for the health and well-being of all the people (UNECA 1975).

In order to maximize the utilization of Nigeria's human resources, it would appear that at least four steps should be taken:

(1) In the process of universalizing primary education, special emphasis should be placed on getting girls through that phase of schooling. As was stated by UNECA, it is vital that those who are most directly responsible for the overall health and well-being of the nation, namely the present and future generations of mothers, receive at least a basic education.

(2) Provision should be made for women to have equal access to the channels leading from the basic education level to higher levels of education. Realities of life in Nigeria are such that even with policies of open enrollment, young women will probably not go on to higher education in as large numbers as young men, and those who do go on will probably exhibit a higher attrition rate for reasons directly related to gender-role patterning in the society at large. It will be necessary therefore to establish special supportive services for women to ensure that as many as possible of those who enter higher-level institutions will complete the courses they start. Given the history of male bias in the existing institutions, it is likely that without supportive counseling and academic services, many women will not have the motivation or the training necessary to succeed.

(3) With respect to occupational and career counseling, it would seem desirable to encourage everyone to enter those fields for which they have aptitude and in which they have interest. Gender-role stereotyping should be discouraged throughout the educational process and in all other institutions. However, if for various reasons women continue to select or to be channeled into certain fields, one aim of governmental policy could be to ensure that these fields not become or not remain "second-class" occu-

pations by virtue of the differential rewards attached to them. Societies can and do determine the remuneration and rewards to be attached to the various occupational roles within them. There is no *a priori* reason why physicians, for example, should earn more than twice as much as nurses, or why elementary-school teachers should earn one-tenth of the salary of university professors. The prestige and rewards that attach to occupations are culturally manipulable. So long as discussions of gender-role differentiation in occupations and education *presume* the continuation of a political and economic order which thrives on inequalities of various sorts (that deriving from gender being only one), the solution to the problem of the injustices caused by these inequalities will continue to be elusive.

(4) Any program aimed at the maximization of the utilization of human resources that focuses solely on formal educational institutions can only reach a minority of Nigeria's population. Perhaps the most important programmatic thrust should be in the direction of vigorous and imaginative nonformal continuing education for women (and men) in the places where they work and in the communities at large. In fact, such programs should be planned and funded alongside programs for basic education because it is through the extra-classroom educational experience that literacy and computational and technological skills can be taught to the women (and men) who constitute today's parental generation.

CREATING A NEW TECHNOLOGICAL AND SOCIAL ORDER

One of the social-science fictions of the twentieth century is the dictum that technological change determines the direction of social change. It has been the case that certain social institutional changes have occurred in the wake of certain technological changes. However, planned social change is possible, and societies or nations may choose to institute social orders just as they institute new technological orders. The task of "social engineering" is extremely difficult, especially for those societies that disavow authoritarianism; however, if the possible social correlates of technological change are systematically explored, and desired alternatives promoted through educational and other channels, directed social change will occur.

The maximum utilization of women in technological development in Nigeria or elsewhere in Africa need not lead to the androgynization of roles, as is advocated by some groups in the West. There are a number of institutions in Nigeria—including the extended families, lineages, and same-gender associations or sodalities—that thrive on gender-role distinctions and division of labor along gender lines. The challenge facing Nigeria, in which gender-role differentiation exists in the context of the subordination of women, is to create a new social order in which the positive features of same-gender solidarity and of gender-role complementarity can be combined with social justice and political and economic equality for females and males alike.

PART IV

AFRICAN AMERICAN WOMEN: BUILDING ON THE STRENGTH OF OUR MOTHERS

"Historically, the strength of Black mothers has been demonstrated by their ability to hold their families together over successive generations. It is no wonder that so many Black high achievers credit their mothers with their success."

"Even though African American women are proportionally fewer than African American males in the public domain, they are well known as leaders in the fields of endeavor they have chosen public service and education, being among the most notable. This leadership tradition is not new: it is rooted in our African heritage, particularly that of West Africa, where women were conspicuous in high places."

Niara Sudarkasa, "African American Women —
A Case of Strength Without Power?"
(*Infra*, pp. 304, 305)

AFRICAN AMERICAN WOMEN:
A LEGACY OF LEADERSHIP

*Brothers, Sisters, and Friends...*I am here today to talk about African American women—past, present, and future. We did not come here without a past. Africa, of all continents, had women in high places—Queen Mothers, Queen Sisters, women chiefs who headed all the women in their towns, who sat with councilors and ministers; women who headed commercial guilds; warriors, military geniuses—the Amazons of Dahomey, Queen Nzinga of Angola. Women were prominent in the economy—as farmers, traders, craftswomen, weavers, food processors, and specialists of all types. Even in America— on the plantations—we worked in fields and in the homes of the so-called "masters." As mothers and grandmothers, we looked after the children—ours *and* theirs.

Today, I have been asked to talk to you about some of the women of our past who should inspire us to a greater future. There are so many women I could talk about...

I could talk about *Harriet Tubman,* who was born in 1826 and lived until 1913—eighty-seven long, hard years. Harriet Tubman, the Moses of our people...herself a fugitive who had been enslaved in Maryland, a woman who dared to escape bondage and then over a ten-year period in the 1850s made twenty trips into the slave states to free hundreds of enslaved men and women. I could talk to you about General Harriet Tubman, who had a bounty on her head. But, with a bountiful and courageous heart, and with faith in her God, Harriet Tubman went forth without fear, and inspired others to be fearless as they crossed that imaginary Mason-Dixon Line—so close to our own Lincoln University—that spelled the difference between slavery and freedom.

I *could* talk to you about Harriet Tubman.

I could talk to you about educators: *Lucy Laney*, born in 1854 in Georgia, the daughter of a Presbyterian Minister who himself had purchased his own freedom from slavery and that of his wife. Lucy Laney was a graduate of the first class at Atlanta University in 1873, and little more than ten years later, in 1886, she established Haines Normal and Industrial Institute in Augusta, Georgia. One of her protegées, who taught at Haines Institute, was none other than *Mary McLeod Bethune*, who later went on to found a school of her own.

I *could* talk about Mrs. Bethune *herself*, born in 1875, who in 1904 founded the Daytona School for Girls. In 1922, it merged with the Cookman School for Boys and became known as Bethune-Cookman College, related first to the Methodist Episcopal Church and subsequently to the United Methodist Church. I could *talk* to you about Mary McLeod Bethune because she has always been a heroine of mine. When I was growing up in Fort Lauderdale, Florida, my grandmother made me to know that the greatest women in the world were Mrs. Eleanor Roosevelt and Mrs. Mary McLeod Bethune. When I was about seven years old, my grandmother said something that stayed with me all my life—it filled me with hope, with dreams: she said that she felt that one day I could grow up to *be* another Mrs. Bethune. I still remember how my grandmother looked when she said it. I still remember how I felt. Nothing that has ever been said to me since has made me feel so proud. I believe it was then that I promised myself to do all I could to live up to my grandmother's dream.

I could talk to you about the time I *heard* Mrs. Bethune in Piney Grove Baptist Church in Fort Lauderdale. I was struck by how plain she looked, in an ordinary dress, and ordinary shoes that all the older women wore. But I remember how she *glowed* when she spoke, how she transported me to Switzerland with her words when she spoke of the beautiful gardens in Geneva, gardens with blooms of all different colors—her great interracial gardens, she called them. The first essay I wrote when I got to college was about that speech. I *could* speak to you of Mary McLeod Bethune.

But today, I want to take a little more time to talk to you about the woman who *started* it all—our first Freedom Fighter, our first Champion of Justice— Sojourner Truth.

Sojourner Truth was known as the Black Joan of Arc; but if Joan of Arc had lived in the same period as Sojourner, she would have been known as the White Sojourner Truth. This woman, large in stature and in spirit—was a warrior. She was a minister. She was a child of God, doing his bidding.

Sojourner Truth was born into slavery in New York in 1797. She gained her freedom in 1826, one year before slavery was abolished in New York. This woman, known then as Isabella, said that it was God who called her to a life of labor on behalf of her people mired in slavery. Like the Apostle Paul, she was transformed, she became *Sojourner*—a name which means one who goes from place to place, and stops for only a little while...and *Truth*—one who would speak the truth without fear of any man. Sojourner went from place to place, using her powerful oratory to speak out against slavery. It was said that she electrified her audiences with her words and her wisdom.

Sojourner was one of the strongest abolitionist voices, and after President Lincoln issued the Emancipation Proclamation in 1863, Sojourner concerned herself with support for the freed Blacks. In 1864, she staged the first sit-in in President Lincoln's office to suggest ways of handling freed, unemployed former "slaves."

Sojourner was a crusader; she rode street cars in Washington, when Blacks were not supposed to. She was forcibly removed and later sued the company and was awarded damages for the incident.

Sojourner was one of the first champions of women's rights as well as African American rights. In 1867, when she was 70 years old, Sojourner Truth was a leader in forming the American Equal Rights Association to eliminate both "white" and "male" from the voting rights regulation in New York state.

Sojourner Truth labored for 57 years for the cause of freedom—from 1826, when she was freed, until 1883, when she died at the age of 86. She was a warrior; she was a crusader; she was a pioneer; she was a visionary; she was a preacher; and she was a woman and a mother. And when she heard white men talking about what they wanted for their women, Sojourner made one of her most famous speeches.

Nobody ever helps me into carriages, or over mud puddles, or gives me any best place. And ain't I a woman? Look at me! Look at my arm! I have ploughed, and planted, and gathered into barns, and no man could head me! And ain't I a woman? I could work as much and eat as much as a man—when I could get it—and bear the lash as well. And ain't I a woman? I have borne thirteen children, and seen most all sold off to slavery, and when I cried out with my mother's grief, none but Jesus heard me! And ain't I a woman?

Sojourner Truth was a woman of yesterday who spoke for tomorrow. Her message, spoken across this land more than a hundred years ago, is still timely today. This woman who died 107 years ago, before the dawn of the twentieth century, speaks *to us* in a language that will take us into the twenty-first.

We who are women can be *proud* of her strength; we can *follow* her example. You who are men can heed her call for an end to male domination and discrimination against women. You can heed the wisdom in her call for full equality and justice for all, male and female. For, as Sojourner Truth said at the age of 80, speaking of the fact that women had no voice in the legislatures and in the courts: "If it is not a fit place for women, it is unfit for men to be there."

She ended her famous *Ain't I A Woman* speech with words that I leave you with today.

...then that little man in black up there, he says women can't have as much rights as men, because Christ wasn't a woman! Where did your Christ come from? Where did your Christ come from? From God and a Woman! Man didn't have nothing to do with him...

...If the first woman God ever made was strong enough to turn the world upside down all alone, these women together ought to be able to turn it back, and get it right side up again! And now they are asking to do it. And the men better let them.

AFRICAN AMERICAN WOMEN—
A CASE OF STRENGTH
WITHOUT POWER?

INTRODUCTION

There is both the stereotype and the reality of the strong Black woman. Historically, we have had outstanding women leaders of the nineteenth century, such as Harriet Tubman and Sojourner Truth. Twentieth-century women who gave reality to the legendary "strong Black woman" include the late Mary McLeod Bethune and—one of our departed contemporaries—Fannie Lou Hamer.

The portrait of the strong Black mother was epitomized in the almost mythological grandmother figure described by E. Franklin Frazier (1939), ruling the roost during slavery. Single mothers, as exemplified by the hardworking mother in Lorraine Hansberry's *Raisin in the Sun*, have often been portrayed as larger than life. But mothers in two-parent families—such as the character "Florida" (played by Esther Rolle) on the TV show "Good Times"—could also be depicted as strong, powerful women (especially when defending their husbands and children). Of course, at various points, even women like "Florida" had to face the societal barriers such as poverty, periodic unemployment, and limited education that restricted their upward mobility.

When one looks at African American women in the workplace, one also encounters the myth and the reality of strong Black women. Historically, one of the myths about Black women was that they were the primary breadwinners in the family while Black men sat idle. The reality was something quite different. Historically, both males and females in the enslaved African American population worked without pay for as long as they could be compelled to do so. After slavery officially ended, Black men and women worked whenever and wherever they could. In some places and at some periods, women may have been able to find work when men could not. However, except for the past three or four decades, Black men were ubiquitous at the bottom of the employment ladder—working two and sometimes three menial jobs so that they could do more than just "make ends meet." Black women were also working outside the home during this period, oftentimes as domestics, taking care of white people's homes and children.

During the 1970s, statistics caught up with the myth of the economically "better off" Black woman, and writers described her situation as one of double or triple jeopardy. On income measures, African American women as a group were shown to earn less than white males, white females, and black males. According to this paradigm, race, gender, and class combined to place Black women in a position of "triple jeopardy"—bereft of strength and devoid of power.

Today, we see some data that appear to give credence to the "strong black woman" legend, and other data that support the idea that Black women constitute a group "suffering from triple jeopardy." In the first instance, we note that African American professional women constitute a group that is growing at a much faster rate than that of Black males. This is attributable to the fact that since the 1980s, Black women have outnumbered Black men at all levels of higher education. Nationally, female undergraduates collectively outnumber males by a mere two-percent margin (51% versus 49%). By contrast, African American female undergraduates outnumber male undergraduates by a full 20 percent (60% vs 40%). At the graduate level, also, male students as a whole just barely outnumber female students (52% vs 48%); among Blacks, however, female graduate students far outnumber males— 62 percent versus 38 percent.

On the other hand, we see a number of trends that make us

less sanguine about the position of African American women. First, there is the sobering fact that proportionally, they and their children are the largest group living in poverty. When we look at "big businesses" owned by Blacks, we see to that most of those at the helm are men. Although the number of African Americans in high-ranking positions in corporate America is very small, most Blacks who are there are men. When we look at the numbers of African Americans in political office, we see that Black males still far outnumber females as mayors, state legislators, members of congress, etc. Similarly, when we look at employment in higher education, we see that men make up the overwhelming majority of the top administrators and the highest professorial ranks. Again, although Blacks as a whole occupy less than five percent of these top positions outside the Historically Black Colleges and Universities (HBCUs), Black males do outnumber Black females in such positions. They also greatly outnumber African American women in leadership positions in the HBCUs.

Overall, Women constitute about 12 percent of America's college and university presidents, and of those only about ten percent are African American women. Thus, African American women constitute only about one percent of those who head America's higher educational institutions. What do we make of these trends? What do we say by way of interpreting the "power position" of African American women in this country vis-a-vis African American males? What about their position in relation to white females and white males?

THE STRENGTH OF AFRICAN AMERICAN WOMEN

If we look for a moment at the roles and relationships of African American women in the home and in the public domain, we undoubtedly see evidence of the strength of these women. In the home, such strength is evidenced in their roles as mothers. Over 40 percent of them are single mothers—but it is important not to equate this statistic with that of single teenage mothers or mothers who have never married. Most of these women are mature adults who are separated, divorced, or widowed. Some are grandmothers rearing children belonging to their daughters. Some fall into other categories.

The strength of women in single-parent households is phenomenal. Most of them are women who are working *and* rearing their children. Despite propaganda to the contrary, those on welfare at any given time constitute a small percentage of African American single mothers. Historically, the strength of Black mothers has been demonstrated by their ability to hold their families together over successive generations. It is no wonder that so many Black high achievers credit their mothers with their success.

Black female-headed households are generally misunderstood. Until recently, all but a small number of these have been built around small clusters of related adults, rather than around a single mother figure. The most common pattern was that of a group of related females, such as sisters or a mother and her adult daughters (and some adult sons) living together with the dependent children of one or more of the women in the group. Together, the adult core group would support the family (although they tended to have separate responsibilities rather than pool their resources). They provided a network of child support and child rearing, and a general mutual support network for each other.

In two-parent households, historically, African American women have also tended to have more egalitarian relationships with their husbands than have white women. One reason for this is that African American women have always worked outside the home and, thus, with the exception of a very small number of them, they were not economically dependent on their husbands in the manner that most white American women were. Even now, the income gap between African American women and their husbands is far less than that between white women and theirs. Studies have shown that when African American women stop working, the household loses about half its income, whereas when white women stop working their households lose only about one-third of theirs. (Incidentally, a number of Black economists have pointed out that this is one reason that the status of "middle class" is such a precarious one among African Americans. The unemployment of one of the breadwinners can easily result in the family's slip down the income ladder and out of the middle class.)

Among African Americans, women have a tradition of outspokenness in domestic situations. They not only "talk back" and speak up for themselves, but also have strong voices in household decisions. Women are just as often the disciplinarians in the home as are their husbands or male companions. Although this is harder to document, there seems to be far more separate ownership within African American marriages than is the case with whites. There seem to be more instances of separately held property, especially high-priced items such as automobiles. Women have traditionally been responsible for purchasing their own clothes and other personal items. No doubt, this is a reflection of the fact that male earnings have not allowed them to provide more than about half of what their families needed. These observations, and many others documented in studies of African American male/female relationships within marriage and other domestic situations confirm the reality that African American women have traditionally had a strong position within the home.

In the public domain, even though African American women have been tradi-tionally underrepresented compared to their men, historically, they have always had some very strong voices to speak out for them and for African Americans as a whole. Leaders such as Harriet Tubman, Sojourner Truth, and Mary McLeod Bethune, whom I mentioned earlier, were mighty leaders—not only of Black women, but of Blacks as a whole.

Today, even though African American women are still out-numbered by men in public offices and other high profile positions, those who are there have very strong voices on the public scene: Dorothy Height, C. Dolores Tucker, Betty Shabazz, Mary Berry, Marian Wright Edelman, Eleanor Holmes Norton, Maxine Waters, Carol Moseley Braun, and Johnnetta Cole, are examples that immediately come to mind. Thus, even though African American women are proportionally fewer than African American males in the public domain, they are well known as leaders in the fields of endeavor they have chosen, public service and education being among the most notable. I must repeat that this leadership tradition is not new: it is rooted in our African heritage, particu-larly that of West Africa, where women were conspicuous in high places.

The great disparity in college-going rates of Black women and men suggests that African American women will increasingly assume those leadership positions typically occupied by persons with college degrees and professional backgrounds. As we approach the twenty-first century, we can expect to see a closing of the gap between Black males and females in such leadership roles. To the extent that the programs now being mounted to "rescue" Black male youth turn out to be successful, the gains by women could be slowed down, but it is unlikely that they will be obliterated.

STRENGTH VERSUS POWER

The latter points I have made about African American women in the private (i.e., domestic) and public domains raise the issue of their strength versus their power in the African American community and, particularly, in the wider society. Relative to their numbers, African American women have had strong voices in the public domain, but they certainly have not had power commensurate with their numbers in the society. I have already pointed to their underrepresentation in leadership roles in politics, business, and education. This relates to the overall male dominance in American society.

Women in general have had and continue to have far less power in decision making than do men. One has only to recall the American faces we saw on television in the recent Middle East crisis (code-named Desert Storm). With the exception of the wives of the leaders and wives and mothers of the troops—who were shown from time to time to give their men folk a "human side"— the only woman seen occasionally was the one who serves as deputy spokesperson for the State Department. And she obviously could only communicate what her male bosses told her to. This conflict, like others in the past, was an all-male decision. It is interesting that women did not speak out for a right to have a voice in the decision, but rather simply for the right to fight and die to carry it out.

It is not just African American women who have virtually no power in the public domain in our society—it is women generally who constitute the majority, but who have yet to trust themselves with the exercise of power. Perhaps one reason why this is the case is that when it comes to political and economic organizing, race and ethnicity, and to a lesser degree class (as in the case of labor groups), have been and continue to be the primary bases for recruitment and action. Let me put that another way: gender has historically ranked last behind race, ethnicity, and class as a criterion for organizing political and economic groupings in this country. There are only two possible majorities in America at the present time: that is a majority made up of whites and a majority made up of women. The white majority is being rapidly undermined by the increasing number of people of color in the population. But the majority made up of women is strengthened rather than diminished by the changing demographics.

Women, whether they are African American, Latino American, Asian American or white American, will not have power commensurate with their numbers unless and until they see themselves as having *common interests* that need to be addressed with a *common voice*. It is interesting to observe that men manage to reach across the divides of race and ethnicity—and even class—to keep their numbers in key positions. And, more importantly, they have persuaded women that it is in the women's own interest to allow them to continue to do so! Hence the support that women give to men, rather than to other women, in electoral politics, in business, in community leadership, and in other arenas.

I started with the proposition that African American women represent a case of strength without power. In reflecting on this reality, I moved to the observation, in passing, that this formulation holds true for women in general, even though African American women lag behind white women in virtually every category on which socioeconomic status is usually based.

I end with a question: Can women reach across the divides of race, ethnicity, and class, to find common cause in pursuit of the public agenda that concerns us? Obviously, in the last three decades we have made some progress in this regard, but at the rate we're going, at the end of the twenty-first century, women will still be trying to find a way to claim their rights as the country's majority population.

Black Women in Higher Education: Movin' Up But Payin' the Price

Education has traditionally been the primary vehicle for African American upward mobility and economic enhancement. And to the extent that we can speak of Black power, education has been one source of that empowerment. Nevertheless, African Americans are still languishing from the nation's unfulfilled promise of educational equality. From kindergarten through college, there is underrepresentation; unequal opportunities for access; unequal chances for success.

Over the past two decades in the area of higher education, we have taken a few steps forward but several steps backward. Despite the high school dropout rates in inner cities, *nationwide* the proportion of Blacks graduating from high school has been on the rise: 67.5% in 1976; 75.6% in 1985. But, over the same period, the proportion of Black high school graduates going on to college declined from 33.5% to 26.1%. And the overall percentage of Blacks enrolled in higher education decreased from 9.4% in 1976 to 8.6% in 1986.

Faced with these data, and having been asked to lead off this Symposium on *The Empowerment of Black Women* by speaking on Black Women and Education in the 21st Century, I fully expected to speak to you, in the brief time allotted, about the manifest problems of inequity and underrepresentation that Black *women* face in higher education. For, make no mistake about it, in relation to our numbers in the population, both Black women and Black men are seriously underrepresented at all levels in our colleges and universities. Correspondingly, their numbers are very low among bachelors, masters, doctorate, and professional degree recipients.

Yet, when I looked past the aggregate statistics on Blacks in higher education for the purpose of understanding participation rates of Black women, and of projecting these into the 21st century, I was completely taken aback by what I found.

All of us in higher education have been aware for some time that the numbers and percentages of Black males in colleges and universities have been declining, but I for one was totally unprepared for the statistics I uncovered as I began to look for some "hard data" to back up my brief presentation to you this morning.

What I found completely changed the focus of my remarks. So alarming is the plummeting of Black male enrollment in higher education, that it must be a key factor in any discussion of the future of Blacks in education or the future of Blacks as a consequence of education. There is no question but that this downward spiral of Black male participation in higher education has serious implications for the future of Black women, for the Black family, and our overall socioeconomic and political future as African Americans moving into the 21st century - as African Americans moving into the third millennium.

Specifically in the context of this symposium, it is important to bear in mind the implications of the declining enrollment of Black men in higher education for any discussion of the prospects for the empowerment of Black women in our society.

It was against the backdrop of these considerations, that I decided to entitle these brief remarks "Black Women in Higher Education: Movin' Up But Payin' the Price."

May I ask you to please lend your attention for a moment to the following trends in Black male and female enrollment in higher education. *In 1984, nationwide, men constituted 48.5% of the undergraduate enrollment and women constituted 51.5%.* Among white undergraduates, the percentage was virtually the same. By contrast, Black undergraduate women made up 59% of the Black students, and Black men 41%. Of the nation's *graduate students* in 1984, men constituted 52% and women 48%. For white graduate students, the numbers were 49.5% males and 50.5% females. Among Blacks, men constituted 38% of the graduate students, and women 62%.

For brevity's sake, I can only give you a snapshot of the data, taken from one point in time. If one looks at the trend over the past decade, it is clear that the gap is widening between the participation rates of Black males and Black females and between Black males and all other groups.

As can be predicted, the data on degrees conferred show a parallel trend. In 1985, 51% of the bachelors degrees awarded nationwide went to men, and 49% to women. If one excludes all peoples of color and looks only at white degree recipients, the numbers are reversed: 49% of the bachelors degrees awarded to whites went to men and 51% to women. Compare this with the case of African Americans where 60% of the bachelors degrees were awarded to women and only 40% to men. If we look at masters degrees, we see that in 1985, Black men earned only 37% of the masters awarded to Blacks, while women earned 63%. Even at the doctoral level, in 1985, Black men earned 49% of the doctorates and Black women earned 51%. Ten years earlier, in 1976, *Black men* had earned 64% of the doctorates awarded to Blacks.

What are the implications of the growing disparities in Black female and male enrollment in higher education? What do we conclude from these data? What do they foretell about interpersonal and sociopolitical dynamics in Black communities? What do they foretell about future employment patterns among Blacks in America?

The first point to be made emphatically is that these data do not permit anyone to conclude that Black women are advancing at the expense of Black men; nor do they indicate that Black women are "to be blamed" for the plight of Black men. The trends in Black male and female enrollment are the consequences of forces operating in schools, in families, and in communities to compel Black males to drop out in alarming numbers at every level on the educational ladder. The data cry out for analysis and for intervention. As Barbara Sizemore said in the symposium on education at the Black Caucus Weekend, it is in the self-interest of all of us, female as well as male, to reverse this pattern of destruction of Black men.

It should be patently obvious that the empowerment of Black women is directly tied to the empowerment of Black men. Can there be any empowerment of Black women in the 21st century if we continue to lose capable Black men who should be in school to unemployment, drugs, crime, and imprisonment? Where is the empowerment when those Black women who do succeed through education have to bear the economic burden of their families while at the same time trying to help their less fortunate sisters who are struggling with theirs at the bottom end of the economic spectrum?

Some will look at the data on Black women in higher education and say that we are "makin' it." I look at these data and emphasize once again that even though the percentage of Black women in colleges and universities has been on the rise, their numbers are still far fewer than they should be, given the numbers of Blacks graduating from high school. The numbers of Black women in colleges and universities look even more paltry when compared with their numbers in the college age population. Black women are of course underrepresented in virtually every field of endeavor, thereby contradicting any claim that they are "makin' it." But most of all, as I have tried to show in these brief remarks, Black women in higher education are now—and will be into the 21st century—paying the price of their relatively higher numbers among the educated professionals by having to shoulder burdens that should be shared by educated Black men, whose numbers are declining fast.

Last, but by no means least, those Black women who have had the benefit of a higher education will pay severe social costs unless Black people as a group reach out to embrace many of these Sisters who will find themselves unmarried and childless, and often unloved, because we live in a society whose mores about mating, marriage and motherhood belong to the 19th century when we are moving into the 21st! Statistics show that Black professional women have fewer children on the average than any other group of women in this country. This does not bode well for us as a people. We have got to lead the Black community in evolving patterns of living and loving that will truly undergird our empowerment as women—our empowerment as a people. It is only when our social structure can embrace us all without stigmas, it is only when we can overcome artificial barriers such as income and occupation to find love and security, that we can build the families that will sustain us as we seek the economic and political empowerment we deserve.

COMMENTS ON THE NATIONAL CENTERS FOR AFRICAN AMERICAN WOMEN, WITH SPECIAL REFERENCE TO THE INTERNATIONAL DEVELOPMENT CENTER

INTRODUCTION

We have come to expect great things from Dr. Dorothy Height and the National Council of Negro Women. Today, Dr. Height, you have heard a chorus of praises, in unison and in harmony, for this brilliant and timely idea of establishing The National Centers for African American Women in Washington, D.C. We not only applaud you and applaud our organization, we pledge our total support.

You have asked me to speak about the significance of the international dimension of these Centers, and to say a word about the significance of one of its components, the International Development Center. I am pleased to be able to do so.

ACTION AND HISTORY: HISTORY IN ACTION

The National Centers are clearly designed as Centers for action. They are future oriented, policy based, programmatic in their thrust, pragmatic in their aims and approaches. They seek to be both national and international in their outreach and impact. We cannot overstress the importance of the international dimension of the Centers' work, particularly that of strengthening links to Africa and the African diaspora in the Caribbean, South America, and elsewhere.

First, we must understand the relevance of our history as women of African descent to the very conceptualization of these Centers. To fully understand the history of our activism as women in America, the history of our roles as women in both the domestic (i.e., private) and public domains, we must begin with an appreciation of the roles of women in African societies.

Thus, in order to understand the evolution of Black families in America, especially the roles of women within them, we must understand the African family structures from which ours evolved. Secondly, in order to understand our history as American women who have always had a high level of participation and visibility outside the family in the *public* domain, we must understand the traditional roles of women in the economic and political spheres of African societies. Our traditions—of working outside the home, of assuming leadership roles in our communities, of promoting self-help organizations—are traditions that go back to the societies from which our ancestors were captured and transported to these shores in chains.

I know it is customary to look no further than the institution of slavery for an explanation of our roles in the family, in the world of work, and in other aspects of the public domain. But we must understand that we brought with us from Africa a tradition of leadership roles in our families as well as in our communities. We brought with us a tradition of economic self-reliance through work outside the home. The institution of slavery forced us to adapt those traditions to its repressive and restrictive conditions. However, we must know that the historical roles of African American women were influenced by their African past just as much as they were molded by slavery. Sojourner Truth and Harriet Tubman, and countless unnamed women leaders from the period of our enslavement, were women in the tradition of the great women leaders of Africa.

We must be aware that in precolonial Africa, more than in any other part of the world, women were conspicuous in high places. They were queen-mothers, queen-sisters, princesses, chiefs, and holders of other offices in towns and villages. In some societies they were warriors; in one well-documented African kingdom, a woman was the supreme monarch. Invariably, African women were (and are today) prominent in the economic life of their countries. Historically they were farmers, traders, and craftswomen; today they are entrepreneurs, corporate officials, and professionals in many fields as well as farmers, traders, and craft workers in the tradition of their mothers.

Why is this knowledge and understanding important to the conceptualization of the National Centers for African American Women? It is important because it helps us to locate ourselves in history. That, in turn, provides an accurate and authentic point of departure for our research on African American women and their families; for our research on African American women entre-preneurs, and on research in many other areas. It gives us insight into the values and structures that we can use as models, as we seek to intentionally create families that can rescue and sustain those of us who need new directions for the twenty-first century.

Equally importantly, the knowledge of the African traditions out of which we evolved will help us to understand the status and roles of women in Africa and in the African diaspora today. When we reach out to African women, to explore ways in which we can collaborate with them in programs to further their educational, economic, and social development, we will understand that we are dealing with women with a history of taking responsibility for themselves and their children; women with a history of leadership in their communities; women who may not speak our language, but who can certainly hold their own when speaking theirs.

We will approach these women with genuine respect and in a spirit of sisterly collaboration, rather than from a Western position of condescension that we find so prevalent in attempts to aid and assist women of Africa and other parts of the non-Western world.

By understanding the traditional roles of African women, we will also appreciate how much the colonial regime, with its Eurocentric emphasis on male dominance, served to undermine the economic, political, and social status of women in Africa. This is a point made in the early sixties by the political anthropologist Annie Lebeuf in a volume edited by Denise Paulme, entitled *Women of Tropical Africa*. It was elaborated in the early seventies by the economist Ester Boserup, in her pioneering book entitled

Women's Role in Economic Development. By understanding the traditional roles of African women, we see how the colonial system created and/or widened disparities between male and female. All too often, policy makers and scholars in the colonial era then portrayed those disparities as part and parcel of the African tradition. To the extent that the colonial regime provided any opportunities for Africans through education, employment, and political participation, those opportunities were mainly afforded to men. Thus, from the 1860s to the 1960s, one sees a "divide-and-conquer" pattern of enhancing the status of African men and a corresponding disempowerment of African women.

CONCLUSION

These brief remarks are intended to stimulate our thinking as we prepare to discuss plans for the development of the international component of the National Centers for African American Women. I hope my remarks indicate how important it is for us to focus on creating partnerships *with* women of Africa, the Caribbean, and other parts of the diaspora, rather than focus on developing programs *for* these women. With our help and support, they can develop programs for themselves.

I know that our Centers will be an inspiration to our Sisters abroad. We should hope that it will not only inspire these women, but will assist them in creating similar institutions in their own countries or regions. In the meantime, we should afford some of them the opportunity to work with us in the development and the implementation of our International Development Center so that we may benefit from their insights as much as they benefit from ours.

Finally, I hope that my remarks underscore how important it is for us to appreciate the significance of our history as Africans as well as our history as Americans in conceptualizing and implementing all of the programs of the National Centers. This history is not just relevant in planning for the International Development Center. It is imperative, for example, to have an accurate historical orientation for all the research and publications produced by the proposed Research, Advocacy and Policy Center. The policies we advocate will be no better than the information on which they are based. We must know from whence we have come in order to know where are going, and more importantly, where we *can* go.

REFLECTIONS ON THE POSITIONS AND PROBLEMS OF BLACK WOMEN IN AMERICA

INTRODUCTION

I wish to express my thanks to the Sisters for inviting me to speak today. It is a challenge and an honor for me to share with you some of my reflections on the positions and problems of Black women in America.

Obviously this is a subject that is most difficult to cover in a short time. The very phrase "the position of Black women" is likely to call to mind several important topics, each of which could occupy all the time I have allotted to me. For example, one could discuss: (1) the position of Black women in the economic, political, and educational spheres relative to Black males, white females, and/or white males; or (2) the question of the historical position of Black women *vis-a-vis* Black males within the family; *or* (3) the position of Black women *vis-a-vis* various liberation movements with which women of different strata or circumstances see themselves allied.

When one mentions the "problems" of Black women, our minds naturally move to issues such as: (1) their right of access to education and employment; (2) the problem of obtaining equal pay for equal work; (3) the problems of the working mother—how can she adequately combine her roles within the home and those without?

Rather than try to discuss any of these issues in isolation, what I will try to do in this address is to suggest a *strategy for the analysis* of our positions and problems. It is my view—and it has been that of many of our heroines and heroes in the forefront of the Black movement in different eras—that one of the responsibilities of the academic or the intellectual is to help clarify the positions from which we struggle. Today I shall try to place the problems and positions of Black women in a historical perspective. My over- all thesis is that in order to deal most effectively with our problems as women we must make a holistic, systemic appraisal of our position as Black people. That done, we should be in a position to chart a course of action that is complementary to—and undertaken in collaboration with—Black men.

In America, the socioeconomic status of all Black people is defined primarily by reference to race. Historically, African males and females were brought here together in captivity, and the patterns of brutality, exploitation, denigration, and degradation which characterized slavery were extended to male and female alike.

Even though gender provided one basis for the division of labor among the enslaved Africans, it nevertheless does not seem to make sense historically to say that Black women were *either* more or less exploited than Black men. Both genders were brutalized to the degree, and in the manner, that it was possible in a given situation. The fact that Black women were raped is neither more nor less an outrage than the fact that Black men were beaten, castrated, or lynched.

The fact that Black men were denied the right to live out the role of husband to the women they chose as wives or the role of father to their children, is no less an abuse nor any less critical to an understanding of the future development of Black families than is the fact that many Black women, of necessity, had to assume the role of family head.

After Blacks were officially declared "emancipated" from slavery, it was race rather than gender that continued to be the dominant criterion by which their access to resources, opportunities, or occupations was determined. The fact that in some parts of the country, during certain specified periods, access to jobs or education might have been easier for either Black women or for Black men is really quite beside the point. *All* black people were severely circumscribed and discriminated against in their quest for equality in America.

It is absurd to claim (as some have done) that, historically, white males and Black women are the two groups who have always been free in America. I would challenge anyone who makes such a statement to document the area in which Black women have occupied positions of authority, exercised power, been accorded rights and privileges, had access to economic opportunities or otherwise exhibited the freedom which was and is characteristically afforded to white males.

It is equally misleading, in my view, to claim that Black women are *more* oppressed than Black men because of the (so-called) "double jeopardy of racism and sexism." Those who espouse this view appear to me to be substituting analogy for analysis. The mere fact that we are female and Black does not mean that our plight has been any worse than that of Black males. For every instance of denial of rights to Black women, a comparable instance of denial of rights to Black males can be cited. The fact that the income of Black women is less than that of Black men is certainly not proof that they are "more oppressed" than Black men. The systematic imprisonment and murder of Black males, particularly those in the age group of 18 to 30, is unsurpassed as a weapon of oppression and a means of undermining the survival of Blacks in America. In the past, it was Black men, not Black women, who were systematically hunted and eliminated, and this is as important to note as is the fact that a Black woman might be denied a job which would be given to a Black man. The systematic elimination of Black males, which has been documented by the sociologist Jacquelyne Jackson and others, is as important a fact of our history as is the legacy of sexual exploitation of Black women by white males.

The point is that we Blacks have been beguiled into debating the quality and quantity of the oppression meted out against us rather than recognizing the necessity to take a united stand against individuals and institutions that would perpetuate that oppression. I am reminded, whenever I hear these debates, of the fact that as a people we are all too ready to allow others to formulate the issues that will concern us; and determine the priorities in our lives as well as in our political movements.

In the 1950s and early 1960s, we were drawn into debates as

to whether slavery in Latin America was more humane than slavery in the United States; in recent times we have spent a lot of time arguing as to whether, historically, Black families in America were mainly headed by single parents or by two parents. In both cases, I ask myself: So what? I doubt that the enslaved Africans in Latin America, grovelling under the whip of their Brazilian or Colombian masters, appreciated the fact that their enslavement was "more humane" than that in the United States. Whether Blacks had mainly two-parent-headed families or one-parent-headed families is far less important than the fact that it was *the flexibility of our family structure* that allowed us to survive and to thrive in America. As scholars, we should try to understand how we can maintain such adaptability in our institutions in the face of a hostile environment.

A similar point can be made with respect to arguments over whether Black women are more oppressed or less oppressed than Black men. The fact is that we are a people entering the twenty-first century in virtual bondage in some places and virtually without equality anywhere. The reversal of this situation requires conscious commitment, sustained struggle, and continuous collaboration and cooperation on the part of Black men and women, old and young.

What are some of the implications of a perspective such as the one I have presented here for the direction of Black women's activism?

The first and most obvious point is that I do not consider it possible to divorce Black *women's* liberation from Black *people's* liberation any more than Black male liberation can be divorced from Black female liberation.

Many Sisters make the mistake of attributing their lack of equality to Black males. This is as myopic a view as that which blames Black women for the attempted emasculation of Black men. It is incontrovertible that historically Black *people* were subjugated by white people. The fact that *some* Black men and some Black women were (and are) instruments in the systematic discrimination against our people must be incorporated into any analysis and into any plan for change. *However*, the fact of the existence of Black agents of discrimination cannot be construed to mean that they are the source of that discrimination.

Not only must Black people clearly recognize where we must place our emphases if we want to effect change, we must also appreciate the systemic nature of the inequities we face. One of the effects of our absorption into this system of inequities and inequalities is the inculcation in us of many of that system's values. Thus, certain segments of the Black population, male and female, emulate or espouse the patterns of interaction and the values of the very power groups that sustain these inequalities.

Some Black men, for example, have consciously or unconsciously adopted attitudes toward Black women that echo the attitudes that white men have historically exhibited toward their women. This is a complicated matter, but the fact that some of the most militant of Black males of the 1960s could advocate that Black women occupy a position distinctly behind or underneath Black males, indicates the extent to which the perspective of some white males on domestic and interpersonal relations had been adopted by some Black male leaders. Despite the fact that these Black males said they were looking to their African heritage as a guide to societal building for the future, the domestic and political philosophy they espoused reflected more of a Victorian English heritage than it did an indigenous African heritage. For in most of the African societies from which most Blacks in the Americas were taken, women have traditionally occupied roles that were conceptualized as complementary rather than subordinate to those of men. West African women were involved in the production and distribution of vital goods and services in their societies; they had political structures and occupied political offices which paralleled those of men; in their roles as mothers, wives, sisters, and daughters, they were intricately involved in decision making within both "domestic" and "public" groups within their societies.

This point leads me to the second major implication of my analysis of the situation of Blacks in America, and that is that Black women cannot, indeed will not, accept the notion that Black liberation depends upon Black women's subjugation. As Linda LaRue (1970), Maulana Ron Karenga (1975a; 1975b), and a number of others have argued, Black women must be encouraged to perform various strategic functions in our society rather than be confined to stereotypical roles which white men defined for white women and against which white women themselves are presently rebelling.

This is not to say that I advocate "doing your own thing" as a viable tactic in the strategy for Black liberation. Sisters and Brothers must realize that the "do your own thing" mentality is a hallmark of the individualism which undergirds the economic and political system that has oppressed us. The liberation of Black people, in my view, will unquestionably necessitate our building communities and societies around values that derive from our African past. As Professor Victor Uchendu recently pointed out in a lecture here at the University of Michigan, *the African world-view stresses a person's obligation and duty as well as his or her rights and privileges.* This means that in Africa, in the area of economic activities as in the area of domestic or political affairs, personal choices, and personal decisions were (and to a great extent still are) made against the background of consideration of duty to one's family, community, or society. In other words, in Africa, one did not (or does not) "do one's own thing" in the sense that one does in the U.S.A.

Thus, while I do not accept the notion that Black women must be forced into exclusively domestic roles or be limited to pursuing professions stereotypically earmarked for those of our gender, I do recognize that *the family is an institution that has a critical role to play in Black liberation.* As such, the family will demand the continued support of Black women as well as Black men. As women, we have historically been a pivotal force in the family and we should continue to be.

One of the most critical roles that Black women have to play within the family involves the socialization of Black children. It is imperative that we inform ourselves in order to enlighten our children; it is imperative that we understand our position as a people in America and in the world in order to educate our children to their position; it is imperative that we involve ourselves in the effort to change that position in order to inspire our children to follow our example.

A third major point that follows from my assessment of the position of Blacks in America is that any analysis which we make of a particular aspect of the life of Black women or of a particular problem that faces Black women, should be made in the context of our overall situation as Black people. For example, one of the issues which most incenses Black women and men is the issue of what is euphemistically termed "family planning." On the one side are the Brothers and Sisters who argue that white America is using birth suppression techniques as a genocidal weapon against Blacks. On the other side are Blacks who maintain that Black women must be allowed to "control their own bodies," which means among other things that they must be able to prevent or eliminate unwanted pregnancies.

It would seem to me that Black women who are concerned about our right to control our own bodies should also maintain that as a people we must have the right to decide to have children as well as the right to determine when we will stop having them. We should have the right to decide if, and under what circumstances we want to utilize contraceptives or to have abortions. At present too many Black women are *forced* to practice birth suppression in the name of "family planning." The situation is compounded by the fact that Black women (here and in Africa) often become virtual guinea pigs on whom pills, drugs, and other devices are forced even though the effects of these drugs and devices are by no means well researched.

The position which I take here does not deny an individual Black woman the right to choose, in consultation with others or by herself, to prevent or to abort pregnancies. At the same time, it recognizes the potentially injurious effects of linking social services needed by Black women to policies that virtually force them to submit to birth suppression programs if they are to get the wherewithal for their daily survival.

I might add, incidentally, that white women who are concerned with control over their bodies might stop to ask why it is that some of the same people who are against abortion and birth control for whites (including poor whites) are in favor of such programs among the Blacks in general, and poor Blacks (who "cannot afford large families") in particular. The fact is that if Blacks had equitable access to jobs, if historically they had been given fair compensation for their labor, if the opportunities in this country were equally available to all, then many of those who are poor could afford the families they desire to have. In the whole equation, more weight must be given to attaining economic parity and less attention given to "family planning" in isolation from other factors.

I would remind you of my reason for referring to the debate

over "family planning" within the Black community. It was (and is) my contention that the analysis of any particular issue that relates to Black women should be approached from a holistic, systemic point of view. What I suggest is that this issue should be looked at in its historical context and from the point of view of the group as a whole as well as from the point of view of the individual.

In general, I have tried to make a case, in this relatively brief talk, for the fact that the treatment of women of African descent in America derives fundamentally from the fact of our blackness, not from the fact of our being women. In fact, as I often state, following Linda LaRue (1970:38), Blacks and some other non-whites in America have experienced what can be called oppression—i.e., systematic, cruel, and inhuman deprivation. White women in America have experienced what can be called suppression—they have been restrained and restricted, but as a group they have not experienced oppression.

Both racism and sexism represent facets of the same drive toward dominion that characterizes the predominantly male, Euro-American power structure. Historically, Black women's exploitation and abuse by white men and women was primarily an expression of racism, with sexism as an added dimension. (Black females were not even regarded as women in the same sense as their white "mistresses.") White women were the victims of sexism, primarily perpetrated by men of their own group. Yet, there is no denying that the ideology of male dominance was (and is) pervasive throughout the society, and accepted, therefore, by the majority of Black males as well as white males. Sexism was (and is) displayed by Black men as well as by whites.

Nevertheless, the predominance of racism over sexism in America is evidenced by the fact that Black men were (and still are) required to show the utmost respect for white women, and usually paid with their lives for acts of abuse, alleged or real, against them. On the other hand, the disrespect and/or abuse of Black women by Black men, and even more so by white men, was (and is) often ignored. Sometimes, in some places, it even was (and is) encouraged.

The predominance of racism over sexism in America has made it difficult for Black women and white women to agree on what constitutes "women's liberation." To say this is not to say that Black women cannot find common cause with white women on certain issues. To the extent that white women are genuinely prepared to incorporate demands of equality for all women into their programs for change, then of course Black women can support such programs. However, in my experience, I have found that white women rarely work for equal justice for all women even though they usually verbalize such a sentiment. When affirmative action programs for "women" are established, these are usually headed and staffed primarily by white women, whereas non-white women are usually forced to turn to the minorities' advocates for assistance. This illustrates the fact that *race and not gender is still the primary demarcator of groups in this country* and in many other places throughtout the world. One would hope that with the maturity of the women's movement, race will no longer be a source of privilege *or* persecution, at least not in our half of the world.

Let me conclude by amplifying a point which I made at the beginning. Black women, like Black men, in all walks of life can play a strategic role in our advancement and liberation. Those of us who are ensconced in academia should repay those Blacks over whose sweat and, in some instances, over whose blood we were put here, by utilizing our skills to help in the analysis of our situation, and by directing our skills toward the transformation of that situation.

I see the work of this Conference as falling entirely within that charge. I hope that we will take our tasks seriously and that we will approach our deliberations in the spirit of Sisterhood.

BIBLIOGRAPHY

A. Articles Included in this Volume

1. **Value Premises Underlying Black Family Studies and Black Families.** Originally published as: "An Exposition on the Value Premises Underlying Black Family Studies and Black Families," *Journal of the National Medical Association* 67, 3 (May 1975):235-239. [First presented at the 77th Annual Convention of the National Medical Assn., Kansas City, Missouri, 1972.]

2. **Dispelling the Myths About Black Families.** Originally published as: "Reassessing the Black Family:Dispelling the Myths, Reaffirming the Values," *Sisters Magazine* 1, 1 (Summer 1988). [Published by the National Council of Negro Women, Inc.]

3. **Female-Headed African American Households—Some Neglected Dimensions.** Originally published in: Harriette P. McAdoo, ed., *Family Ethnicity:Strength in Diversity* (Newbury Park, Calif.: Sage Publications, Inc., 1993a). Earlier versions of this chapter were presented at the Conference "Woman to Woman: Single Parenting from a Global Perspective," sponsored by Delta Sigma Theta Sorority, Inc., Nassau, Bahamas, 1987, and at the symposium "Women of Color," at Virginia Commonwealth University, 1989.

4. **Speaking up for Single Mothers.** Unpublished presentation, February 27, 1990.

5. **African American Families and Family Values.** Previously published in: N.Sudarkasa et al., eds., *Exploring the African-American Experience,* Lincoln University Press, 1995; first published in the Harper Collins edi-

tion of that volume (1994); also to be published in: Harriette P. McAdoo, ed., *Black Families,* 3rd ed. (Newbury Park, Calif.: Sage Publications, Inc., forthcoming).

6. **Roots of the Black Family: Observations on the Herskovits-Frazier Debate.** Originally published as: "Roots of the Black Family: Comments on the History of a Debate on History," *LSA Magazine* [University of Michigan, Ann Arbor], Spring 1982.

7. **African and African American Family Structure.** Originally published in: *The Black Scholar* 12, 2 (November/December 1980); reprinted in: Johnnetta B. Cole, ed., *Anthropology for the Eighties* (New York: The Free Press, 1982) and in: Johnnetta B. Cole, ed., *Anthropology for the Nineties* (New York: The Free Press, 1991).

8. **Interpreting the African Heritage in African American Family Organization.** Originally published in: Harriette P. McAdoo, ed., *Black Families,* Beverly Hills, Calif.: Sage Publishing Company, 1981 [1st ed.] and 1988 [2nd ed.].

9. **Timeless Values for Troubled Times: Strengthening Today's African American Families.** Extracted from keynote addresses presented to the National Council of Negro Women, in Washington, D.C., on December 1, 1989 and the Nationwide Family Meeting Teleconference, National Council of Negro Women, in Washington, D.C., January 27, 1990.

10. **Planning *for* the Family versus "Family Planning"—The Case for National Action in Nigeria.** Originally published as "National Development Planning for the Promotion and Protection of the Family" in: E. Akeredolu-Ale, ed., *Proceedings of the 1975 Conference on Social Research and National Development in Nigeria* (Ibadan, Nigeria: Nigerian Institute for Social and Economic Research, 1977).

11. **The "Status of Women" in Indigenous African Societies— Implications for the Study of African American Women's Roles.** Originally published in: *Feminist Studies* 12, 1 (Spring 1986):91-103; expanded version (which is included in this volume) was published in: Rosalyn Terborg-Penn, ed., *Women in Africa and the African Diaspora* (Washington, D.C.: Howard University Press, 1987).

12. **The Changing Roles of Women in Changing Family Structures in West Africa: Some Preliminary Observations.** Originally presented at the Conference on Women in the African Diaspora: An Interdisciplinary Perspective, Association of Black Women Historians, Howard University, Washington, D.C., June 12-14, 1983.

13. **In a World of Women: Field Work in a Yoruba Community.** Originally published in: Peggy Golde, ed., *Women in the Field:Anthropological Experiences* (Chicago: Aldine Press, 1970); 2nd ed. published by the University of California Press, Berkeley, Calif., 1986.

14. **Female Employment and Family Organization in West Africa.** Originally published in: Dorothy McGuigan, ed., *New Research on Women and Sex Roles* (Ann Arbor: University of Michigan Center for

Continuing Education for Women, 1976); reprinted in: Filomina S.
Steady, ed., *The Black Woman Cross-Culturally* (Cambridge, Mass.:
Schenkman Publishing Company, 1981).

15. **Women and Migration in Contemporary West Africa.** Originally
published in: Wellesley Editorial Committee, ed., *Women and National
Development:The Complexities of Change* (Chicago: University of Chicago
Press, 1977); also published in: *Signs* 3, 1 (1977).

16. **The Effects of Twentieth-Century Social Change, Especially
Migration, on Women of West Africa.** Originally published in: Patricia
Paylore and Richard Harvey, eds., *West Africa Conference,
1976:Proceedings* (Tucson: University of Arizona, 1976).

17. **Gender Roles, Education, and Development in Africa.** Revised from
a paper titled "Sex Roles, Education, and Development in Africa" originally published in *Anthropology and Education Quarterly* XIII, 3 (Fall
1982).

18. **Male/Female Disparities in Education and Occupations in Nigeria:
Implications for Technological Development.** Originally published in:
Moyibi Amodo and C.D. Tyson, eds., *Technological Development in
Nigeria* (New York: Third Press International, 1979).

19. **African American Women: A Legacy of Leadership.** Originally presented at The Women's Day Program, Camphor Memorial Church,
Philadelphia, Pa., March 18, 1990.

20. **African American Women—A Case of Strength Without Power?**
Originally presented at The Women's History Month Program,
Millersville University, Millersville, Pa., March 8, 1991.

21. **Black Women in Higher Education: Movin' Up But Payin' the
Price.** Originally presented at: Spelman College Inaugural Symposium
for the inauguration of Dr. Johnnetta Cole, on the Empowerment of
Black Women, Atlanta, Ga., October, 1988.

22. **Comments on the National Centers for African American Women,
with Special Reference to the International Development Center.**
Originally presented at the National Council of Negro Women Council
of Advisors on the National Center, Chantilly, Va., June 11 and 12,
1993.

23. **Reflections on the Positions and Problems of Black Women in
America.** Keynote address presented to the Conference on Perspectives
on Black Women, sponsored by the Center for Continuing Education of
Women and the Center for Afroamerican and African Studies, The
University of Michigan, Ann Arbor, Mich., March 20, 1976

B. Works Cited in this Volume

Agbasegbe (Demerson), Bamidele. "Is There Marriage between Women in Africa?" In: J.S. Williams, et. al., eds., *Sociological Research Symposium, V.* Richmond, Va.: Commonwealth University Department of Sociology, 1975.

——. "The Role of Wife in the Black Extended Family: Perspectives from a Rural Community in Southern United States." In: Dorothy McGuigan, ed., *New Research on Women and Sex Roles.* Ann Arbor, Mich.: University of Michigan Center for Continuing Education of Women, 1976.

——. "Some Aspects of Contemporary Rural Afro-American Family Life in the Sea Islands of Southeastern United States." Presented at the Annual Meetings of the Association of Social and Behavioral Scientists, Atlanta, Ga., March 1981.

Aldous, Joan. "Urbanization, the Extended Family and Kinship Ties in West Africa." In: Pierre van den Berghe, ed., *Africa: Social Problems of Change and Conflict.* San Francisco: Chandler Publishing Co., 1963.

Allen, Walter R. "The Search for Applicable Theories of Black Family Life." *Journal of Marriage and the Family* 40, 1 (1978):117-129.

——. "Class, Culture, and Family Organization: The Effects of Class and Race on Family Structure in Urban America." *Journal of Comparative Family Studies* 10 (Autumn 1979):301-313.

Amin, Samir, ed. "Introduction." In: *Modern Migrations in Western Africa.* Oxford: Oxford University Press, 1974.

Aschenbrenner, Joyce. "Extended Families Among Black Americans." *Journal of Comparative Family Studies* 4 (1973):257-268.

——. *Lifelines: Black Families in Chicago.* New York: Holt, Rinehart, & Winston, 1975.

——. "Continuities and Variations in Black Family Structure." In: D.B. Shimkin, E.M. Shimkin, and D.A. Frate eds., *The Extended Family in Black Societies.* The Hague: Mouton, 1978:181-200.

Aschenbrenner, Joyce, and C.H. Carr. "Conjugal Relationships in the Context of the Black Extended Family." *Alternate Lifestyles* 3 (November 1980):463-484.

Awe, Bolanle. "The Iyalode in the Traditional Yoruba Political System." In: Alice Schlegel, ed., *Sexual Stratification: A Cross-Cultural View.* New York: Columbia University Press, 1977.

Awosika, Keziah. "Nigerian Women in the Labour Force: Implications for National Economic Planning." Paper presented to the National Conference on Nigerian Women and Development, University of Ibadan, 1976.

——. "Nigerian in the Informal Labor Sector." Paper presented at the Conference on Women and Development, Wellesley, Mass., 1976.

——. "Women in the Urban Labor Force—Implications for Manpower

Planning in Nigeria." Paper presented at the Nigerian Economic Society Conference on Urbanization and National Development, Kaduna, 1977.

Bascom, W.R. "The Principle of Seniority in the Social Structure of the Yoruba." *American Anthropologist* 44, 1 (1942):37-46.

——. "The Esusu: A Credit Institution of the Yoruba." *Journal of the Royal Anthropological Institute* 82 (1952):63-69.

Bauer, P.T. *West African Trade.* Cambridge: Cambridge University Press, 1954.

Bender, D.R. "A Refinement of the Concept of Household: Families, Co-Residence, and Domestic Functions." *American Anthropologist* 69 (October 1967):493-504.

Billingsley, Andrew. *Black Families in White America.* Englewood Cliffs, N.J.: Prentice Hall, 1968.

——. *Climbing Jacob's Ladder.* New York: Simon & Schuster, 1992.

Blassingame, John W. *The Slave Community: Planation Life in the Antebellum South.* New York: Oxford University Press, 1972, 1979.

Boserup, Ester. *Woman's Role in Economic Development.* London: Allen & Unwin, 1970.

Boulding, Elise. *Handbook of International Data on Women.* Beverly Hills, Calif.: Sage Publications /New York, N.Y.: John Wiley & Sons, 1976.

Bowen, Elenore Smith. *Return to Laughter.* New York: Harper & Row, 1954.

Bracey, John H., August Meier, and Elliott Rudwick, eds. *Black Matriarchy: Myth or Reality.* Belmont, Calif.: Wadsworth Publishing Co., 1970.

Busia, K.A. *The Position of the Chief in the Modern Political System of the Ashanti.* Oxford: Oxford University Press, 1951.

Caldwell, J.C. "Determinants of Rural Urban Migration in Ghana." *Population Studies* 22, 3 (1968):361-377.

——. *African Rural-Urban Migration.* Canberra: Australian National University Press, 1969.

Carper, Laura. "The Negro Family and the Moynihan Report." *Dissent* March/April 1966. [Reprinted in: Robert Staples [ed.?], *The Black Family: Essays and Studies.* Belmont, Calif.: Wadsworth Publishing Co., 1971.]

Codere, Helen. "Power in Rwanda." *Anthropologic* 4 (1962):45-85.

Cohen, Abner. "Cultural Strategies in the Organization of Trading Diaspora." In: Claude Meillassoux, ed., *The Development of Indigenous Trade and Markets in West Africa.* Oxford: Oxford University Press, 1971.

——. *Customs and Policies in Urban Africa: A Study of Hausa Migrants in Yoruba Towns.* London: Routledge & Paul Kegan, 1969.

Cole, Johnnetta B., ed. *Anthropology for the Eighties.* New York: The Free Press, 1982.

Colson, Elizabeth. "Family Change in Contemporary Africa." *Annals of the New York Academy of Sciences* 92, 2 (1962):641-52 [citations: John

Middleton, ed., *Black Africa*. New York: The Macmillan Co., 1970].

Committee to Study the Status of Women in Graduate Education. "The Higher, the Fewer." In: *The Graduate School*. Ann Arbor: University of Michigan, 1974.

Demerson, Bamidele Agbasegbe. "Family Life on Wadmanlaw Island." In: M.S. Twining and K. Baird, eds., *Sea Island Roots*. Trenton, N.J.: Africa World Press, 1991.

DuBois, W.E.B. *The Negro American Family*. Atlanta: Atlanta University Press, 1908 [citations: New American Library edition, New York, 1969].

Eades, Jeremy. "Kinship and Entrepreneurship among Yoruba in Northern Ghana." In: William A. Shack and Elliott P. Skinner, eds., *Strangers in African Societies*. Berkeley: University of California Press, 1979.

Elkins, Stanley. *Slavery: A Problem in American Intellectual Life*. Chicago: University of Chicago Press, 1959 [citations: Universal Library edition, Grosset & Dunlap, 1963].

English, Richard. "Beyond Pathology: Research and Theoretical Perspectives on Black Families." In: Lawrence E. Cary, ed., *Social Research and the Black Community: Selected Issues and Priorities*. Institute for Urban Affairs and Research, Howard University, Washington, D.C., 1974.

Fortes, Meyer. "Kinship and Marriage Among the Ashanti." In: A.R. Radcliffe-Brown and D. Forde, eds., *African Systems of Kinship and Marriage*. Oxford: Oxford University Press, 1950.

——. "The Ashanti Social Survey:A Preliminary Report." *Rhodes- Livingstone Journal* 6 (1948):1-36.

——. "The Structure of Unilineal Descent Groups." *American Anthropologist* 55 (January-March 1953):17-41.

——. *The Web of Kinship Among the Tallensi*. Oxford: Oxford University Press, 1949.

——. "Time and Social Structure: An Ashanti Case Story." In: M. Forest, ed., *Social Structure:Studies Presented to A.R. Radcliffe-Brown*. Oxford: Oxford University Press, 1949.

Fortes, Meyer and E.E. Evans-Pritchard, eds. *African Politcal Systems. Oxford: Oxford University Press, 1940.*

Frazier, E. Franklin. *The Negro Family in the United States*. Chicago: University of Chicago Press, 1939 [citations: 1966 edition].

Furstenberg, Frank, T. Hershbert, and J. Modell. "The Origins of the Female-Headed Black Family: the Impact of the Urban Experience," *Journal of Interdisciplinary History* 6 (1975):211-233.

Genovese, Eugene D. *Roll Jordan Roll: The World the Slaves Made*. New York: Random House, 1974.

Gil, B., A.F. Aryee, and D.K. Ghansah [and the Ghana Census Office]. *Ghana 1960 Population Census, Special Report "E": Tribes in Ghana*. Accra: Ghana Census Office, 1964.

Goody, J. *Production and Reproduction: A Comparative Study of the Domestic Domain*. Cambridge, Mass.: Cambridge University Press, 1976.

Gould, W.T.S. "International Migration in Tropical Africa: A Bibliographical Review." In: W.T.S. Gould, ed., *International Migration in Tropical Africa*. [Special Issue of] *International Migration Review* 7, 3 (1974):347-65.

Green, Vera. "The Black Extended Family in the U.S.: Some Research Suggestions." In: D. Shimkin, et al., eds., *The Extended Family in Black Societies*. The Hague: Mouton, 1978.

Gugler, Josef. "The Impact of Labour Migration on Society and Economy in Sub-Saharan Africa: Empirical Findings and Theoretical Considerations." *African Social Research* 6 (1968):463-486.

Gutman, Herbert. *The Black Family in Slavery and Freedom: 1750-1925*. New York: Random House, 1976 [citations: Vantage edition, 1977].

Haley, Alex. *Roots: The Saga of an American Family*. Garden City, N.Y.: Doubleday & Co., 1976.

Hatchett, Shirley and James S. Jackson. "African American Extended Kin Systems." In: Harriette P. McAdoo, ed., *Family Ethnicity*. Newbury Park, Calif.: Sage Publications, Inc., 1993.

Herskovits, Melville J. *The Myth of the Negro Past*. New York: Harper & Brothers, 1941 [citations: Beacon Press edition, Boston, 1958].

Hill, Polly. *The Migrant Cocoa Farmers of Southern Ghana*. Cambridge: Cambridge University Press, 1963.

——. "Hidden Trade in Hausaland." *Man* 4, 3 (1969):392-409.

——. "The Occupations of Migrants in Ghana." Ann Arbor: University of Michigan, Museum of Anthropology, Anthropological Papers, 1970.

——. "Two Types of West African House Trade." In: Claude Meillassoux, ed., *The Development of Indigenous Trade and Markets in West Africa*. Oxford: Oxford University Press, 1971.

Hill, Robert. *The Strengths of Black Families*. New York: Emerson Hall Publishers, 1971.

Hodder, B.W. "The Yoruba Rural Market." In: P. Bohannon and G. Dalton, eds., *Markets in Africa*. Evanston, Il.: Northwestern University Press, 1962.

Jaynes, Gerald D. and Robin M. Williams, Jr., eds. *A Common Destiny: Blacks and American Society*. Washington, D.C.: National Academy Press, 1989.

Jackson, Jacquelyne J. "But Where are the Men?" *The Black Scholar* (December 1971):30-41.

Jelin, Elizabeth. "Migration and Labor Force Participation of Latin American Women: The Domestic Servants in Cities." In: The Wellesley Editorial Committee, eds., *Women and National Development: The Complexities of Change*. Chicago; The University of Chicago Press, 1977.

Jewell, K. Sue. *Survival of the Black Family: The Institutional Impact of U.S. Social Policy*. New York: Praeger Publishers, 1988.

Johnson, Charles S. "In the Shadow of the Plantation." Chicago: University of Chicago Press, 1934.

Karenga, Maulana Ron. "In Love and Struggle: Toward a Greater Togetherness," *The Black Scholar* 6, 8 (March 1975).

——. "In Defense of Sis. Joanne: For Ourselves and History (the Joanne Little Case)." *The Black Scholar* 6, 10 (July-August 1975).

Katzin, Margaret. "The Jamaican Country Higgler." *Social and Economic Studies* 8, 4 (1959):421-440.

——. "The Role of the Small Entrepreneur." In: M.J. Herskovits and M. Harwitz, eds., *Economic Transition in Africa*. Evanston, Il.: Northwestern University Press, 1964.

Kennedy, Theodore R. *You Gotta Deal With It: Black Family Relations in a Southern Community*. New York: Oxford University Press, 1980.

Kenyatta, Jomo. *Facing Mt. Kenya: The Tribal Life of the Gikuyu*. [1938] Vintage edition, 1965.

Kerri, James, N. "Understanding the African Family: Persistence, Continuity, and Change." *The Western Journal of Black Studies* 3, 1 (1979):14-17.

King, James R. "African Survivals in the Black American Family: Key Factors in Stability." *Journal of Afro-American Issues* 4, 2 (1976):133-167.

Kuper, Hilda, ed. *Urbanization and Migration in West Africa*. Berkeley: University of California Press, 1965.

Ladner, Joyce. *Tomorrow's Tomorrow: The Black Woman*. Garden City, N.Y.: Doubleday & Co., 1971.

Landman, R.H. "Language Policies and Their Implications for Ethnic Relations in the Newly Sovereign States of Sub-Saharan Africa." In: B.M. duToit, ed., *Ethnicity in Modern Africa*. Boulder, Co.: Westview Press, 1978:69-90.

LaRue, Linda. "The Black Movement and Women's Liberation." *The Black Scholar* 1, 7 (May 1970).

Lebeuf, Annie. "The Role of Women in the Political Organization of African Societies." In: D. Paulme, ed., *Women of Tropical Africa*. The Hague: Mouton & Co., 1960.

Linton, Ralph. *The Study of Man*. New York: Appleton-Century, 1936.

Little, Kenneth. *African Women in Towns*. Cambridge: Cambridge University Press, 1973.

——. *West African Urbanization*. Cambridge: Cambridge University Press, 1965.

Lloyd, Peter C. "Craft Organizations in Yoruba Towns." *Africa* 23, 1 (1953):30- 44.

——. "Divorce among the Yoruba." *American Anthropologist* 70 (February 1968):67-81.

——. "The Yoruba Lineage." *Africa* 25, 3 (1955):235-51.

Mabogunje, Akin. "Migrants and Innovation in African Societies: Definition of a Research Field." In: N. Sudarkasa, ed., *Migrants and Strangers in Africa*. [African Urban Notes, Series B, No. 1.] East Lansing: Michigan State University, African Studies Center, 1974.

——. "Migration Policy and Regional Development in Nigeria." *Nigerian Journal of Economic and Social Studies* 12, 2 (1970):243-262.

——. "Regional Mobility and Resource Development in West Africa." [Keith Callard Lectures.] Montreal: McGill-Queen's University Press, 1972.

———. "The Yoruba Home." *Odu: Journal of Yoruba and Related Studies* 5 (1958).

Malveaux, Julianne. "The Economic Statuses of Black Families." In: Harriette P. McAdoo, ed., *Black Families*. Second edition. Newbury Park, Calif.: Sage Publications, 1988.

Manns, Wilhelmina. "Supportive Roles of Significant Others in Black Families," In: Hariette P. McAdoo, ed., *Black Families*. Second ed. Beverly Hills: Sage Publications, 1988.

Maquet, J.J. "The Premise of Inequality in Rwanda." Oxford: Oxford University Press, 1961. Translated from: *Le systeme des relations sociales de l'ancien Rwanda*. [Memoires-Collection in 8.Sciences del'Homme. Ethnologie, Vol. 1.] Tervuren: Academie Royale des Sciences Morales et Politiques, 1954.

———. *Civilizations of Black Africa*. London: Oxford University Press, 1972.

Marshall, Gloria A. [Niara Sudarkasa]. "Benefit Societies in the British West Indies: The Formative Years: 1793 to 1846." [Unpublished Master's Thesis.] New York: Columbia University, 1959.

———. "The Marketing of Farm Produce: Some Patterns of Trade Among Women of Western Nigeria." *Proceedings of the 1962 NISER Conference*. Ibadan: Nigerian Institute for Social and Economic Research, 1963.

———. "Woman, Trade and the Yoruba Family." [Ph.D. dissertation.] New York: Columbia University, 1964.

———. "Marriage: Comparative Analysis." In: *International Encyclopedia of the Social Sciences*. New York: Macmillan Co. / The Free Press, 1968.

———. "Interpersonal and Institutional Relationships in African Society" and "Integrative Elements in African Social Life." In: *Black Perspectives in the Social Sciences*. [Video lecture series.] Kent, Ohio: Kent State University, Institute for African American Affairs, 1970.

Martin, Elmer P. and Joanne M. Martin. *The Black Extended Family*. Chicago: University of Chicago Press, 1978.

Mathis, Arthur. "Contrasting Approaches to the Study of Black Familes." In: Peters, Marie, ed., *Special Issue:Black Families*. [Special issue.] *Journal of Marriage and the Family* 40, 4 (Nov. 1978).

Mauss, Marcell. *The Gift*. Transl. by Ian Cunnison. London: Cohen and West, Ltd., 1954.

Mazrui, A.M. "Gandhi, Marx and the Warrior Tradition: Towards Androgynous Liberation." *Journal of Asian and African Studies* 12(1977):1-4.

Mbilinyi, Marjorie. "The 'New Woman' and Traditional Norms in Tanzania." *Journal of Modern African Studies* 10, 1 (1972):57-72.

Mbiti, John. *African Religions and Philosophy*. New York: Praeger, 1969.

———. *Love and Marriage in Africa*. London: Longman Group Ltd., 1973.

McAdoo, Harriette P. "Factors Related to Stability of Upwardly Mobile Black Families." *Journal of Marriage and the Family* 40, 4 (1978):761-776.

———. *Extended Family Support of Single Black Mothers*. [Report No. NIMH 5R01 MN32159.] Rockville, Md.: Department of Health and Human

Services, Public Health Service, Alcohol, Drug Abuse and Mental Health Administration and National Institute of Mental Health, 1983.

———, ed. *Black Families.* Beverly Hills, Calif.: Sage Publications, 1981; Second ed. 1988.

McAdoo, John L. "The Roles of Black Fathers in the Socialization of Black Children," In: Harriette P. McAdoo, ed., *Black Families.* Second ed. Beverly Hills: Calif.: Sage Publications, 1988.

McCall, Daniel F. "The Effect on Family Structure on Changing Economic Activities in a Gold Coast Town." [Ph.D. dissertation.] New York: Columbia University, 1956.

Mintz, S.W. "The Jamaican Internal Marketing Pattern." *Social and Economic Studies* 4, 1 (1955):95-103.

Moynihan, Daniel Patrick. *The Negro Family: The Case for National Action.* Washington, D.C.: U.S. Government Printing Office, 1965.

Murdock, George Peter. *Social Structure.* New York: The Macmillan Co., 1949.

Nadel, S.F. *A Black Byzantium.* Oxford: Oxford University Press, 1942.

Nobles, Wade. "African Root and American Fruit: The Black Family." *Journal of Social and Behavioral Sciences* 20, 2 (1974):32-63.

———. "Africanity: Its Role in Black Families." *The Black Scholar* (June 1974b):10-17.

———. "Toward an Empirical and Theoretical Framework for Defining Black Families." *Journal of Marriage and the Family* 40, 4 (1978):679-688.

Nyerere, Julius. "Education for Self-Reliance." In: I.N. Resnik, ed., *In Tanzania: Revolution by Education.* Arusha, Tanzania: Longmans of Tanzania, 1968.

O'Brien, Denise. "Female Husbands in Southern Bantu Societies." In: Alice Schlegel, ed., *Sexual Stratification: A Cross Cultural View.* New York: Columbia University Press, 1977.

Ogunsheye, F.A. "Formal Education and the Status of Women in Nigeria." Presented to the National Conference on Nigerian Women and Development in Relation to Changing Family Structure, University of Obadan, 1976.

Okediji, Peter Ade and Okediji, F. "Marital Stability and Social Structure in an African City." *Nigerian Journal of Economic and Social Studies* 8, 1 (1966):151- 163.

Okediji, Peter Ade. "A Psychosocial Analysis of the Extended Family: the African Case." *African Urban Notes* [Series B] 1, 3 (1975a):93-99. [African Studies Center, Michigan State University.]

———. "Developing a Measure of Extended Family and Kinship System." *Nigerian Journal of Sociology and Anthropology* 2, 1 (1973b):75-79.

Onwuejeogwu, M.A. *The Social Anthropology of Africa: An Introduction.* London: Heinemann, 1975.

Oppong, Christine. *Marriage Among a Matrilineal Elite: A Family Study of Ghanaian Senior Civil Servants.* Cambridge, Mass.: Cambridge University Press, 1974.

Ottenberg, Phoebe. "The Changing Economic Position of Women Among the Afikpo Ibo." In: W. Bascom and J.J. Herskovits, eds., *Continuity and Change in African Cultures*. Chicago: University of Chicago Press, 1959.

Owens, Leslie H. *This Species of Property: Slave Life and Culture in the Old South*. New York: Oxford University Press, 1976.

Pala, Achola O. "The Role of African Women in Rural Development: Research Priorities." [Discussion Paper 203.] Nairobi, Kenya: University of Nairobi, Institute for Development Studies, 1974.

——. *African Women in Rural Development*. Washington, D.C.: Overseas Liaison Committee, American Council on Education, 1976.

Paulme, Denise, ed. [H.M. Wright, trans.] *Women of Tropical Africa*. Berkeley: University of California Press, 1963.

Perdue, C.L., Jr., T.E. Barden, and R.K. Phillips. *Weevils in the Wheat: Interviews with Virginia Ex-Slaves*. Bloomington: University of Indiana Press, 1980.

Perlman, M., and M.P. Moal. "Analytical Bibliography." In: Denise Paulme, ed. [H.M. Wright, trans.], *Women of Tropical Africa*. Berkeley: University of California Press, 1963.

Peters, Marie. "Notes from the Guest Editor." M.F. Peters, ed., *Special Issue: Black Families. Journal of Marriage and Family* 40, 4 (Nov. 1978) *[Special issue]*.

Phillips, H.M. *Basic Education—A World Challenge*. New York: John Wiley & Sons, 1975.

Piel, Margaret. "The Expulsion of West African Aliens." *Journal of Modern African Studies* 9, 2 (1971):205-229.

——. "Ghana's Aliens." In: W.T.S. Gould, ed., *International Migration in Tropical Africa*. [Special Issue of:] *International Migration Review* 7, 3 (1974):347-365.

Powdermaker, Hortense. *After Freedom: A Cultural Study in the Deep South*. New York: Viking Press, 1939.

Radcliffe-Brown, A.R. "Introduction." In: A.R. Radcliffe-Brown and D. Forde, eds., *African Systems of Kinship and Marriage*. London: Oxford University Press, 1950.

Radcliffe-Brown, A.R. and Daryll Forde, eds., *African Systems of Kinship and Marriage*. London: Oxford University Press [for the International African Institute], 1950.

Rainwater, Lee and William Yancey. "The Monynihan Report and the Poling of Controversy." Cambridge, Mass.: The M.I.T. Press, 1967.

Rattray, R.S. *Ashanti Law and Constitution*. Oxford: Clarendon Press, 1929.

Rivers, W.H.R. *Social Organization*. Alfred A. Knopf, New York: 1924.

Robertson, C. "Ga Women and Socioeconomic Change in Accra, Ghana." In: N.J.Hafkin and E.G. Fay, eds., *Women in Africa: Studies in Social and Economic Change*. Stanford: Stanford University Press, 1976.

Rodney, Walter. *How Europe Underdeveloped Africa*. Washington, D.C.: Howard University Press, 1972:288.

Rosaldo, Michelle. "Woman, Culture, and Society: A Theoretical Overview."

In: M. Rosaldo and L. Lamphere, eds., *Women, Culture, and Society*. Palo Alto, Calif.: Stanford University Press, 1974.

Rosaldo, Michelle and Louise Lamphere, eds., *Woman, Culture and Society*. Palo Alto, Calif.: Stanford University Press, 1974.

Rouch, Jean. "Migrations in Ghana." *Journal de Societe des Africainee* 1956.

Rousseau, Ida Faye. "African Women: Identity Crisis? Some Observations on Education and the Changing Role of Women in Sierra Leone and Zaire." In: R. Rohrlich-Leavitt, ed., *Women Cross-Culturally*. The Hague: Mouton, 1975.

Ryan, William. "Savage Discovery—The Moynihan Report." *The Nation* November 22, 1965. [Reprinted in: Robert Staples, ed., *The Black Family: Essays and Studies*. First edition. Belmont, Calif.: Wadsworth Publishing Co., 1971.]

Sacks, Karen. "Engels Revisited: Women, the Organization of Production, and Private Property." In: Michelle Z. Rosaldo and Louise Lamphere, eds., *Woman, Culture, and Society*. Palo Alto, Calif.: Stanford University Press, 1974.

Sahlins, Marshall. "The Segmentary Lineage: An Organization of Predatory Expansion." *American Anthropologist* 63 (1961):322-343.

———. *Stone Age Economics*. Chicago: Aldine Publishing Co., 1972.

Sanday, Peggy. "Female Status in Public Domain." In: M. Rosaldo and L. Lamphere, eds., *Woman, Culture, and Society*. Palo Alto, Calif.: Stanford University, 1974.

Schildkrout, Enid. "The Fostering of Children in Urban Ghana." Presented in a Symposium on Transactions in Parenthood at the Annual Meeting of the American Anthropological Association, Toronto, 1972.

Shimkin, Dimitri, Edith M. Shimkin, and Dennis A. Frake, eds., *The Extended Family in Black Societies*. The Hague: Mouton Publishing, 1978.

Shimkin, Dimitri and Victor Uchendu. "Persistence, Borrowing, and Adaptive Changes in Black Kinship Systems: Some Issues and Their Significance." In: D. Shimkin, et al., eds., *The Extended Family in Black Societies*. The Hague: Mouton Publishing, 1978.

Shorter, E. *The Making of the Modern Family*. New York: Basic Books, 1975.

Skinner, Elliott. "Labour Migration and its Relationship to Socio-cultural Change in Mossi Society." *Africa* 30, 4 (1960):375-401.

Smith, R.T. "The Matrilocal Family." In: J. Goody, ed., *The Character of Kinship*. Cambridge, Mass.: Cambridge University Press, 1973.

Smock, Audrey. "The Impact of Modernization on Women's Position in the Family in Ghana." In: Alice Schlegel, ed., *Sexual Stratification: A Cross-Cultural View*. New York: Columbia University Press, 1977.

Stack, Carol. *All My Kin*. New York: Harper & Row, 1974.

Staples, Robert. "The Black Family Revisited." In: Robert Staples, ed., *The Black Family Essays and Studies*. Second edition. Belmont, Calif.: Wadsworth Publishing Co., 1978.

Steady, Filomina Chioma. *The Black Women Cross-Culturally*. Cambridge,

Mass., Schenkman Publishing Company, Inc., 1981.

Stone, L. "The Rise of the Nuclear Family in Early Modern England: The Patriarchal Stage." In: C.E. Rosenberg, ed., *The Family in History.* Philadelphia: University of Pennsylvania Press, 1975.

Sudarkasa, Niara. *Where Women Work: A Study of Yoruba Women in the Marketplace and in the Home.* Anthropological Papers, No. 53. Ann Arbor: Museum of Anthropology, University of Michigan, 1973.

——. "Commercial Migration in West Africa, with Special Reference to the Yoruba in Ghana." *African Urban Notes* [Series B] 1, 1: 61 (1974):103. (East Lansing, Mich.: Michigan State University, African Studies Center, 1974.)

——. "The Economic Status of the Yoruba in Ghana Before 1970." *The Nigerian Journal of Economic and Social Studies* 17, 1 (1975):93-125.

——. "Family: African Roots," In: J. Salzman, D. Smith, and C. West, eds., *Encyclopedia of African American Culture and History,* Volume 2. New York: Simon & Schuster Macmillan, 1995.

——. "From Stranger to Alien: The Socio-Political Status of the Yoruba in Ghana, 1900-1970." In: William Shack and Elliott P. Skinner, eds., *Strangers in African Societies.* Berkeley: The University of California Press, 1979.

——. "The Role of Yoruba Commercial Migration in West African Development." In: Beverly Lindsay, ed., *African Migration and National Development.* University Park, Pa. and London: The Pennsylvania State University Press, 1985.

Tetteh, P.A. "Marriage, Family and Household." In: W. Birmingham et al., eds., *A Study of Contemporary Ghana.* Vol. 2. London: Allen & Unwin, 1967.

Tilly, L.A. and J.W. Scott. *Women, Work, and Family.* New York: Holt, Rinehart & Winston, 1978.

Uchendu, V. *The Igbo of South-Eastern Nigeria.* New York: Holt, Rinehart & Winston, 1965.

United Nations Economic Commission on Africa. Human Resources Development Division. African Training and Research Center for Women. "Women and National Development in African Countries: Some Profound Contradictions." *African Studies Review* 18, 3 (1975).

United Nations Trusteeship Council, T/1538. Visiting Mission to Trust Territories in East Africa, 1960. Report on Rwanda-Urundi.

U.S. Department of Health and Human Services. *Report to Congress on Out-of-Wedlock Childbearing.* DHHS Pub. No. (PHS) 95-1257. Hyattsville, Maryland, September 1995.

Valentine, Charles A. *Culture and Poverty.* Chicago: Chicago University Press, 1968.

Van Allen, Judith. "Women in Africa: Modernization Means More Dependency." *Center Magazine* [Santa Barbara, Calif.] 1974.

Ware, Helen. "Polygyny: Women's Views in a Transitional Society, Nigeria 1973." *Journal of Marriage and the Family* 41, 1 (1979):183-195.

Watson, R.L. "American Scholars and the Continuity of African Culture in the United States." *Journal of Negro History* 63, 4 (Fall 1978): 375-386.

Whitehead, Tony L."Residence, Kinship and Mating as Survival Strategies:A West Indian Example." M.F. Peters, ed., *Special Issue:Black Families.* [Special issue of:] *Journal of Marriage and Family* 40, 4 (November 1978):817-828.

Whyte, Martin K. *The Status of Women in Preindustrial Societies.* Princeton, N.J.: Princeton University Press, 1978.

Wilson, William Julius. *The Truly Disadvantaged.* Chicago: University of Chicago Press, 1987.

Woodson, Carter G. *The African Background Outlined.* Washington, D.C.: Association for the Study of Negro Life and History, 1936.

Young, Virginia H. "Family and Childhood in a Southern Negro Community." *American Anthropologist* 72, 2 (April 1970):269-288.

Zwane, Benedict. "Overpopulation and Economic Growth in the Developing Countries." *Transition* l, 9, No. 49 (July/September 1975).